Telling Women's Lives

Telling Women's Lives

Subject/Narrator/Reader/Text

Judy Long

NEW YORK UNIVERSITY PRESS

New York and London

NEW YORK UNIVERSITY PRESS
New York and London

© 1999 by New York University

Chapter 6: Excerpts from Letters from Jenny reprinted by
permission of Harcourt Brace; excerpts from The Fantastic Lodge
reprinted by permission of Houghton Mifflin; excerpts from Social
Science and the Self reprinted by permission of Rutgers University
Press.

Library of Congress Cataloging-in-Publication Data
Long, Judy.
Telling women's lives : subject/narrator/reader/text/ Judy Long.
p. cm — (Feminist crosscurrents)
Includes bibliographical references (p.) and index.
ISBN 0-8147-5074-5 (alk. paper)
ISBN 0-8147-5975-3 (pbk. : alk. paper)
1. Women—Biography—History and criticism. 2. Autobiography. I.
Title. II. Series.
CT3203 .L65 1999
809'.39592072—dc21   99-6297
                            CIP

New York University Press books are printed on acid-free paper,
and their binding materials are chosen for strength and durability.

Manufactured in the United States of America

10 9 8 7 6 5 4 3 2 1

This book is for Reba Rose Tapper
1904–1991

Contents

Acknowledgments

When I undertook the telling of a woman's life, it seemed a peculiar thing for a sociologist to do. Although I felt impelled to do it, the task was alien to my training and to my professional community. As I struggled to tell one woman's life, my questions took me to the disparate literatures of autobiography and biography, oral history and life history. I read for the first time the contributions of scholars in literary theory and criticism. New questions took me back to an old interest in feminist methodology and epistemology. These strands began to converge with the great stream of feminist scholarship in which I had been swimming for many years, particularly the extensive literature in the sociology of sex and gender. In formulating a method for telling women's lives, I have interrogated literatures across the disciplines and juxtaposed traditions that are strangers to each other. I hope this work will be of use to all those who want to write lives. The trespasses and solecisms that resulted are entirely my responsibility.

This book would not have been possible without the work of several generations of feminist scholars—some outside the academy and some within. I am conscious of the bulwark of this research, growing deeper and more powerful over a quarter-century. Consequently, my debt is enormous. The names of those I owe appear on every page. In addition, several colleagues took time from demanding schedules to read several chapters of *Telling Women's Lives* in various drafts. I particularly want to thank Kathy Barry, Marj DeVault, and Shula Reinharz. The next generation is also an important part of this project. I want to acknowledge the members of my graduate seminar in Sociological Life History in 1992, who assured me that S/N/R/T made a euphonious acronym and showed me what could be done with the framework: Susan Adair, Alex Antypas, Susan Belair, Mary Croft, Zhan Gao, Michael Hovey, Rose Imperato, Jan Lambertz, Joy Meeker, Thalia Mulvihill, Raji Swaminathan, Lynn Woehrle, and Nina Wright.

It is no secret that writing a book can make a person crazy. When it takes longer than expected, and a few things go wrong, it can make a person crazier. The lucid intervals I have enjoyed are due to the efforts of Dan Tapper who, with the Beastie Girls, kept my feet on the ground, and provided a foundation of love and hilarity. I thank them.

Telling Women's Lives

1

Telling Women's Lives

> We must reinscribe for their subjects the hidden texts within their work, the tension between their writings and the traditions in which they are written, above all the anxieties of authorship at a time and place where permission to be authors is not granted women, and cannot readily be seized.
>
> —Carolyn Heilbrun (1985, 12)

This book germinated in my fascination with another woman's life,[1] and my need to grasp what would be involved in telling it. Propelled by these two forces, I entered upon a journey of discovery that many other readers and writers are making in the last decades of the twentieth century. At first my subject herself filled my focus; she was a fascinating individual who, then in her middle seventies, had been living in Mexico as a "political refugee" for thirty years. The first mystery that attracted me was the challenge of subjectivity. I was awed by Lini's life and the consciousness that shaped it—a reaction reported by many others who work with women's narratives. Lini de Vries was unique, heroic, a model for women of any age. My first introduction to Lini had been through her autobiography. As I got deeper into the mystery of subjectivity I became interested in the spectacle of a woman's enacting the subject of an autobiographical narrative, the problematics of self-presentation, and the calculus of publication. I came to appreciate multiple narratives (and multiple audiences). I found myself reading intensively in autobiography as a genre, as well as in its theoretical and critical literature.

Lini de Vries was an admirable individual, whose life had been adventurous and oppositional. But not unique. As I read on, I changed my mind about what I was discovering. I had not really discovered Lini (after all, she had published an autobiography). My real discovery was that the unremarked lives of women concealed such bravery, drama, and virtue—and this was not rare. Like others who have read and written women's biography and life history, I went on to discover many admirable women's lives. This realization turned me toward a second mystery: why had such outstanding figures been hidden from me? How had my elite education encompassed such an omission? Pursuing this question, I learned that personalities who impressed me so deeply might be dismissed as ordinary or "obscure" lives. I began to ask, what is an admirable life, and who decides? I had arrived at one of the major constraints on telling women's lives (and a third mystery): the institutions of genre and the canon, where evaluation and gatekeeping are joined.

While my explorations of canons and convention led me away from individual women's lives, they also led me back to my first concern, the need for a method adequate for telling *women's* lives. In seeking women's lives through a range of genres and disciplines, I examined the gains and distortions found in established methods. None of these fit women's lives; each would need expansion and reformation for the telling of women's lives.

After exploring the challenges of autobiography, I moved on to the dilemmas involved in telling another's life: I read extensively in biography, oral history, and life history. In my search for the elements of a feminist method for telling women's lives, the narrator became an important figure. I found as a narrator (and also as a reader) that different accounts could relay different truths about the same events and persons. This multiplicity provided a clue to the plural subjectivities involved in writing another's life, and the possibility that authorship could be shared by subject and narrator.

The questions involved in telling lives cross disciplinary and generic boundaries—as do the readers who are seeking answers. People who read biography and autobiography are also devouring diaries and letters, journals, life history, oral history and memoirs. I wanted *Telling Women's Lives* to encompass some of this diversity: to explore certain traditions in depth, but also to stray across their borders. I wanted to introduce the reader to many women—not just "Great Women." And I wanted to keep alive the dynamic linking readers and writers. Subject and narrator each have one foot in the world of print. I entered upon my journey as a reader; now, as I write, I am aware that others are beginning similar journeys of discovery and dismay. I hope that *Telling Women's Lives* will meet the needs of such readers and writers.

Plan of the Book

The organization of *Telling Women's Lives* reflects the transformations of my own inquiry. The partnership of subject, narrator, and reader provides the framework of this book. I begin with the female subject, and the nexus involving female subjectivity, women's self-writing, and the shape of women's lives. Three chapters deal with aspects of women's autobiography. Chapter 2 deals with the collision between the female life and the "generic" tradition of autobiography. The reader can take it as read that parallel critique applies to the genres of biography and life history that are taken up in later chapters. Chapter 3 examines the autobiographical impulse and narrative strategies that women adopt in telling their lives. Chapter 4 focuses on some of the distinctive content women write about, and the struggle to find language for writing it.

Moving on from autobiography, later chapters focusing on other traditions take for granted an infrastructure dictated by genre and discipline. A second thread of the book takes up the problematics of telling another's life, as in life history and biography. Four chapters deal with biographers' dilemmas and the question of a narrator's subjectivity. Chapter 5 emphasizes the face-to-face relationship between subject and narrator and the reciprocal nature of influence. Chapters 6 and 7 take up the presence and responsibilities of the narrator, dilemmas of biography, and challenges of female biography. Chapter 6 examines three classical life histories of women by sociological narrators. Chapter 7 deals with feminist biography. In the final chapter I outline an emerging methodology for telling women's lives, pulling together themes from the content of women's autobiography, principles of feminist praxis and the theory of the narrator with examples from feminist research.

Subject/Narrator/Reader/Text: A Framework for *Telling Women's Lives*

In the context of intersubjectivity, I am aware that the boundaries among narrator, subject and reader are not fixed. Moreover, the terms I employ for the S/N/R/T framework have contested meanings. I am using the terms "subject," "narrator," "reader," and "text" in specific ways. When I speak of the subject in this text I mean the biographical individual whose life is being told; when that life is told by another, that other is called the narrator. I am using the term "subject" in a sociological sense: the subject as agent. I hope that no reader will view the subject in this book as "the" subject, a unitary, monolithic, or universal construction. I use the term "subject" to mark a source of action, a site of subjectivity, the nature of which is not determined in advance, but is only apparent when set in motion by a particular act of telling. Moreover, the understanding of the subject that the reader creates is, like the narrator's understanding, a unique emergent colored by her biographical particularity and her active exercise of empathy. Different narrators and readers can create different subjects from the same life.[2] A third partner, the reader, exists for the subject as the intended audience for her self-revelation. The reader often influences the narrator's efforts as well.

A second focus of *Telling Women's Lives* is the narrator. The narrator is a second subjectivity, involved with the subject, whose agency is essential for the creation of life history and biography. Adopting the novel term "narrator" is a way of keeping the relationship between the subject and the narrator central and visible. It is this relationship that determines the existence, the development, and the outcome of the research encounter. In a sense the idea of a narrator refers to a moment in the production of a text. It is a function that continues to exist only as long as subject and narrator are in relation, rather than a permanent "role" independent of the situation. With relationship paramount, I chose a term that implies some of the commitment and passion narrators often bring to their task. This theory of the narrator will prove controversial. It breaks decisively with the tradition of the "objective" researcher and the authoritative third-person voice.[3] Another dimension of the narrator's role also deserves mention. For even as she establishes the all-important relationship with the subject, the narrator is also involved in another relationship with a different significance for telling women's lives. Often the narrator has strong allegiance to the traditions of genre or discipline; he/she may be thinking of readers quite different from those the subject is seeking. The subject's encounter with genre is often mediated by the narrator's relationship with her/his public.

The third partner in telling women's lives is the reader, the intended and essential audience of the subject. Reaching out to a reader is a pervasive theme in women's autobiography, which communicates a lively sense of a female readership as a lifeline to the woman writing her life.[4] In journals, diaries, and letters, too, the subject often explicitly invokes her reader. But critic Susan Schibanoff reminds us that this relationship is two-edged. Since medieval times, literature has recognized two classes of readers, differing in their significance for women. The common reader is an appreciative consumer of writing, while the primary reader is a gate-keeper or critic. The subject of autobiography often looks to the common reader for understanding or "rescue," while the "primary reader" is the focus of the apprehension women suffer in writing their lives. This more complex view of readership is important in thinking about the project of telling women's lives.

The fourth element in the framework of *Telling Women's Lives* is the text.[5] Although this book focuses on written texts, in a real sense the oral account is the avatar of all methods of telling women's lives. Life-telling as discourse originates in communication. The paradigm for the com-municative act is not the written text but the face-to-face encounter, in which person and relationship are paramount. In societies where the oral tradition is more influential than is literacy, the connection between tellers or singers and their listeners forms a discourse. I view the written text as a point in a process of communication. The text is the concrete expression of a relationship between subject and another, representing their discourse in altered form. When I speak of texts, I mean to include nonwritten narratives and when I speak of readers, I include hearers.

The text, like the reader, has a double life. In addition to its relation-ship with subject and narrator, a text stands in relation to the company of texts. It acquires a secondary existence separate from the relationship that gave it life and becomes implicated in the politics of genre and prob-lematics of language.

The organization of the book has its roots in certain distinct litera-tures, which are then linked by questions regarding subject, narrator, reader, and text. Each of the established traditions tends to highlight one or more of the vital relationships among subject, narrator, reader and text, and to slight or obscure others. None of the established genres illu-minates all the relationships. Autobiography spotlights the subject and presents the reader with a first-person account of her life and her con-cerns. In biography the relationship between the subject and the narrator is of paramount importance—but the text conceals the person of the nar-rator, who does not appear as a separate subjectivity. In life history the narrator functions as the essential "second person" to whom the subject tells her life. When the text is produced, however, that second person is hidden behind an authoritative third-person voice. These traditions fail to provide a model for telling women's lives.

In addition to the pattern provided by genres and the S/N/R/T frame-work, the book is unified by other concepts and concerns that run throughout: connection, diversity, reading for gender, the encounter with genre, and issues of voice. In this book the idea of connection appears in a number of places, under a number of names: empathy, identification, intersubjectivity, fusion, even contamination. The project of telling lives is made possible, in the first place, by the human connection that links the subject, narrator, and reader. The strength and multiplicity of these connections are telling us something important: not that we are the same, not that we are one, but that each of us is all of these. In the context of literate Western societies, we are all subjects *and* readers *and* narrators. Each of us has a life history, acts as an audience for others' life stories, and actively elicits them. Each of us reads, in part, to know another's re-ality. As subjects we struggle to express our subjectivity; as readers we resonate with records women have made of their lives. As narrators we are inspired to rescue other women's lives from obscurity, to enthrone them in history, and in so doing to preserve the link between women's lives.[6] Processes of identification and social comparison are fundamental building blocks of social relations; they link all the partners in life-telling and underlie activities of criticism and biography, among others. The psychological link between the biographer and her subject has frequently been noted. Less commonly recognized is the influence of identification in critical judgment. The framework of S/N/R/T, which emphasizes the relations among all these terms, gives intersubjectivity a central place. The examination of the traditions of autobiography, biography, and life history leads to a method based on intersubjectivity.

The issue of method is central to this book. Existing methods provide only a partial answer to the challenge of transforming a life. For living a life does not automatically prepare one for telling that life. Our lives as lived are "haphazard, make-do, minding-one's-own-business kind of af-fairs" (Bittner 1980, 2). The task of telling lives brings distinctive dilem-mas. Scholars tend to agree that the brute facts of a life—the "life as lived"—are not directly accessible to us. We must invent a plausible ac-count for that which we can observe. All accounts are therefore con-structed, and bear an indistinct relation to verifiable events. All are fic-tions, whether they are told by the subject or a "third person." Every ac-count reflects the subjectivity that birthed it.

In addition, making a life story from a life requires multiple transfor-mations. Order, coherency, and pattern are introduced into the life only through the creation of a narrative. In telling women's lives, we are forced to confront the problematic relation of women subjects to their culture's storehouse of narratives. Genres collect and contain these narratives, raising issues of access and legitimacy. Inevitably genres constitute a symbolic environment with which the narrator must come to terms. That encounter is decisive in telling women's lives.

Voices for Telling Women's Lives: First Person/Third Person

Our interest in subjectivity leads us to take autobiography as the starting point for this study, privileging first-person accounts over third-person accounts. We read women's self-writing for knowledge about women's collective situation, daily lives, and consciousness, information that is not to be found in other documents.[7] The lack of official notice of women, reflecting the politics of gender, bears on the issue of voice. In the absence of a public reality or history, women's personal narratives become their representatives. First-person accounts are essential for understanding the subjectivity of a muted social group.

Third-person accounts are no substitute for the missing first-person accounts, nor can the fiction of the generic person bridge the gap. Problems of third-person accounts include distortions introduced by abstraction and unjustified generalization, exacerbated by an androcentric tradition. In addition, where third-person constructions are defined from the perspective of the dominant group they serve ideological purposes. Aspects of femaleness that are of use or value to men dominate such images; other dimensions are obscured. Too often in third-person accounts women are represented by conventional masks resembling acceptable stereotypes of womanliness.[8] The imaginative construction "Woman" is distant from the collective experience of women.

Among third-person constructions, the convention of the generic subject may mask the absence of women by the use of "inclusive" or "generic" language. Following this convention may involve the absurdity of "averaging" over the fundamental social categories of woman and man. More often the "generic" person is abstracted from male experience alone, rendering women's lives invisible. Essentialism distorts the picture of women still further, narrowing and simplifying representation of women. Today there is widespread recognition that omission of women has produced a fundamentally limited understanding of human experience. We are now at a point where history and theory need to be grounded in women's reality (Barry 1988, 360). First-person accounts of women's experience are required to rebuild the database for scholarly activity in many fields.

First-person accounts can overcome many of the limitations of the third-person voice.[9] In deciding to take first-person accounts as a starting point for this book I situate myself as a feminist reader, with a feminist critique of a third-person literature about women. It is an unusual move for a social scientist to relinquish the surety of the authoritative third-person voice and step aside to give precedence to first-person voices. But it is only through woman-centered inquiry that we can discover what experiences women are trying to communicate, and what they have to say.

In seeking the female subject in autobiography, we begin with a tradition that speaks with a first-person voice. In so doing we begin with a paradox. Autobiography is personal and private writing—but third-person representations are never absent. Inescapably, when women think and write reflexively, societal images and stereotypes of women are present in their minds. Women are surrounded by third-person definitions of who they are, cultural prescriptions that are transmitted in oral tradition and private writing as well as written and published work. Even when they avoid published autobiography, women subjects do not escape the impact of these normative formulae. The constraints operating on women's space and women's voices are reflected in the narratives women create.

The Encounter with Genre

This book concentrates mainly on three traditions for narrating lives: autobiography, life history, and biography. Despite their differences, these genres have certain features in common. All three have narrative conventions, a canon, theory, gatekeepers, and partisans. Each tradition demonstrates a lack of fit with the texts by or about women. Although they do not deal explicitly with gender, the established genres limn a masculine experience. The masculinity of the traditions makes it difficult for the narrative of female experience to find a berth and a reading. Each genre (along with the critics and professors who maintain its boundaries) has functioned in the past to disqualify and hence exclude much writing that centers on women's lives. The application of generic standards operates to restrict the range of accepted writing, enforcing limits via reward and punishment. The activity of exclusion is carried out by critics, who perform public and published acts of evaluation. Their disavowal of identification enhances their claims to objectivity, which in turn buttress the social control function of genre. In this book I take autobiography as a prototype of social control in androcentric literary production.

Reading for Gender

Gender shapes the subject's narrative and the narrator's text. Equally, gender colors the reading and interpretation of the narrative. Understanding women's experiences, or accounts of them, requires one to read the code of gender. The reader must recognize how women and men write gender into their accounts, and into their accounts of lives. Personal narratives of women provide a portrait of gender arrangements that are invisible in the dominant discourse and that yield to a gender-sensitive reading. Inevitably, women's personal narratives "tell on" the gender arrangements of their society. In reading (or writing) about women, the collective situation of women, as revealed in personal narrative, must be taken as context. Reading for gender means understanding women's place in society and history (Smith 1976). As a muted social group, women's collective experience is understated or omitted in official representations, recognized identities and traditions of their society (Ardener 1975).

Although gender is a fundamental principle of social organization, it remains untheorized in much scholarly writing. We as readers have the task of uncovering the dynamics of gender in lives we read. And since gender is an attribute of narrator and reader as well as subject, we must extend our reading for gender beyond the subject. Finally, we must situate ourselves, as well as those "others" in the S/N/R/T framework. This dictates an expanded role for first-person accounts of subjects, narrators and readers. The goal of this study is to discover a method for telling women's lives that is situated, embodied, gendered and speaks in the first person.

Diversity

Gender, race, class and age are fundamental principles of social organization, their intersection defining the individual's social location. Distinctive women's concerns spring from specific configurations of sex, race and social class. The intersection of race and sex has attracted much attention during the past ten years.[10] The contribution made by first-person accounts is illustrated by the autobiography of Anne Moody (1968), who tells of her experiences as a young person in the civil rights movement. Moody[11] recounts her discovery of race in an unforgettable encounter with white boys who turn out to be her brothers. Her account of working as a white woman's maid could only have come from the experience of a person who was African American and female. And she records her participation in the earliest actions of the Civil Rights Movement, a historical moment has already been written as though the only participants were men.[12]

The intersection of class and sex has received less attention. Often in first-person accounts the subject cannot state her class position clearly. Most theoretical (third-person) formulations of the class system deal with women by subsuming them under the class locations of male relatives. Yet present-day demographics demonstrate that women do not always share in the resources of their male relatives or spouses, and may experience striking instability as a consequence of marital disruption. The constraints under which wealthy women live also need to be analyzed.[13] Too often writers employ a theory of class uninflected by gender, and assume women have the same amount of freedom, privilege and power as do men of their class. The complexities of dealing with gender within class and class within sex call for the offices of a narrator—but that narrator must be adept at reading for class and gender.

Sexual orientation creates other, invisible partitions. Narrators need to be particularly aware of conventional perspectives here. A subject-positioning that defines women by links to men is especially inadequate for understanding lesbian lives. Women who live outside these linkages are invisible to the male eye, and underdocumented in official literature. In fact, lesbian narratives are particularly illuminating with reference to gender and to the formation of identity. Lesbian "coming out stories" recount the conquest of personal and social identity in resistance to the heterosexual order. These constitute a self-referential canon that is almost entirely neglected by scholars writing on autobiography.[14]

Subjects who are not implicated in female-male relations can produce particularly clear accounts of gender arrangements. Coming out stories can be read as narratives of women exiting from patriarchy (Zimmerman 1983, 1984, 1990). In addition, lesbian narratives illuminate relations between women that are obscured when women are separated from each other and grouped into heterosexual pairs. For example, female communities and female linkages between generations, both invisible from the perspective of patriarchy, are repeatedly documented in lesbian writing.[15] Other aspects of women's experience that are routinely understated in the "generic" literature include women's multiple identities and the occurrence of bonding across categories. Dialogues between women are rare in the official discourse that defines "knowledge" and shapes the disciplines (Bulkin et al. 1988).

The diversity of women would seem to be a fact that is impervious to essentialist or other distorting constructions. Women are differently located in streams of experience that are structured by class, by race, by age, by sexuality. We have lived in different polities, different centuries and indeed, in different history. We have lived singular, married, indentured, enslaved; in religious communities, lesbian communities, utopian communities; in concubinage, in families, in prisons. These differences can divide us, or can be manipulated so as to divide us.

The personal remains political: today the inscription and interpretation of women's personal narratives is the focus of controversy centered on difference. Thinkers and writers who have explored the deep commonalities in women's experience have been attacked for "essentialism," for proposing or seeking universals in women's experience.[16] Such formulations are read as denying or invalidating diversity. But writers have rarely claimed that commonalities among women negate or override the specifics of multiple identity. Rather, writers accused of universalizing may simply be taking for granted a feminist discourse that allows them to hear diversity and expect complexity.[17] The controversy can, however, direct us to the importance of how we read, as well as write. Reading individual lives provides a correction to the tendencies toward abstraction and generalization in the scholarly literature, but awareness of diversity must be part of the reading. Part of the narrator's task is to situate the subject in the structures of her society. Situating the subject recontextualizes sex, race and class. The reader and narrator of women's lives must similarly situate themselves. Beyond that, there remains the task of writing diversity. Inventorying the diversity of women is not a practical project. Rather, in writing diversity the goal must be to invoke a discourse spacious enough to include voices from a vast range of experiences and leave room for future comings-to-voice.

In telling women's lives, writing diversity has its own history. At an earlier stage in the development of feminist discourse, North American writers were unself-conscious about the cultural assumptions they brought to the study of women's lives. They have been criticized for being color-blind, and classist in their premise of classlessness. The corrective for these limitations has come from three sources: from critique by women of color, from the voices of women of color writing as subjects, and from the reflexivity of Euro American women writing as narrators. Writing by women of color has contributed to the situating of Euro-American women writers, marking the limits of their work and stripping it of unwarranted generalization.[18] The discourse gained complexity when women of color talked back to the narrator (Gluck and Patai 1991).[19] Other narrators talk back to the Euro-American reader.[20] The discourse expands further as women of color continue to write as subject and as narrator.[21]

The diversity of women writing has expanded the discourse still further as they put narrative to new uses. Writers combining subject and narrator roles have begun to tell the story of a relationship, a group, a social category of which they are a part. Sociologist Joyce Ladner (1972), positioning herself as a black woman, tells the adaptations of young black women from urban housing projects. Lois Benjamin (1991) recounts how racism affects the lives of successful African American adults. Joann Faung Jean Lee (1991) presents short life histories of Asian Americans of many origins and generations. James Diego Vigil situates life histories of Latino street gang members in the essential context of group membership and group identity (1988). Adeola James (1990) brings together first-person narratives of women writers from diverse African countries: within the multivalent rubric of a continent, the particularity of individuals within peoples can be heard. Helen Codere attempts to create a portrait of an entire country, Burundi, through a group of autobiographies (1973). Kath Weston uses coming out narratives of lesbians and gay men to illuminate the way family ties are negotiated (1991). Catherine Reissman uses divorce narratives to reveal how social relations of courtship and marriage are constructed differently for women and men (1990).

Women are so diverse, and live in such varied cultural, racial, and economic circumstances, that we cannot pretend to speak in a single voice. By listening to a plurality of voices in different corners of the planet and across centuries we strengthen our ability to resist demeaning power structures without risk of being coopted (Lionnet 1989). It is in this spirit that this study includes the voices of women who have lived in different countries and different centuries, and who occupy social locations that are separated in terms of race and class. I make no attempt to tame or smooth over the diversity of women's self-writing. I do not seek to create a single narrative. On the contrary, the picture becomes more complex as we add the diversity of narrators to the diversity of subjects.[22] I aimed to create a mosaic of women's voices, in the hope that the reader will carry forward the sound of a multitude that interrogates the established traditions and invites diverse narrators.

Dilemmas of Female Autobiography

Most lives that are chronicled in history, anthropology, sociology, or political science fail to reflect women's experience. Autobiography and biography tend to catalogue Great Lives of Great Men. The life history tradition in sociology has included few women. Women's lives are less rare in ethnographic life history, but they are portrayed in stereotyped ways. The relative neglect of women's first-person accounts is a fundamental problem of the autobiographical tradition today.

The collective history of women's lives is largely lost to the tradition of autobiography. One widely accepted history of autobiography begins with St. Augustine, and progresses through a canon defined by Jean Jacques Rousseau, Henry James, and Benjamin Franklin (Sayre 1964). If we accept this history we remain ignorant of "Lady Sarashina," a Japanese woman of the Heian period, whose book survives from the eleventh century. We overlook Margaret Cavendish and Dame Julian, two early English autobiographers. We fail to consider slave narratives, oral histories, and the *testimonio* of Domitila, a Bolivian tin-miner's wife (Barrios de Chungara 1977). The male canon has no place for Carolina de Jesus' moving account of her life in a Brazilian *favela* (slum); no niche for the poet alta's attempt to write the life she was living as a welfare mother. It does not recognize the value of lesbian "coming out stories."

A second dilemma of autobiography relates to unorthodoxy of form. Many women have neither the time nor the skills to write contemporaneous accounts of their lives. Few women can command the conditions required by the conventional autobiographical subject: leisure, privacy, and "a room of one's own." Consequently women's self-writing rarely takes the form of standard autobiography.[23] Some women's lives are told only in letters to family and intimates, and survive unnoticed in family archives. Today, oral history and ethnographic life history bring into existence narratives that would never otherwise have been written. These factors militate toward a diversity and eccentricity of form that create problems for women autobiographers.

When an individual positions herself as subject she confronts the tradition of autobiography, and distinctive expectations come into play. The tradition exerts pressure on the subject to tell her life a certain way; the norms are shaped to male lives. If the subject has a public life, her autobiography must focus on that; if she has visible work, she is expected to emphasize that and suppress the account of her daily work at home.[24] Tradition requires the autobiographical subject to see herself as someone special, and her life as exceptional. This kind of public assertion is difficult and uncomfortable for many women. A woman may wish to record her life, yet shrink from the presumption that implies.[25]

The norms defining the autobiographical subject are clear enough. However a "double standard" (or double bind) applies to the female subject in autobiography, biography, and life history. She must qualify for inclusion in the list of notable men, but she must also prove herself as a female.[26] Her qualifications for each disqualify her for the other.

The relation between the female subject and the autobiographical tradition is thus marked by constraint. Much of her unease stems from the character of the genre. In the next chapter we examine the puzzling nature of a genre that paradoxically effaces and silences women's experience while appearing to transcend gender.

2

Gender and Genre

. . . . the circle of those present
draws upon the work
of those speaking from the past
and builds it up
to project it
into the future.

—Dorothy Smith (1979, 137)

Some theoretical and critical work on autobiography reads as
though the autobiographical impulse translates unproblematically into
action, with the text emerging automatically. Upon inspection, such
work without exception assumes a male subject. To invest oneself with
historical significance, to claim the attention of the reading public, to follow the model of previous notable lives—all are positionings more easily
attained by male than female subjects. The interlocking prerogatives of
maleness and subject-ness facilitate the connections between the self and
history, man and society. Women's trepidation about committing themselves to writing autobiography has everything to do with the unacknowledged masculinity of the genre. In this chapter I examine autobiography as a discourse of institutionalized androcentrism. In order to do
this, I must first explore the nature of genre, and then how masculinity
came to be embedded in the lineaments of genre.

The established traditions of scholarship tend to rely upon written
texts to the exclusion of other forms of expression. Texts are classified by
genre, and forms of expression are ranked hierarchically. Each genre is a
social construction, continuously shaped by its own conventions. Genres
exert force by means of their institutional and normative status. Genres
are by their nature conservative. They represent established conventions,
anchored in a discursive community, that help define "what is permitted

a writer and expected of a reader" (Bruss 1976). Concrete mechanisms of genre routinely reproduce the androcentric discourse from year to year, from generation to generation. Such mechanisms—the canon, its gatekeepers, and the related control of publication and access to posterity—act as filters for inclusion and exclusion. From a sociological perspective, genres have the function of social control, limiting the range of acceptable behavior and invoking the possibility of sanction. Further, they serve to link men's lives with the ongoing literary tradition that perpetuates the formulae and indeed, legitimizes exemplary lives.

In the case of autobiography, the genre consists of rules for transforming the life as lived into the literary form called autobiography.[1] These rules create an apparently generic subject and a generic tradition of autobiography. These processes can be described in sex-neutral terms; but I will show that the seeming gender neutrality of genre masks a double-distilled masculinity that impedes the inclusion of women. The particular is made generic and the generic universal by means of processes of abstraction and generalization.

Framing an autobiography means relinquishing the particularity of the life and merging with the genre. Shaping a life into an autobiography evokes earlier texts and the readers who controlled their selection. A process of matching and shaping connects the subject's writing with the tradition in print. In this way the subject and his readers are parties to an autobiographical pact: they agree to assume a correspondence between the life and the Life.[2] Genre, with its power of convention, implicates all the parties to life-telling in the transformative processes of abstraction and generalization. The subject transforms her life, the reader relies upon the autobiographical account for knowledge of the subject, and the critic magnifies commonalities and "universal themes" found in the text. In the case of women's autobiography the autobiographical pact is more complex than has previously been supposed, for different pacts may govern the subject's relationships with her common reader and her critic/reader.

In the first transformation, the male individual is transmuted into the generic subject. The particularity of sex is traded for claims of worth and affirmations of continuity with the tradition. The subject consults his culture's storehouse of narratives and shapes his writing accordingly. A second transformation, from generic to universal, requires the essential agency of a critic. He officially brokers the connection with the tradition and publicly vouches for the worth of the text.

In scholarly genres, the selected masterworks that comprise the canon are commonly characterized in terms of universal value or significance. In fact, however, the established traditions are circumscribed by masculinity. They are created by male critics and scholars who cite works by men that chronicle events and issues of concern to men. Far from being universal, this is a parochial literature. The presumption of critical objectivity enhances the perception of universality in a particularly potent way. For this reason it is relevant, in examining how genre works, to read criticism for gender.

The universalizing dynamic cements a link among the male subject, male culture, and patriarchy. The critical claim to universal value cloaks the sense of connection based on shared masculinity. The "universality" of the generic subject masks the masculine nature of his experience, and gender goes underground. The denial of affinity, in turn, permits the masculinity of the tradition to remain unanalyzed. Consequently gender is not problematized, nor difference.

The substitution of the autobiographical subject for the individual and the generic for the particular have consequences for reading and writing women's lives. When masculine experience defines the norm, while at the same time gender is disavowed, work that reflects women's experience is doubly stigmatized. When we as readers accept the conventions of generic autobiography, we are giving permission for the generic and autobiographical subject to be used interchangeably. We give our consent to the universalization of male experience.

This concentration of male subjects and male critics gives a masculine cast to the canon of autobiography. However, autobiography is masculine in a second sense as well. An underlying dynamic of gender shapes literary genres, as it does other institutional forms. Gender scripts at the societal level are linked at a deeper level with masculine personality, and with the scholarly genres in which men reflect themselves to each other. In research on masculine personality, separation is equated with independence, maturity, integrity, and identity. In turn, the characteristic elements of the male autobiography bear a remarkable correspondence to the male sex role script, valorizing significance, objectivity, and distance (Juhasz 1980, 222).[3] The life is transformed into autobiography following separative principles that mirror masculine culture. What is not acknowledged is that these are masculine rules for shaping a male genus out of men's lives. What the reader encounters is a canon in which exemplary men become the model and standard for each other.

Telling Men's Lives: The Making of a Genre

The androcentric tradition of autobiography was untroubled by gender until 1980. In that year Estelle Jelinek disturbed the smooth surface of generic autobiography by contrasting male autobiography with female autobiography. The recognition of gender in autobiography cast a new light on the difficulties women have in inscribing themselves in the genre (Jelinek 1980; Neuman 1991). Most often, the critic/reader is implicitly asking how well women's narratives conform to male autobiography. The common features of men's autobiographies—pattern, destination, a "significant" (public) life, solitariness, "universal" themes, and the suppression of the personal—become the criteria for evaluating women's narratives. Consequently, emphasis on these themes contributes to the invisibility of women's narratives.

The subject constructs his autobiography by imposing pattern upon his life. Northrop Frye associates the issue of selectivity with that of agency in autobiography, which is

> inspired by a fictitious impulse to select only those events and experiences in the writer's life that go to build an integrated pattern. (1957, 307)

Frye emphasizes a selectivity that reflects the maker's will and purpose. He seems to assume that pattern is apparent to the subject, who has no difficulty in actively grasping and using it. The male subject participates in a tradition of authorship and authority that emphasizes his agency,[4] but the requirement of agency may be more problematic for the female subject. Common devices used to order recalled experience include the adoption of a chronological, linear narrative, which is well suited to accounts of career and of war but resonates less readily with women's daily lives.

Pattern in autobiography also involves repertoires of narratives, access to them, and the related question of discourse as a community based on similarity and liking. A pattern is "built" or "discovered" by human agency, for it is a fiction, not a fact. Patterns for telling one's life originate outside one's life experience; they are imported from the cultural storehouse. Differences in individuals' access to cultural "plots" or narratives have implications not only for writing lives but for reading them. "Generic" plots may have the effect of obscuring or effacing the story the female autobiographer has to tell.

Narratives function as sense-making structures, bridging the gap between the subject's mind and that of the reader. Concurrence between these patterns makes for a satisfying experience of reading. Conversely, absence of shared patterns or failure of concurrence creates a dysphoric experience. Sex differences in subjects' accounts or readers' expectations may make for problems of "intelligibility." Texts that employ the accepted narratives of the discourse receive judgments of good form, with intelligibility taken for granted. Writing that employs recognized patterns and narratives engages the reader. Rachel Blau DuPlessis, in *Writing Beyond the Ending* (1985), argues that typical sequences of action and response are "psychically imprinted," making them expected and accepted as we read along in the narrative. DuPlessis contends that established plots are "seductive paths of feeling that are culturally mandated, internally policed, hegemonically poised" (1985, 5). She views narrative structures of this sort as a type of infernal engine that reproduces meanings reflecting the dominant ideology. Ideology integrates collective codes of action and individual desire by combining emotional and cognitive structures.

Nancy Miller, in *The Heroine's Text* (1980), notes that the culture underwrites only certain narrative strategies, an observation that applies to all the traditions of life-telling, including autobiography. Writers who essay "going beyond the ending," who consciously or inadvertently adopt a deviant narrative strategy, may reap negative critical judgments.

A second element of male autobiography is the idea of a destination. Published autobiographies celebrate lives that can be seen to have a destination, often in public life. Reading autobiographies of men, one is struck by a sense of easy and legitimate entrée into the public sphere and a lack of barriers. In writing his life, the male subject can simultaneously position himself in history and lay claim to a public heritage. Linking himself to a reality "larger" than his personal life, the subject magnifies his own significance.[5] The element of destination fits well with the principle of agency in men's autobiographies. The shaping of the account reflects the sense that the subject shaped his life toward its destination. Retrospective narration can enhance the "self-evidence" of this goal.

A third cardinal attribute of male autobiography is the solitary subject. The Hero Quest is a familiar narrative featuring a solitary hero en route to his destiny. The hero's solitariness emphasizes both self-reliance and worthiness; themes of achievement and worth are prominent. The hero in modern literature is little influenced by others. Paradigmatic autobiographies minimize connectedness between the hero and others, hewing to a fiction of individualism.[6]

The suppression of emotion and inner life constitutes a fourth identifying feature of male autobiography. In the distinguished autobiographies of the canon, self-revelation and intimacy are surprisingly absent (Jelinek 1980, 10ff.). Given the gendered nature of autobiography, the subject's excising parts of his self and life is significant, and it is significant which parts they are. Painful and/or intimate happenings are suppressed, as well as romantic attachments, familial relations, and personal idiosyncrasies. In the generic autobiography, the world of emotions, of home, of relationships, the processes of work and struggle in relationships—in short, the "female heart"—are minimized. A striking example is the autobiography of Henry Adams. Following the suicide of his beloved wife Clover, Adams tells his life without any mention of the event or his reactions. This radical exclusion falls within the conventions of generic autobiography. Indeed, the exclusion may be seen as enhancing Adams's attempt to fuse his life with history and achieve objectivity.[7]

Gatekeepers of Autobiography

Gatekeeping for the domain of autobiography is one of the functions of criticism. But Dorothy Smith might have been describing any of the genres when she wrote

> Men attend to and treat as significant what men say and have said.
> The circle of men whose writing and talk have been significant
> to one another
> extends back in time as far as our records reach.
> What men were doing has been relevant to men,
> was written by men
> about men
> for men.
> Men listened and listen to what one another say.
> A tradition is formed,
> traditions form,
> in a discourse of the past with the present.
> The themes, problematics, assumptions, metaphors and images
> form
> as the circle of those present
> draws upon the work
> of those speaking from the past
> and builds it up
> to project it
> into the future.   (1979, 137)

This "circle effect" is in fact a closed circle. It supports the claim to universality by suppressing difference.[8]

The projection of maleness to universality pervades the literature on autobiography. Critics confess an intense interest arising from a sense of connection between themselves and the autobiographical subject. A sense of identification based on similarity is fundamental not only to the critic's motivation but to the development of the genre: a congenial mirroring effect is central to the formation of the canon. Themes of attraction to like and rejection of unlike are manifest in critics' writing about autobiography. The critic's identification with the male subject, his selection of male lives, and his valorization of masculine narratives enhances his work of boundary-maintenance. In the professional literature the deep connections between subject and reader at the level of motivation are sometimes conceded but not theorized. Roy Pascal notes that autobiographer and critic are drawn into the same orbit (1960).

A conscious identification with the subject plays a significant role in the work of James Olney, a senior critic in the field of autobiography. Olney is

> interested in why men write autobiographies, and have written them for centuries, and in why, after the lapse of those centuries, we continue to read them. (1972, vii)

Olney sees the attraction of the reader to autobiography primarily in terms of self-discovery. Of all forms of literature, Olney thinks, autobiography means the most, because of the increased awareness of ourselves that we derive from understanding another's life. The understanding we seek, he emphasizes, is not of the other but of ourselves.[9] From autobiography, he says, we can learn

> what man has been, what forms have proved possible to humanity, which is a knowledge that one seeks with the intention more particularly of knowing what man is. (1972, xx)

Any remaining ambiguity about the universality of the autobiographical canon is resolved by examining the lives Olney chooses to study—all men. In the same passage Olney links the critic/subject, the author/subject, and the generic subject of autobiography.

> And this knowledge is again, to each of us, necessary for a very particular reason: behind the question, "What is man?" lies another, more insistent question—the ultimate and most important question, I should think, for every man: "How shall I live?" (1972, xi)

Olney admits that "literary criticism . . . can be seen as autobiography reluctant to come all the way out of the closet" (1972, 5). Without explicitly addressing the issue of gender, Olney provides a striking illustration of its influence. He cites as formative influences in his own intellectual history a curriculum emphasizing "Concepts of Man [*sic*]" and the reading of (men's) autobiography. In *Metaphors of Self* the generic language that Olney employs does not conceal the masculinity of the text. He defines the focus of his work as "a study of the way experience is transformed into literature . . . a humanistic study of the ways of *men* and the forms taken by *human* consciousness" (1972, 10; italics mine).[10] Underscoring the patriarchal message, Olney proceeds to regale the reader with an extended metaphor of his literary defloration.

Olney's gendered discourse illustrates the powerful hold masculinity has on the genre, and the surprising blindness of respected scholars to issues of gender. This is no personal idiosyncrasy: the prevalence of sex-biased citation practices elevates gender blindness to a failing of the genre—that is, to the level of institutional practice. The role of the critic as the source of authoritative definitions reinforces this solipsistic tradition.

The critic's prerogative of selection, and its implications for building the genre, are illustrated by Robert F. Sayre in a book devoted to the "best and most revealing" of American autobiographies. Sayre chose Benjamin Franklin, Henry Adams, and Henry James as his subjects, individuals who are compelling for Sayre because they "comment profoundly on the American experience." The female reader wonders how profound an understanding can be gained when it leaves out half the American experience. How valuable is a critical assessment for which universalizing "*the* American experience" remains unproblematic?

The production of faulty scholarship is a predictable consequence of the masculinization of autobiography. Estelle Jelinek has documented the neglect of women subjects in the literary tradition of autobiography (1980, 1986). Women are even more scarce as critics than as subjects of autobiography. The critical literature exhibits a pronounced asymmetry: in the literature of any particular period, the reader will find that work on women's autobiography (the "special case") scrupulously reviews the corpus of masculine and "generic" autobiography. However, authors writing about men (the generic or inclusive treatment) fail to cite even the contemporaneous scholarship that deals with women. The one-sidedness apparent in the critical literature on autobiography has a biasing effect

on scholarship. The neglect of women's lives is so entrenched that succeeding generations of scholars assert, counterfactually, that there are no
female autobiographies (e.g., Krupat 1985).[11]

Autobiography as Battleground

Despite the weight of institutionalized masculinity, the accumulating volume of women's autobiography and its critical commentary are putting
increasing pressure on the genre.[12] Innovation in autobiography is incidental to the quest to inscribe the female subject. Invention arises in a
space created by feminist scholarship, with its feminist critique and trans-
disciplinary tradition. Even without explicit critique, however, woman-
centered scholarship appears to have a destabilizing effect on the field.

Woman-authored texts have been rediscovered and celebrated. As the
female counter-canon comes into view, it rises to haunt and reproach the
genre that has excluded it. The feminist critique has problematized the
conventional nature of autobiography as a genre, and the constraints it
imposes on female life-telling. Feminist critics have spotlighted the intersection of gender and genre, viewing autobiography as a generic contract
that reproduces the patrilineage (S. Smith 1987, 82).

In the battleground that is contemporary autobiography, critics are
occupied with a number of issues concerning the conceptualization of the
subject, interpretation of narratives, and the relative restrictiveness or
openness of criteria of form.[13] Contemporary women's autobiography
embodies fundamental challenges to genre and its enforcers, and to the
tradition of a generic subject in literature. The whole system of genres is
being questioned. In their preoccupation with stratification and the politics of inclusion and exclusion, genres mirror the patriarchal gender system (Stanton 1984).

The nature of the autobiographical pact is a perennial site of contestation. The limits of the taken-for-granted notion of the subject have
been extensively discussed (Ryan 1980; Lang 1982; Jay 1987). Addi-
tional reservations arise from woman-centered research. Increasingly,
women writers and critics have turned away from the standard of the
generic subject and from comparisons with it.[14] In seeking ways of rendering the subject that reflect a multidimensional, open-ended, connected, tentative and complex subjectivity, many women writers have become indifferent to the earlier controversies. The forms and subjects of

female autobiography have diverged from the template for generic auto-biography. The self-in-relation and the plural subject contradict the sep-arated self, the solitary subject.[15] An emphasis on multiple themes, on process and on open-endedness conflicts with the simple trajectory and known destination of male autobiography.

The familiar dichotomy of public and private occupies a prominent section of the battleground. Since feminist critique has problematized the polarization of public/private, the "personal" quality of women's narra-tives invites reinterpretation.[16] This reversal requires a more complex reading of women's narratives, raising the question of critics' familiarity with female narratives and feminine codes of self-representation.

Critics also diverge on issues of form: should a personal narrative be lopped and chopped, shaven and shorn to fit the Procrustean bed of genre, or should the form be expanded to encompass the accounts that exist?[17] Critics' positions on these questions are determined, at least in part, by how well traditional forms have served them.[18] A number of women writers and critics are consciously advocating new forms shaped to the complexity of women's lives (see, e.g., Kolodny 1980c; Juhasz 1980). Some writers explicitly reject the dominant conventions of auto-biography (Jelinek 1980) and narrative. A major point of contestation concerns how "messy" autobiography is or should be.[19] Messiness ver-sus control is a trope for concern about inclusion and exclusion. Some critics suspect that women and other outsiders may be drawn to this genre precisely because of its messiness (Olney 1980).

Given the territorial nature of defined genres and disciplines, argu-ments about form are often about defending boundaries and the author-ity of critics. In contemporary autobiography,

> Here all sorts of generic boundaries *and even lines dividing discipline from discipline* are simply wiped away, and we often cannot tell whether we should call something a novel, a poem, a critical dissertation, or an auto-biography. (Olney 1980, 4; italics mine)

The genre of autobiography has historically privileged some self-referen-tial accounts and excluded others.[20] Currently, white male critics are being forced to do battle on their own turf. In the contemporary battle-ground of genre, it is significant that the ranks of critics have themselves been breached, and that members of previously excluded groups are now wielding the power of critical judgment.

The politics of publication and posterity are apparent in the history of published autobiographies of women. Early works of autobiography have been "disappeared," permitting male scholars to assert their nonexistence. Some of the most exemplary autobiographical works of women have been known to prior ages, and have only become "invisible" in our own time. For example, the journal of a Heian lady known to us as "Lady Sarashina" has been the subject of scholarly discussion since the eleventh century, but many contemporary authorities fail to mention it.[21] The autobiography of Margaret Cavendish, Duchess of Newcastle, one of the earliest in the English language, has been similarly submerged. And few authors can have been discovered as often as Christine de Pisan.[22]

The impression that a women's autobiographical tradition does not exist is readily dispelled.[23] Activity in women's history, in literature, and in the social sciences has, over the past twenty years, reversed the impression of absence, and pointed to an important lesson. Genre has limited our access to the female subject (and hers to us). Knowing women's lives thus requires a revisionist method of reading that is open to a broader range of narratives.

Conclusion

In analyzing autobiography I have emphasized its character of institutionalized masculinity. The generic/male subject nests within a masculine canon built upon commentary from male critics. Male experience is foundational. Correlatively, in almost all cases males are selected to typify knowledge, culture, and history.[24] A mutual magnification operates among these elements that acts to naturalize the hegemony of the male subject and the male canon. Female subjects are correspondingly diminished. The same critical processes that elevate the male subject disadvantage the female.

The female autobiographer, staring into the mouth of the canon, confronts a number of distinct difficulties. First, the invisibility of women's autobiography is an impediment to women's self-writing.[25] Women's writing does not appear in the canon, is not held out to aspiring writers as exemplary literature, is not manifest as the standard to be met or extended. As Joanna Russ observes, women denied access to the feminine literary tradition carry the heavy burden of having to reinvent it in every generation (1983, 63ff.). A second, related difficulty is the painful perception that there have been no "great" women writers.[26] A third is that women's writing is pushed to the periphery of every tradition, and its content devalued.

The proactive effects of the masculine tradition constitute a fourth problem: male models cast an inescapable shadow over women considering, attempting, or struggling to write their own lives. Women who seek to emulate those models are like Cinderella's stepsisters, lopping off their toes to fit into the glass slipper. Fifthly, female autobiographers suffer penalties at the hands of male critics. The evaluation of women's autobiography, and its possibilities for publication and of inclusion in the canon are affected by its failure to fit the gendered template of the genre.

A sixth consequence of masculinized autobiography is the perpetuation of faulty scholarship. Biased citation practices in favor of male autobiography ensure that work on women fails to become more acceptable over time, and young scholars interested in telling women's lives are encouraged to seek other topics.[27] The promulgation of the error of male bias by authorities blinds all but the most independent-minded scholars, and the reliance of scholars on authority makes the correction of error highly unlikely. Writing her life propels the female subject into the realm of genre with all its institutional ramifications. Her "personal" narrative is inextricably bound up with the dynamics of power: through her "private" writing the female subject engages the forces of patriarchy. As we take up women's autobiographical impulse and the forms of autogynographical narratives in the chapters to come, we recognize that they are framed by the gendered arrangements of institutional autobiography. Women's trepidation about committing themselves to writing autobiography reflects the masculinity of the tradition, in which barriers to difference are continuously reinforced through the routine operation of the mechanisms of genre.

3

Scribbling Women

To create seemed to me such an assertion of the strongest part of
me that I would no longer be able to give all those I love the feeling
of their being stronger, and they would love me less.

—Anaïs Nin (in Goulianos 1974, 302)

Female autobiography is not autobiography as usual. Women's
self-writing is animated by the tension between external control of women
and the assertion of female subjectivity, a tension visible in women's personal narratives of whatever form. For the woman autobiographer, the
process of self-discovery is accompanied by a sense of contestation and
risk. Autobiographical strategies employed by women convey some degree
of challenge to the all-male tradition of autobiography and often a feeling
of threat. Women subjects anticipate difficulty in being "read" or "heard"
by a male audience. And women writing their lives for a public cannot escape the terrors and penalties of trespassing on male turf. Women subjects
are at risk because the requirements of autobiography and the requirements of femininity are at odds. Patricia Meyer Spacks states

The propriety of feminine autobiography is dubious. Autobiography is
self-display, opposed to the female virtues of modesty and concealment.

(1972, 249)

Sidonie Smith (1987) observes that feminine reputation or virtue is
founded upon silence. Women's life and its particulars are shrouded in silence. Metaphors of space and place also help to define female autobiography as trespass. In history's scheme the good woman is defined by her
absence. She does not assert herself in public speech, nor is she talked
about by others. Public spaces are for business, politics, and the rigors of
citizenship; women's sphere is out of sight and sound. The public/private

polarity is a fundamental trope for the gender system. Writing a woman's life involves a pointed inversion of the conventional relations of public and private, and symbolizes a fundamental challenge to gender relations defined in these terms.

These contradictions provide the context for female autobiography. So recording her life plunges the woman subject into a dilemma that is not of her making. The constraints operating on women's space and women's voices are reflected in the narratives women create. In thinking about women's autobiography, therefore, the autobiographical impulse cannot be separated from the assessment of external and social constraints on women's self-writing. In this chapter, I focus on the sources and the vicissitudes of the autobiographical impulse in women.

Varieties of Autobiographical Impulse

A major theme of women's self-referential writing is the desire to be known, which springs from many sources. A woman's desire to write her life may be inspired by the desire to document her life, to "make sense" of it, to celebrate it, to assert her unique subjectivity. Personal narrative may be formed by secrecy, the need for catharsis, or the yearning for a reader. It may express solidarity with other women and serve the function of resistance. In many instances, the autobiographical impulse reflects the subject's desire to make contact with others.

One elemental motivation for women's self-referential writings is self-assertion or self-celebration. Sometimes an autobiography reflects a woman's desire to express herself and leave a mark. An individual who takes pleasure in herself, her life, and her subjectivity may seek to extend that subjectivity beyond her lifetime. Sometimes a subject's sheer exuberance demands an audience. One of the earliest autobiographies in English was that of Margaret Cavendish, a seventeenth-century Englishwoman, who did not want to be "a spectator rather than an actor." She explicitly craved fame (and by this she meant posterity):

> I am very ambitious; yet 'tis neither for beauty, wit, titles, wealth, or power, but as they are steps to raise me to Fame's tower, which is to live by remembrance in after-ages. (Spacks 1972, 177)

The diary of Marie Bashkirtseff is another document that celebrates the self. Bashkirtseff, a young painter of Russian birth who lived in Vi-

enna, Nice, and Paris in the nineteenth century, is often cited for the unabashed egoism of her diary. Its subject desired "to conquer time" by
sending a record of a self down through the ages (Moffat and Painter
1975, 47). The destiny Marie imagined for herself included an early
death, fame, and a fascinated posterity. Marie had maintained her diary
from the age of nine. Her retrospective preface, quoted below, was written at age twenty-four, not long before her death from tuberculosis in
1884:

> Of what use were pretense or affectation? Yes, it is evident that I have the
> desire, if not the hope, of living upon this earth by any means in my power.
> If I do not die young I hope to live as a great artist, but if I die young, I in-
> tend to have my journal, which cannot fail to be interesting, published. . . .
>
> If I should not live long enough to become famous, this journal will be
> interesting to the psychologist. The record of a woman's life, written down
> day by day, without any attempt at concealment, as if no one in the world
> were ever to read it, yet with the purpose of being read, is always interest-
> ing; for I am certain that I shall be found sympathetic, and I write down
> everything, everything, everything. Otherwise why should I write? Besides,
> it will very soon be seen that I have concealed nothing.
>
> (Moffat and Painter 1975, 47)

This kind of self-assertion—desiring posterity, claiming that her life has
significance—is often disavowed in women's public utterances, and even
in their private writings. Marie Bashkirtseff is rare in expressing confidence in the positive judgment of future readers. More commonly,
women anticipate censure for autobiographical assertiveness.

A slightly different motivation for writing one's life is the desire to
convey the reality of that life. A major goal of much autobiographical
writing of women is to make a record. Mary Mason has examined some
of the earliest English-language autobiographies, including those of Margaret Cavendish and Margery Kempe.[1] Mason notes that a meticulous
concern with accuracy and verification characterizes both accounts. Of
Kempe Mason says, "In creating her book she was creating her proper
image, in creating her text she was creating her exemplary life." Indeed,
Kempe was "obsess(ed) with getting it right" (1980, 221). Deborah Norris Logan, a member of a distinguished eighteenth-century Pennsylvania
family, created a record for herself and for future generations. In 1815,
at the age of fifty-four, she began a diary that ran to seventeen volumes
and four thousand pages (Barr 1985, 15, 22).

Secrecy is an important theme in many women's narratives. The sub-

ject seeks to be honest and to know herself, but these goals may be proscribed in her life as regulated by society. Much of women's self-writing
originates as the private adjunct to the observable life. The contradiction
between woman's observable life and her subjectivity is managed by a
practice of secrecy. The writing is often meant to remain private, and is
not intended for publication. Women's private writings reveal that their
life as lived is fraught with disingenuousness. The perception of danger
gives rise to defensive subterfuge. In some instances the subject specifies
external sources of threat. In other texts she expresses a conflict that has
been internalized. That which is most honest must not be expressed publicly. Anaïs Nin, the writer and artist, contrasts the accepted falsity of her
outer life with the truth of her diary:

> I only regret that everyone wants to deprive me of the journal, which is the
> only steadfast friend I have. . . . In the journal I am at ease. Playing so many
> roles, dutiful daughter, devoted sister, mistress, protector, my father's new
> found illusion, Henry's needed, all-purpose friend, I had to find one place
> of truth, one dialogue without falsity. This is the role of the diary.
>
> (Nin 1966, ix)[2]

Secrecy, in this kind of writing, has the significance of permitting self-
expression without fear or penalty. An honest account requires a private
and protected means of expression. Without this protection the process
of self-discovery might be too risky. Many autobiographers seek self-in-
sight as a product of self-writing. Their work conveys a passionate commitment to make themselves known, first of all to themselves.[3] In the
context of contradiction and constraint, self-knowledge involves a complex struggle. Self-revelation is not achieved by simply recording one's
personal thoughts. An honest account must be achieved by dint of effort.
It is in this rigorous mood that Marie Bashkirtseff sounds the note of piti-
less honesty as the standard by which autobiography should be judged.
Sophie Tolstoy's (1928) goal of "objectivity" was a parallel aim. And
Florida Scott-Maxwell, an American writer and pyschotherapist, is willing to embrace the dreaded label of selfishness in asserting her interest in
herself:

> But who is it that knows me so well and has to endure me? There is the I
> that has to bear all the other I's and can assess them correctly; and there is
> the I who feels such sick distaste and drunken elation at being itself, all its
> selves, who is even thankful for the opportunity of having been itself, un-
> comfortable as it has been. Is the judging I a separate entity, and who can

this wise I be? It feels higher, greater than I. I fail it, it scorns and rebukes me. Then who is it? I feel like a hierarchy, and perhaps I am one. I am my chief interest because to me I am life. My curiosity, delight, pain tell me about life itself. This makes me a monster of egotism, but that is what I am and have to be, for how else do I know, really know anything? I observe others, but I experience myself.   (1979, 18–19)

Another motive for women's private writings is the immemorial function of catharsis. Fanny Fern[4] urged women to write, for the sake of sanity. Fern felt that the domestic round into which women were locked, and the overlooking of their finer sensibilities in marriage, could lead to madness without the outlet of writing. Fern thought writing would be a safe outlet for thoughts and feelings that could not be heard even by those nearest and dearest to the writer. She felt it was not safe to repress so much, but that men made poor confidants for what women saw in their world (Wood 1971, 18–19).

Anthologists have recognized that self-writing has survival value for women (e.g., Hoffman and Culley 1975). A diary or journal may act as a safety-valve or sanctuary, a vital adjunct to a daily life of constraint and self-restraint. Often women's self-writings are not intended to be read. They may constitute a very personal and private refuge. Marie Bonaparte was a French psychoanalyst and writer who, at the age of seven, wrote a diary in her "secret" language. Incorporating and reflecting upon these childhood writings when in her sixties, after psychoanalysis, she wrote,

in writing them I found unspeakable relief, a supreme catharsis. I fled into an imaginary world, far from this world with its torments, its conflicts and its disappointments. . . . This reflex of taking refuge in writings whenever I have been hurt by life has remained with me. Disappointment or grief, so far from preventing me from working, always drives me irresistibly to seek solace in literary or scientific creation.   (Spacks 1972, 36l)

In this context the secrecy of a woman's self-referential writing may reflect a condition of isolation, if there is no-one in her face-to-face world with whom her thoughts can be shared. This was the condition in which Beatrice Webb[5] found herself by the time she was twenty-six. The only unmarried sister of eight, Beatrice felt isolated from people her own age as she cared for her father. She used her diary for self-communion, a habit that went back to childhood.

It would be curious to discover who it is, to whom one writes in a diary? Possibly to some mysterious personification of one's own identity, to the

Unknown, which lies below the constant change in matter and ideas, constituting the individual at any given moment. This unknown was once my only friend; the being to whom I went for advice and consolation in all the small troubles of a child's life. Well do I remember, as a small thing, sitting under the damp bushes, and brooding over the want of love around me (possibly I could not discern it), and turning in upon myself, and saying, "Thou and I will live alone and if life be unbearable we will die."

(Spacks 1972, 366)

In addition to catharsis, women's secret writings can carry the significance of resistance and potential revenge. Fanny Fern reveals the fantasy of vengeance in predicting the reactions when the secret diary is posthumously read and women's writing accuses the men who ignored or brutalized them.[6] The perceived power of the written word is evident in women's fantasies of revenge by pen, a weapon often officially proscribed for women. The fantasy revenge succeeds through the tactic of breaking down the walls between the personal and the public life of women, and spilling the secret.

A diary or journal can be a refuge not only from private miseries, but from external conditions that systematically oppress women. In her private writings a woman can find not only sanctuary and consolation, but also a foundation for protest. A woman who dares not speak out can still speak up in her secret writings. In private she can oppose, accuse, spurn, revile, curse and threaten, doubt and challenge. She can lay down upon the page hurts she must conceal each day, despair she cannot declare, anger she must dissemble. The secrecy of a woman's self-writings can have a special significance of solidarity with other women. Her writings may be part of the enslaved woman's compact with herself—and with the potential army of allies, other women. In Fanny Fern's thinking, secret writings of women constitute the home base for an underground of resistance (Wood 1971). Sometimes it is only their common fate, and a commitment to making it known, that induces women to risk taking up the pen. The subject sometimes overcomes her ambivalence by affirming a connection with other women. It may be easier for a woman to claim autobiographical significance when her act of assertion is seen as part of a collective commitment. Thus Harriet Jacobs, an escaped slave, makes her life known for the sake of mothers who remain in slavery (Jacobs 1987). Domitila Barrios de Chungara, a Bolivian miner's wife, begins her *testimonio* with these words:

I don't want anyone at any moment to interpret the story I'm about to tell as something that is only personal. Because I think that my life is related to my people. . . . I want to make this clear, because I recognize that there have been people who have done much more than I for the people, but who have died or who haven't had the opportunity to be known. . . . I also want to say that I consider this book the culmination of my work in the International Women's Year Tribunal. . . . Finally, I want to clarify that this account of my personal experience of my people, who are fighting for their liberation—and to whom I owe my existence—well, I want it to reach the poorest people, the people who don't have any money, but who need some orientation, some example which can serve them in their future life. (1977, 15)

The making of a record, no matter how secretly intended, evokes an audience. Subjects who require secrecy and privacy for autobiographical writing nonetheless remain entwined with an imagined reader. Even secret writers entertain the hope of a future audience, and many diarists have flirted with the idea of publication. The subject imagines some reader, one capable of reacting to the narrative and its subject. Sometimes the audience is no more than the self: still, a self that participates in the interrogation of experience, that buffers and anchors the subject in her daily rigors. Very frequently the subject expresses the desire or expectation of making a connection with another through her writing. This yearning reaches beyond the private, daily dialogue with oneself. Many diarists and autobiographers have hoped to find a needed friend in an unknown, future reader. Their self-writings express a yearning to be understood, a hope often pinned to an anonymous stranger.

Most often, the intended audience for women's self-referential writing is other women. Women subjects imagine a female reader. Harriet Jacobs, writing the record of her life as a slave woman, expresses her reliance on her intended reader as confidante in June 1857. She includes events she fears will discredit her in the North. Her confession is made bearable only because she knows it is this trusted ally who will be reading it.

There are some things that I might have made plainer—woman can whisper her cruel wrongs into the ear of a dear friend much easier than she could record them for the world to read. I have placed myself before you to be judged as a woman, to come to you just as I am, a poor slave Mother—not to tell you what I have heard but what I have seen—and what I have suffered—and if there is any sympathy to give—let it be given to the thousands of slave Mothers that are still in bondage. Let it plead for their helpless Children that they may enjoy the same liberties that my Children now enjoy. (Sterling 1984, 81)

Elizabeth Foote Washington was wife to George Washington's nephew Lund. The successive passages from her journals reveal, ever more clearly, the desire for connection with a future reader. Initially she took for granted posterity in the form of daughters. When this posterity was denied her, she turned to thoughts of other relatives, and finally strangers. In time her mundane goal of domestic instruction is supplanted by the desire to be known, to connect with another at the level of unique subjectivity.

The Autobiographer's Dilemma of Silence Versus Trespass

The desire to define one's life, and to document it, has a fundamental attraction. For a woman, however, the autobiographical impulse is on a collision course with decorum. One strategy for skirting trespass is therefore to avoid public self-display and confine oneself to private writing. Letters, diaries, and journals—favorite forms of self-expression for women—make no claim to historical significance. They seem not to trespass on the masculine sphere. They do not thrust their authors before the public eye, nor reek of self-assertion. Yet even in private writings, the fear of censure causes women to practice self-censorship. Elizabeth Foote Washington wrestled with this dilemma, as her journal entries indicate. The autobiographical impulse warred with the limits of respectable femininity. Over time, Elizabeth evolved a justification for her activity. One could claim propriety in writing one's life if its purpose were consistent with or instrumental to an approved feminine role. Thus Elizabeth originally intended her writing to instruct a future daughter in household management and upright living. Yet even here the impulse to subjectivity wars with self-censorship, and yields to an acceptable rationale:

> I once had a thought of being more particular, and to have kept a journal of my life,—but that I could not have done faithfully, without speaking of all the ill treatment I ever met with, and that I did not wish to hand down. Therefore, whatever memorandums I have made in times past, I now shall destroy them all, and let only this manuscript book remain,—because should I have children, and especially daughters, it can be no disadvantage to them for to know something of my general conduct in my family.
>
> (Evans 1975, 346)

The trespass of a female self-writer might be mitigated if she restricted herself to a private audience of family or intimates, a posterity limited to a circle of kin. Anne Bradstreet, a poet of the Massachusetts Bay Colony, wrote a brief autobiography that was intended for a family audience (her children). It was created within the collective consciousness of her family life, and she saw it as part of her sacred duty to her family. In further mitigation, Bradstreet's record was undertaken at the instigation of her son, rather than being self-initiated. Her dedication expressly includes the themes of secrecy and posterity so prevalent in women's autobiographical writing:

> This book by any yet unread
> I leave for you when I am dead,
> That being gone, her you may find
> What was your living mother's mind.
> Make use of what I leave in love
> And God shall bless you from above.
> (Mason 1980, 230)

Yet even in their private writings women feel obliged to defend themselves against charges of egoism and presumption. Thus Elizabeth Foote Washington felt it necessary to deny that self-aggrandizement was the motive for writing her life. Writing in 1792 she says,

> Tis certain I have wrote and copied together a great deal, an abundance I have destroyed. But what I have now I shall keep for my own satisfaction and comfort. Let them that comes after me think what they will, I do not keep them with an ostentatious view. (Evans 1975, 354)

Sometimes the best defense is a good offense. Margaret Cavendish opens her account of her life by addressing those who would "scornfully" put the question, "Why hath this lady writ her life?" She defends by taking the offensive against anticipated "carping tongues" and "malicious censurers." She particularly needed to neutralize the criticism that writing about herself signified an inappropriate overvaluing of herself. The irrepressible Cavendish wrote:

> But I hope my readers will not think me vain for writing my life, since there have been many that have done the like, as Caesar, Ovid and many more, both men and women, and I know no reason I may not do it as well as they.
> (Spacks 1972, 249)

It is doubtful whether Cavendish succeeded in disarming her critics by aligning herself with Ovid and Caesar. Indeed, Cavendish violates the conventions of women's self-writing by comparing herself with male subjects.

Familial and personal purposes can be melded in the justification of self-writing. Thus Margaret Cavendish, who has asserted the intrinsic value of her life, also voices a practical motivation for telling her life. Given the realities of social arrangements in which she lived (particularly marriage), her existence might well be obscured and her posterity denied if she failed to write her life. The hope of not being effaced prompted Margaret Cavendish to conclude her twenty-four-page autobiography thus:

> Neither did I intend this piece for to delight, but to divulge; not to please the fancy, but to tell the truth, lest afterages should mistake, in not knowing I was daughter to one Master Lucas of St. Johns, near Colchester, in Essex, second wife to the Lord Marquis of Newcastle; for my Lord having had two wives, I might easily have been mistaken, especially if I should die and my Lord marry again. (Spacks 1972, 245)

Apart from her respectable pedagogical aims, Elizabeth Foote Washington had an interest in her own subjectivity. Writing in 1792, she expresses partiality for a particular volume of her journal precisely because it is steeped in her own subjectivity:

> Somehow I feel a greater desire to have had some one to have given this book to, than I do any of the other. I suppose the reason is because this book is all my own thoughts and reflections. Though I am sensible there is great imperfections in the book. Yet I am desirous some one should have it—oh the weakness of human nature is great. But as I do not expect to have children now, if I leave this book behind me after my death, think I ought before that happens to write it over again, to correct what errors there may be in the diction of it—but whether I shall ever have the time, I cannot say. What pleasure a child would have taken in reading this after their mother was gone—but let me be dumb, and not say another word. (Evans 1975, 357)

Narrative Strategies for Telling Women's Lives

It is easy to see why self-expression in a woman requires strategic calculation: how to enjoy the pleasures of self-expression while avoiding the penalties for self-assertion. So much are women conscious of threat and punishment that this calculus influences the form of their autobiographical writing. Women have sought to encompass the contradiction between trespass and silence by employing a variety of narrative and stylistic stratagems. They have avoided certain audiences and selected others; they have censored their own writings; they have employed disguises, apologies, and disclaimers.

My reading of women's self-referential writings reveals at least three narrative strategies which serve as means of telling one's life in a context of threat. Three strategies used in first-person accounts of women's lives are "telling it slant," "telling it straight," and "telling it messy." Differing dynamics of form, content, and the relationship between them can be seen in the three approaches. Any one writer may employ any or all of them.[7]

Anticipating a hostile critical establishment and an unreceptive literary tradition, a female subject may adopt a "necessary indirection" in her writing (Spacks 1972). Emily Dickinson articulates this strategy, in a poem that speaks to a female audience.

> Tell all the truth but tell it slant
> Success in circuit lies
> Too bright for our infirm Delight
> The truth's superb surprise
> As lightening to the Children eased
> With explanation kind
> The truth must dazzle gradually
> Or every man be blind—
>
> (1935, 1129)

This poem capsulizes a tension in women's self-expression, one that informs Adrienne Rich's (1979) and Tillie Olsen's (1978) writing among others.[8] Women readers react to the poem with instant comprehension. The idea of "telling it slant" relates to the social constraints under which communication takes place. From a sociological point of view, "telling it slant" comprises communicative behavior of a group in a less powerful position vis-à-vis a dominant group (G. Mitchell 1984).

Negation of self, denial of affect, loyalty oaths, and disclaimers of all descriptions—all are ways of "telling it slant," ways by which the female subject seeks to avoid a head-on confrontation with male prerogative. In discussing female traditions of Victorian autobiography, Deborah Nord notes the predilection of women for the humbler memoir, in contrast to the assertive autobiography, detailing the facts of a life without presuming to assert a thematic coherence. Female memoirs retain a discursive, episodic, "unstructured" character which on the one hand corresponds to the daily experience of women's lives, and on the other deviates from the pattern of the inspirational male autobiography (Nord 1985). In this form the subject's narrative does not claim significance for her person, and does not assert a link with History-with-a-Capital-H. Such memoirs appear to skirt the dangerous territory of tabooed self-assertion.[9] Spacks identifies a dampening of assertion in the public women she studied: Eleanor Roosevelt, Golda Meir, Dorothy Day, Emma Goldman, Emmeline Pankhurst. For the most part these women do not admit to taking pleasure in their notable power, ability, and effectiveness. Emma Goldman is the exception; she rejoices in her public successes (but accepts punishing relationships in her private life).

Another way of "telling it slant" is to write fiction rather than autobiography. Some critics have suggested that a woman can tell her life more truthfully in fiction than in autobiography (Huf 1983, 13). Nord suggests that writers of fiction can escape some of the constraints of memoir. The author can avoid accusations of intellectual presumption, unfeminine egotism, and lack of modesty while allowing her female characters to grapple with conflicts proscribed by convention. Writing fiction permits novelists to do this without being identified with and condemned for their characters' unconventionality. Just so, Anaïs Nin expresses a sense of freedom from constraint in using herself as a subject for fiction:

> I was more at ease with myself as a character because it is easier to excavate on one's own property. I could be used for all experiences, was protean, unlimited.
> (Goulianos 1974, 303)

Maxine Hong Kingston, June Arnold, and Audre Lord pursue autobiographical projects in the guise of fiction. Kate Millett's use of fictional forms allows her to violate many conventions of generic autobiography.[10]

Use of denials and disclaimers is another means of "telling it slant." Since Fanny Fern, American women writers have prefaced their work with self-deprecating disclaimers. Early American women in print disclaimed any intention to compete with men, or to pretend to literature. Caroline Lee Hentz, a popular nineteenth-century southern novelist, disavows all literary pretension, all skill, intention, or intellectual effort:

Book! Am I writing a book? No, indeed! This is only a record of my heart's life, written at random and carelessly thrown aside, sheet after sheet, sibylline leaves from the great book of fate. The wind may blow them away, a spark consume them. I may myself commit them to the flames. I am tempted to do so at just this moment.   (1856, 69)

Where women cannot deny their use of the pen, they can disavow its significance, via trivializing language if need be. Margaret Cavendish executes a classic maneuver in contrasting her "scribbling" with the duke's "writing":

Also *he creates himself with his pen*, writing what his wit dictates to him, but I pass my time rather with *scribbling* than with writing, with words than wit.   (Spacks 1972, 248; italics mine)

Another means of disavowal is to minimize the power of the connection between the subject and her female reader. Women writers have sometimes laid claim only to a readership that they define as peripheral and negligible (Marcus 1988). Finally, women defend by undoing, censoring what they have written. Elizabeth Foote Washington engaged in self-censorship; over time she not only modified the purpose of her writing, but edited it severely. She destroyed much of her record, and concealed unacceptable content. Her action reflects her sensitivity to readers' expectations as to seemly female behavior. Deborah Norris Logan[11] also anticipated a censorious future reader. In later life she edited out passages in her journal that were too gossipy, and apologizes to a future reader for some of her actions.

The assertion of subjectivity can also be camouflaged by means of subject positioning. Female autobiography can be disguised by concealing it within or around another type of narrative. Authors of religious memoirs, for example, were protected from accusations of presumption, since their purpose was to draw attention to the Creator and not their humble selves. Another conventional disguise placed a cause or a voyage at the center, weaving an incidental female life into the border. Indeed, this is a common strategy for telling the lives of women who were public figures. Female memoirs are sometimes disguised as biographies of a husband, where the female subject positions herself as appendix or appendage. Beatrice Webb and Elizabeth Barrett Browning both wrote their autobiographies and appended them to their husbands' biographies. Carobeth Laird wrote an autobiography with the ostensible purpose of providing a memoir of her marriages (Kamel 1992). Margaret Cavendish limns her own portrait in a double image of self and husband. Cavendish had a strong impulse to assert her own ego, and an equally strong motive to observe sexual proprieties. Her solution to this conflict was to double her autobiography and then double it again. Cavendish created a double portrait when she wrote a biography of her husband the duke, and appended her own (written ten years before she wrote that of her husband).[12]

When women's fears counsel a need for indirection, one response is "telling it slant." As a strategy, "telling it slant" assumes that male and female readers respond differently to this form of narrative camouflage.

A narrative strategy of "telling it messy" may offer a second means of concealment from the eyes of male critics. Accounts of women's lives state baldly that women's lives are messy: they involve dirt, diapers, infections, blood, repetitive labor, interruptions, lack of closure, obligations, intensity, vigilance, minutiae. Women's nonlinear experience of time cannot be accommodated by a directed trajectory. Equally, women's web of relationships cannot be contained within the outline of the solitary hero of autobiography. Women's work is characterized by endless process with no product, a diffuse and open organization, and a lack of unilateral control.

Over a lifetime and in the daily routines, women's lives tend to show a loose, episodic structure that reflects the ways in which their lives are organized and determined externally to them and the situations they order and control (D. Smith 1987, 152).

"Messy" accounts strive to recreate this consciousness. However, "messiness" creates problems for the male critic/reader. From the critic's point of view, it is not only diapers that are messy. Emotions, emotional interactions, and the expression of feelings can also be "messy." Rules of male socialization and the protocol of literary criticism proscribe such disorder. As a consequence, messy narratives will be discounted. Messy accounts occurring outside literary criticism suffer the same fate as messy memoirs. Carol Gilligan notes that women's morality, with its relativism and faithfulness to context, appears to men as diffuse and inconclusive, vague (and "messy"). Critics of women's plays complain about the lack of plot and loose, episodic structure. Women's poetry is characterized as open, intimate, particular, involved, engaged, committed. The form of the poetry is explicitly seen as an extension of the self.

Feminist social scientists find domestic labor and everyday life compelling topics, while male social scientists generally shy away from them. Social scientists' subject-positioning by gender gives rise to opposing evaluations of significance. Again, "messy" accounts require a particular reading ability, and unite the subject and reader who share this ability, excluding the reader who cannot penetrate its meaning.

A third narrative strategy is "telling it straight." Feminist scholars in many disciplines have become aware of a "line of fault," a discontinuity between women's experience and the established knowledge of their fields. That knowledge often contains distorted images of women. Feminist critique of renderings of women's lives, whether in social science or literature, has given rise to the desire to set the record straight, to correct the distortions, and to create a new, valid body of work. Increasingly, feminist scholars have come to see that an unavoidable part of setting the record straight is exposing the role of their own disciplines in discrediting woman-centered work (e.g., Showalter 1985; D. Smith 1979, 1987). "Telling it straight" thus requires "straightening," the corrective of feminist analysis. One method for "straightening" is simply to move women's experience from the periphery to the center. Woman-centered research of the past two decades has provided a new foundation for scholarly literatures. Telling women's lives is an essential part of this foundation.[13] In addition, today's feminist scholarship claims a freedom from the conventions of androcentric scholarship. A critique of androcentrism is part of feminist scholarship in many scholarly disciplines.

Each of the narrative strategies described here relies upon a sympathetic readership that is capable of reading these female dialects. The ongoing development of the female discourse continually knits reading and writing together, strengthening the link between subject and reader. This continued interaction in turn sustains the female self-referential tradition. The recursive relationship between female author and female reader, linked by a distinct literature, seems to promise safety from the critic's "arrogant eye" (M. Frye 1985).

Subject and Reader in Women's Autobiography

Women's autobiography begins with the subject, but soon inevitably encounters her readers. It is impossible to ignore the partnership of subject and reader when speaking of women's autobiography. The subject relies on her reader to validate the experience she struggles to express. She can achieve her goal of being known only when the reader engages with her. The reader is essential for the completion of the subject's communicative act.[14]

Self-writers employ narrative strategies that actively evoke their readers.

Texts written in code require a particular strategy of reading; the subject's facility at "telling it slant" is met by the reader's ability to read on the slant. Feminist literary critics have suggested that women writers and readers share a common code, based on a separate literature. Narrative strategies of "telling it slant" and "telling it messy" may be a means of communication in code.[15] Subtexts embedded in the ostensible narrative are perhaps more readily discerned by the "resisting reader" than by male literary critics. Male readers will not often be able to read a woman's text in the way that women do. Insofar as communication between women may deal with content that is excluded from the male canon it may be safe from criticism as well. Content dealing with women's daily work, with connection and with emotion-work provide rich vocabularies for speaking in code. These elements may act to maintain the "unintelligibility" of women's self-referential writing.[16] To the extent that women's writing constitutes a self-referential canon that remains outside the awareness of the critical establishment, reciprocation of reading and writing can continue immune from attack.

A second aspect of readership is relevant to the shaping of women's self-writing. As a reader the subject may seek specifically female models for telling her life. Female readers search literature for the inscription of a female destiny that is heroic, that inspires them, that certifies a life of worth (Brownstein 1982, xxiv). Thus women read novels in search of heroines: a woman who is attractive and powerful and significant, someone whose life is worth writing about. The same search leads women to read autobiographies and biographies. The woman reader seeks a world that revolves around her, that makes being the way she is make sense. The autobiographical subject, much as her reader, needs access to women's first-person accounts, and for the same reasons.

A third aspect of readership links the themes of this chapter with those of the next. Women's autobiographies express a powerful ambivalence about their future readership, reflecting posterity's two faces. The smiling face represents the reader who will understand her and affirm her subjectivity, the frowning face the critic who will ridicule her writing and consign her subjectivity to oblivion.[17] Jane Marcus writes about celebrated women who knew about oblivion as a destination for great women. They knew that fame in their lifetimes would not protect them against future obscurity. Quite consciously they resorted to publishing their memoirs as a "hedge against certain deflation of their reputations" (Marcus 1988, 119).

Autogynography

For a number of women, avoiding trespass or escaping detection are not options. In committing herself to a formal autobiography, a story of self written with the intent of dissemination, the female subject makes a claim of significance that cannot be misunderstood. When the female subject defines herself she overruns the restriction of women to private life and private space. The public authority of autobiography means claiming a new space for the female subject. Writing her autobiography positions the female self in the public sphere, in history.[18]

For these reasons Domna Stanton has created the term "autogynography" to refer to what is involved in a woman's writing her life. Stanton defines autogynography as an act of self-assertion that is essential to the denial and reversal of the status assigned to women under patriarchy.[19] In patriarchal writing the male is subject; the female is the inessential other. Women's autobiography represents a movement away from the subject-positioning of a woman. Therefore only autogynography creates the female subject. Creating the subject, an autograph gives the female "I" substance through the inscription of an interior and an anterior. It is a conquest of identity through writing (Stanton 1984). Existing scholarship has largely excluded such entry.

Female autobiography decenters the traditional subject and contests the hegemonic discourse. A number of scholars have pointed out that the idea of subject and its implied individualism involves an exclusively masculine tradition (e.g., Marcus 1988). Taking up the pen signifies dominance. Gilbert and Gubar (1979) have analyzed the way in which writing symbolizes male patrimony.

Conclusion

This chapter began by examining the sources of women's autobiographical impulse, and the narrative strategies subjects adopt in telling their lives. But women do not write their lives in a vacuum. Women's self-writing germinates and takes its shape in a social and symbolic world that fails to welcome female subjectivity. For women, the autobiographical act involves encounter with an alien masculine world and conscious transgression against norms of female conduct. The invisibility of women creates the problem of "voice." Themes of silence and transgression are pervasive. The autogynographic subject operates in a discursive context where heroism, authority, wisdom are all solely masculine virtues. Doubts and division assail a woman seeking to tell her own life, who has as models only male autobiographies, and who is challenged to resonate with male history, theology, social theory, and/or philosophy.

Achieving a woman-centered understanding is a prequisite for reading women's lives.[20] New narratives and new ways of reading are called for. These strategies rely on a different repertoire of plots, different conceptions of the subject, and different forms of narrative. We turn next to a consideration of the distinctive content that women writing about their lives seek to convey.

4

Translating Darkness

And when women write, they translate this darkness. Men don't
translate. They begin from a theoretical platform that is already in
place, already elaborated. The writing of women is really translated from the unknown, like a new way of communicating, rather
than an already formed language.
—Marguerite Duras (1981, 174)

Readers seeking women's narratives will find few in the canon
of autobiography. Women are heavily represented among authors of
"noncanonical," subordinated forms of writing. Readers will be obliged
to adopt a broader definition and look outside the canon—in letters, diaries, fiction, and poetry. For women's lives demand new forms of narrative, shaped by their purposes and the conditions of their lives. In addition to problematics of form, narrators of women's lives have recognized
a problematic of language. As subjects and as narrators women are seeking terms for significant realities that have not previously been inscribed.
As Marguerite Duras says, no language exists for this telling; women
subjects must invent a discourse by "translating darkness." In this chapter I examine some of the distinctive content that gives shape to women's
personal narratives (Duras 1981).

Dailiness

One hallmark of women's narratives is dailiness. This theme subsumes
both the shape and texture of the day and the nature of the work that fills
it. Dailiness in women's autobiography embraces the web of relationships in which women are embedded and the fabric of daily tasks. It reflects the episodic experience of work and relationships, the lack of clo-

sure, and the nonlinear experience of time that characterize women's daily life. It records the interruptions, the "emotion work" that women do, the psychological and emotional insights that animate their practice of "relationship work." Above all, it records and asserts the value of the repetitive work that women do.

Woman's daily life is made up of sites and activities that are usually omitted from the male autobiographical tradition. When women write their lives, the space they devote to women's work contrasts dramatically with the corresponding void in men's accounts. The facts and the significance of their daily work bulk large in many women's self-referential writings. In chronicling their daily lives, women directly challenge the insignificance attributed to these lives in the official, public writings of society. Their daily work is a large part of the reality that shapes women's subjectivity, a reality subjects seek to convey in their writing. In making a record of their daily lives they are making a record of women's consciousness.

Disregarding the conventions of the genre, women's narratives often portray the life as lived, in all its triumphant dailiness. Women's work has been meticulously and concretely recorded in women's journals, letters, and diaries.[1] In conventional accounts (biography and life history as well as autobiography), "mere" repetition is eliminated. But in women's accounts this repetition is not suppressed: repeated actions are repeatedly chronicled. The repetition itself makes a statement: its sheer mass and circumstantial nature make visible the labor involved in "women's work."

Women's work is notable for the degree to which it controls daily life. This work is the lot of all women, not just of wives. The burden of such work can keep a young girl from school, just as family responsibilities restrict the economic participation and artistic production of wives and mothers. From Margaret Davies comes an anonymous account of the domestic ardors that foreclosed the possibility of education for one young girl in 1931.

> When I was ten years old I began to earn my own living. I went to mind the baby of a person who kept a small general shop. My wages were l/6 a week and my tea, and 2d. a week for myself. I got to work at eight in the morning and left at eight at night, with the exception of two nights a week when I left at seven o'clock to attend a night school, one of a number started by Lord Shaftesbury, called Ragged Schools. I was very happy in my place and was very fond of the baby, who grew so fond of me that by the time he was twelve months old he would cry after me when I went

home to my dinner and when I went away to school before he was in bed. I felt very proud of my influence over my baby, and got into the habit of taking him home with me rather than let him cry. But I could not take him to school with me. As it was summer time and his mother could not keep him quiet, she offered me 3d. more a week to give up going to school and stay with the baby. This was a great trial to me. I did not like to feel the baby was crying and being neglected while I was at school. At the same time the teacher was so pleased with my progress and I was so anxious to learn, that I decided to stay at school. This upset my mistress and she made up her mind I should not go to that silly school. The conflict ended with my refusing to work for her, and so we parted.

(Davies 1975, 20–21)

Woman's work also blocked Harriet Jacobs's writing her narrative of liberation. She wrote only in the time unpredictably free from her responsibilities as a house servant. In letters to her trusted ally, Amy Post, a feminist and abolitionist, Jacobs recorded the calculations and stratagems by which she attempted to get time to write. In January 1854 she wrote:

I have kept Louisa here this winter so that I might have my evenings to write, but poor Hatty name is so much in demand that I cannot accomplish much. If I could steal away and have two quiet months to myself I would work night and day. To get this time I should have to explain myself, and no one here accept [*sic*] Louisa knows that I have even written anything to be put in print. I have not the courage to meet the criticism and ridicule of educated people. (1987, 80)

In March 1854 she wrote:

As yet I have not written a single page by daylight. Mrs. W wont know from my lips that I am writing for a Book and has never seen a line of what I have written. I told her in the autumn that I would give her Louisa services if she would allow me my winter evenings to myself but with the care of the little baby and the big Babies I have but a little time to think or write but I have tried in my poor way to do my best and that is not much.

Just now the poor Book is in its Chrysalis state and though I can never make it a butterfly I am satisfied to have it creep meekly among some of the humbler bugs. (1987, 81)

As the daily work of housewifery can block a woman from creative work, so the identity of household worker can mask her subjectivity.

In particular, the intersection of racism and sexism has meant that biographies of black women writers do not parallel those of the male intellectuals who are their peers. Domestic work has been a residual occupation for African American women, and remains one of the largest occupational categories for African American women. Black women artists, unlike their male peers, have been captives of women's work. Poet Phillis Wheatley and writer/ethnologist Zora Neale Hurston are among those who have worked as domestics. Harriet Jacobs labored in the nursery and kitchen by day, writing at night. Her creative work was kept secret from her employer and others who peopled her daily life.[2]

The dailiness of women's accounts can reveal aspects of experience that are ordinarily ignored or denied, unmentionable facts of life such as poverty. Carolina de Jesus (1962), living in a *favela* in Brazil, kept a journal of her daily struggles to feed and clothe her family.

> May 19 I left the bed at 5 a.m. The sparrows have just begun their morning symphony. The birds must be happier than we are. Perhaps happiness and equality reigns among them. The world of the birds must be better than that of the *favelados,* who lie down but don't sleep because they go to bed hungry. . . .
> I broke my train of thought when I heard the voice of the baker:
> "Here you go! Fresh bread, and right on time for breakfast!"
> How little he knows that in the favela there are only a few who have breakfast. The *favelados* eat only when they have something to eat.
> (1962, 42)

> How horrible it is to see a child eat and ask: "Is there more?" This word "more" keeps ringing in the mother's head as she looks in the pot and doesn't have any more. (1962, 46)

> I made a meal. The grease in the frying pan was beautiful. What a dazzling display! The children smile watching the food cooking in the pans. Still more when it is rice and beans—it's a holiday for them. (1962, 51)

Poverty in women's daily lives has further aspects that are rarely mentioned, such as the relationship between marriage and subsistence. The poet alta notes pithily and practically

> the welfare money did not come yesterday; the worker did cut me off like she promised. but the medi-cal & foodstamps ($46 worth for $32) arrived. my first thot was "o good! i dont have to get married. (1974, 33)

Connection

A second theme of women's autobiography is emotional connection.[3] The female subject often situates herself in a web of relationships, or tells her history in terms of relationships. Relationships are important in women's developmental trajectories, as well as at the point of self-writing.[4] This female emphasis on connectivity is more than a narrative stance. The discourse of connectivity does not arise only in response to the challenge of autobiography; it has deep roots in female culture. Women's autobiography makes this theme, easily overlooked in men's autobiography, inescapable. Feminine values valorize connection. Relationship is a deeply held value of women, and is related to female concepts of adulthood and virtue.

Connectivity has many dimensions, as woman-centered research in a number of fields has begun to reveal. The vocabulary of female connectivity is diffuse, and still somewhat tentative. Scholars in different disciplines have employed various terms in a developing discourse on connectivity (Smith-Rosenberg 1975; Abel 1981). Connection includes not only the state of being-in-relation, but also a manner of relating to things or people. Connection is not a passive state of being; it is defined by activity, not sentiment. Florida Scott-Maxwell was living alone, by choice, when she wrote in her journal:

> Although I am absorbed in myself, a large part of me is constantly occupied with other people. I carry the thought of some almost as a baby too poorly to be laid down. There are many whom I never cease cherishing. I dwell on their troubles, their qualities, their possibilities as though I kept them safe by so doing; as though by understanding them I simplified their lives for them. I live with them every minute. I live by living with them. I dwell with the essence of friends so intensely that when they arrive I can be paralyzed by the astonishing opacity of their actual presence.
>
> (1979, 34)

Florida Scott-Maxwell's idea of "cherishing" is not limited to thinking about other people but requires active caring. As Scott-Maxwell writes, by means of her care she seems to ward off ill fortune from those to whom she is committed. It is as though activities of care have the power to prevent aggression.[5]

Research on women's moral development has illuminated an "ethic of care" that centers on the activities of relating (Gilligan 1982). This ethic of care is an expansive orientation, representing women's sense of responsibility and concern for a widening circle. It is a morality not limited to the family or the household; women's leadership in many areas of public and community life is motivated by this ethos. Inclusion is another aspect of care: making sure no-one is left out or isolated (Gilligan 1982, 43). The ethic of care pulls women toward relationships, and makes them take responsibility for these relationships. Indeed, the ethic of care makes women responsible for the well-being of the world: obligation to self and others is extended to an impersonal or oceanic caring.[6]

The valuing of connection, the exercise of empathy and care, the investment in relationship work are not characteristic of all women, nor is there any connection between these values and femaleness. The link, if any, is with female culture and female socialization.[7] Same-sex associations throughout adolescence and young adulthood reinforce patterns of behavior and value that differentiate girls and boys. Research on sex differences suggests that individuals are continuously socialized for connection or for separation, depending on their sex.

"Relationship Work"

The phenomenon of relationship work links the themes of connection and dailiness: caring is work accomplished by repeated activity. "Feeling work" and "relationship work" are commonplace for women, but have attracted little attention from scholars in the social sciences. Hence women's personal accounts constitute the first direct evidence we have of what is involved in relationship work. The emerging picture is that this work involves discipline, insight, persistence, expert timing, risk-taking, and opportunity cost. It requires both skill and motivation, and above all, it takes time and strategy. Dorothy Smith (1979) imports the vocabulary of work organizations to her analysis of homemaking, examining the managerial responsibilities involved:

> A housewife, holding in place the simultaneous and divergent schedules and activities of a family, depends upon a diffuse and open organization of consciousness available to the various strands, which are coordinated only in her head and by her work and do not coordinate otherwise in the world.
>
> (1979, 152)

Social research that chronicles the everyday work of women exposes the cognitive activity required to drive feeling work, revealing the rational calculus women employ in creating emotional climate. Marjorie DeVault (1991) has studied the efforts women exert to create sociability around the family dinnertime. Tillie Olsen (1961) portrays the fusion of emotion work and housework, combining the subject's domestic activity of ironing with an interior dialogue with her daughter's teacher. The housework chore provides an exterior frame for relationship work that is performed in the mother's thought processes.

The work of care resembles women's other domestic work, work that must be continually repeated and may remain invisible and unrecognized. Women have traditionally taken up the burden of relationship work: morale boosting, "maintenance work" on relationships, counseling, advising. They are traditionally held accountable for outcomes of relationship work such as the quality of their marriages and the outcomes of child-rearing. And women conceptualize their efforts as work[8] that creates a product: a "good relationship," a "healthy child." In *Flying,* Kate Millett describes relationship work to which a group of adults committed themselves. This work with an autistic child exemplifies women's ethic of care: from the premise that caring can make a difference follows the commitment to spend one's resources of time and energy to make that difference.

> I saw him first last winter among company upstairs, an idiot carried into the room like an error, doddering in arms. The drool on his mouth. Eyes empty of everything. It was a moment of terrible embarrassment. The thing was obscene. One averted the eyes. . . . Then we began it, this gamble. Going to make Winnie a child. Seeing it work, the eyes beginning to focus, the mind beginning to form. He no longer croons, he looks, actually looks at things and sees them. He is coming alive inside, angry even. I glance again at the crawl box, a wooden slide with ropes across the chute. He is inserted into it twenty-four times a day by main force. Yes, force. Ashamed of ourselves we force him down it, torturing him in his rage. He hates it.
>
> . . . Winnie, his arms and legs moving in rhythm to three adults bored beyond endurance, sweating, waiting for the cigarette break and the next cup of coffee but intent in rhythm together, planting the pattern of the child's crawl that he never learned within a four-year-old body whose mind is over three years behind it. The movement we engrave remorselessly on the lateral nerves, hoping to force the living cells to take over the work of the dead. Paul says he has already gained four months of childhood

through the program. Neurologically eight months to start with, he is now up to twelve.

I thought the whole project American quackery in the beginning. Something they'd fallen for in their despair. But it worked. Exercises, diagrams, wooden structures that Paul and Angus built, charts, tables, timing regulations, rules about food, color, music. A whole bureaucracy. But the results were real. Winnie, at another structure, one he has mastered and can even like now, he stands on his toes walking below the overhead bars, his hands gripping, even the bad hand, the right one. He is smiling, showing me what he has learned while I was gone. Then he falls into my arms. (1990, 349)

Women's autobiographical writings demystify intimacy, making it clear that relationship work is work. Women's autobiography also casts new light on the essentialist theories that defined affective competence as a natural attribute of "the feminine personality."[9]

"Emotion-Work" of Women

Women's willingness to commit to relationship work is linked to emotion-work,[10] a third theme of women's personal narratives. Women relate to emotion (and consequently to emotion work) in a way distinctly different from men. Women are likely to write of emotion as a resource, a source and form of energy, an affirmation of self.[11] In women's culture, feeling can be applied for positive purposes.[12] Emotion as power can be "harnessed" or "managed" in constructive or destructive ways, expressed in a discourse of resources and management. Women sometimes use economic metaphors to record a calculus of investments and yields in the management of resources, and an awareness of a finite supply of psychic energy that is available to be invested.[13] Like any resource, emotion can be squandered or can be profitably invested.

In addition to its constructive employment in the world, emotion can be a valued part of the self. In women, self-affirmation does not require denying or negating emotion. Self-feeling is both empowering and self-affirming. This accounts for the seeming paradox that women, in a socially less powerful position than men, tend to be risk-takers in relationships.

Still, emotions as attributes of the self can be dangerous. Of women's emotions, anger is the most severely proscribed and potentially the most dangerous: it can get you killed. Yet women's anger is also seen as a creative force (Spacks 1972; Gunn 1982). Other feelings that have value include the "narcissism" that motivates the female self-writer (Spacks 1972).[14] Clearly, in a situation where misogyny is institution-alized, a woman's ability to believe in her merit, celebrate herself, and assert herself through writing is emancipatory. The importance of a woman's community in affirming such self-assertion and making it safe is apparent.

The topic of feelings is one where the divide between women and men can be clearly seen. Many women discourse fluently in a language of feelings and of feeling work that is as foreign to men as is the vocabu-lary of hues and colors. A drastically different valuation of feeling helps to maintain the separation between the sexes. Autobiographies and di-aries illustrate the contradiction between men's and women's valuation of feeling. In self-writing men prefer and try to accomplish the suppres-sion of feeling. From a masculine perspective, expression of emotion is a negative occurrence, for in the male culture feeling signifies weakness. Admitting feelings, being preoccupied with them, being wrung by them is shameful. Expressing one's own emotion connotes being out of con-trol and the threat of being overwhelmed. Only when a person has "mastered" his feelings can he "pull himself together." In the male cul-ture, other people's emotions are also threatening. When one feels buf-feted or crowded by someone's emotional display it is hard to maintain the desired separateness from others, the feeling of being in control, of the centrality of one's own ego. Emotion is also threatening when it sig-nals a demand for connection (for empathy, sympathy, responsibility, rescue).[15]

A female sensibility draws together the three themes of dailiness, con-nection, and emotion work, in a passage by alta (1974). She acknowl-edges that the dailiness of women's work eludes telling; asserts a femi-nine valuation of feelings; and overturns the taken-for-granted domi-nance of the husband-wife relationship in privileging the mother-child relationship:

> how could i possibly tell this story. it is too long. 8 years, every day of it, no one could even write one day. the minutes. history is so much simpler. . . . how she would smile & giggle in her sleep & i would bend over her blessed face, letting her laughter bless me. & her father lonely male in his chair with pipe & slippers & evening paper & not an honest feeling in his bones. she & i together. she & i against the world. always.

. . . . it was lori taught me how to love. no man, no adult, it was she who loved me more & more each day & who wanted to be loved more & more each day. if there was any marriage, it was not between me & her father.

(1974, 6)

Women and Autobiography

Jane Marcus has asked, how are women's lives to be told? One answer to this question is to define a form that reflects the life as lived. Women's lives are to be told in narratives that embody complexity, connection, emotion, effort. Inescapably, women's attempt to inscribe self-in-relation produces innovation in form. Writer and poet Kim Chernin, in *In My Mother's House,* positions her mother as a teller of stories, each of which moves the overall narrative along and each of which is embedded in the daughter's own recollection and commentary (1983). In creating a biography of her mother, Chernin also writes her own autobiography. Chernin's own voice is heard in dialogue with her mother, and again when she appears as a storyteller herself.[16] Another source of innovation is a nonlinear sense of time and process that informs some women's narratives.

In addition, women may seek to invent a narrative strategy that retains the lineaments of conversation and its intimacy. Some accounts have a plural subject and hence a plural narrator. Thus Sandra Butler, a writer and trainer, and Barbara Rosenblum, a sociologist, created a chronicle that charted the course of Barbara's fatal cancer.[17] In this book the voices alternate, but the whole is a joint product of two subjectivities.[18] Women have also created plural subjects in trying to express a group identity. Susan Stanford Friedman has suggested that one possible form for women's autobiography is collective.[19] In their writing women subjects sometimes seek to create positive expressions for collectively held identities. In defining herself as subject, a woman may tell the story of her race or her family. This may particularly motivate a woman who is part of a minority or marginalized group. African American women, for example, position themselves in community when telling their lives. Thus Pauli Murray[20] originally intended *Proud Shoes* as a family memoir for a family readership. Karen Fields, a sociologist, began *Lemon Swamp* as an oral history with her grandmother. As an African American woman earning a doctorate at the beginning of the twentieth century she was from the perspective of the dominant culture something of a rarity. In recounting her family's long history as teachers and educators Fields expresses another reality.[21] In texts such as these the subject's (or narrator's) group is an essential part of her autobiography.

The connection between subject and narrator, made visible and audible, means that some of these texts are hard to classify: autobiography shades into oral history, biography into prosopography. Telling women's lives often involves new or mixed genres.[22] Toni Morrison, Maxine Hong Kingston, Audre Lord, and Gwendolyn Brooks have pursued autobiographical projects in the form of fiction. Kate Millett's *Flying* is autobiographical but violates many conventions of generic autobiography. "Messiness" is the shorthand for this content; it is also an element of style. "Messy" accounts make no attempt to streamline the narrative, to corset the subject, to shear the web of connections. The fullness of women's accounts reproaches the leanness of generic autobiography, and contradicts its claim of universality.

"Messy" accounts may be particularly challenging for the critic/reader. From the critic's point of view, it is not only diapers that are messy. Emotions, emotional interactions, and the expression of feelings that can also be "messy" are proscribed by rules of male socialization and the protocol of literary criticism, as discussed in chapter 3. Critics have employed a special vocabulary of misprision to characterize violations of these norms.[23] The suspicion and often derision with which the term "confessional" is used in literary criticism signals the rejection of messiness. "Confessional' writing is often perceived as expression unmediated by craft, unguided by talent. Use of the epithet "soap opera" communicates critics' rejection: to characterize something as "soap opera" is simultaneously to ridicule its intensity and denigrate its content. Similarly, the term "confessional" seems a codeword reserved in literary criticism for women's self-referential writing.[24] It connotes the undisciplined, tasteless outpouring of that which inhabits the disorderly, uncorseted, gross, unpredictable, uncivilized female. Critical judgments along these lines assert a disjuncture between women's self-referential writing and Literature, with a subtext of invidious contrast to the approved masculine form. The masculinity of intellectual culture is reflected in Simone de Beauvoir's squeamishness as she somewhat dubiously characterizes women's writing:

But they have often aptly described their own inner life, their experience, their own universe; attentive to the hidden substance of things, fascinated by the peculiarities of their own sensations, they present their experience, still warm, through savory adjectives and carnal figures of speech.

(Spacks 1972, 21)

The rejection of content is often signaled by critics' judgments of unintelligibility. Kate Millett's *Flying* appeared to one critic "an endless outpouring of shallow, witless comment," interminable, tedious (Kolodny 1980c, 238). It remained for a feminist reading of *Flying* to demonstrate that Millett's "formlessness" was a new form, consciously designed to convey content that had previously been denied entry. Millett has explicitly challenged the critics and confirmed Kolodny's reading.

Not surprisingly, portrayals of women's lives in other genres also include unseemly content, stretch the limits of form, and are judged deviant. Life history, fiction, the visual arts, and biography are sites of contestation along these lines.[25] It is not only critics of autobiography who reject the "messy" content of women's lives, but also critics of women's poetry, art, and fiction. Plath's and Millett's "unintelligible" content involves experience that is uncompromisingly female. They write about experiences that are rarely or never dealt with in men's writing: menstruation, lesbianism, "hissing in the kitchen." In telling this content Plath and Millett disregarded masculine conventions of propriety and provoked judgments of scandalousness (or worse). The early evaluation of Sylvia Plath's work contained a critical rejection of the personal. The reversal of this critical judgment may be traced to the rise of a new way of reading, and the directed action of female readers.[26]

Narratives of women's lives stand in contrast with those of men. Where male subjects portray themselves as separated, women represent themselves as connected. Where men's stories are set in the public eye, women chronicle private scenes. Where men prune their lives down to a terse outline, women's accounts remain "messy." Where men claim a destination, women record process. Where men universalize their experience, women's narratives remain contextualized. Women's autobiographies differ from those of men in terms of plot, content, and form. The content of women's self-referential writing requires us to analyze connection, dailiness, and emotion work. These elements of female autobiography, both form and content, have subversive and emancipatory potential for the genre as a whole. What is learned from women's lives can advance understanding of other lives.

From considering the content of women's personal narratives we have moved to the critical response to them. The forms generated in the search to tell women's lives have the potential for changing autobiography. It seems that beyond a personal conquest of identity, telling women's lives inevitably has a political aspect. Autogynography is an act of assertion that breaches the "line of fault" between the female self and the world of consequence. In so doing it affects the discourse of autobiography. The fact of women's self-assertion changes the position of figure and ground, of subject and other. Ours is the revenge of the dancing dog: if dogs can indeed dance, then thinking about dancing must change, as well as thinking about dogs.

The autogynographical act, once achieved, changes the form and substance of autobiography. It produces unprecedented texts and new methodological precedents. Writing women's lives, whether through the means of autobiography, life history, or biography, has the significance of contestation, and the potential for overturning established genres. In this context, writing about women's daily life has political as well as existential significance. Theoretical upheavals and methodological innovations are an inevitable accompaniment of woman-centered scholarship. Woman-centered thought permits the reversal of figure and ground to place women's lives at the center of the genre.

Orthodox literary criticism is bound to view accounts of women's lives as different, hence deviant, hence positioned at the periphery. Difference can be interpreted as a deficiency or, alternatively, as a signpost to a reality previously unknown. Generally, the unorthodoxy of women's writing provokes the critic and illuminates his subject positioning. The narrative strategy of "telling it messy" further disrupts the procedures that routinely efface the content of women's experience. In responding the critic becomes socially situated; he himself becomes intelligible.

Inscribing women's lives is thus not a simple matter of using existing language, or even of "translating" unfamiliar experiences into familiar terms. Equally, "the" authentic voice of woman cannot be designated; the diversity of women's voices cannot be reduced to one. The voices women find reflect the language that they hear; they are marked by the individual's location in society and history. Women ourselves employ different voices for different messages and different audiences.

The challenge from woman-centered research goes beyond its specific impact on autobiography. The intellectual apparatus as a whole is stressed by woman-centered inquiry. Knowledge based exclusively on men is decentered, and with it a whole apparatus of ancillary concepts, traditional judgments of significance, paradigms, the pantheon of geniuses, and the canon itself.

5

The Second Person in Social Science

> For years the description of events in anthropology and other so-
> cial sciences often occurred as if the investigator were an invisible
> cloud hovering over an event.
> —James M. Freeman and David L. Krantz (1980, 10)

In examining autobiography we focussed on a tradition of
life-telling that emphasizes first-person accounts; biography, in contrast,
emphasizes third-person accounts. In the social sciences we find both
kinds of narrative. While mainstream social science is dominated by
third-person accounts, the tradition of sociological life history provides
an enduring counterpoint in the form of first-person accounts. Putting
our focus on sociology allows us to explore some fundamental issues that
affect an author's choice of first-person or third-person voice and the
consequent shaping of the text. This choice depends heavily on how the
researcher's role is defined.

The goal of this chapter is to recast the social researcher as a narrator:
a biographically real person who interacts face-to-face with human beings in research encounters. This is the second person, so called because
that is how the subject regards him or her. We begin by following the trail
of this elusive second person, who is invisible in the formal writings of
social science, his voice unheard.[1] We know that the second person participates in interviews, or in field observation, as an embodied biological
entity. Then, we find, he disappears. Yet it is face-to-face encounters, and
the intersubjectivity they entail, that hold the key to reconceptualizing
social research and developing a valid methodology for telling women's
lives. So we seek first of all to uncover the second person.

To understand the mysterious disappearance of the second person and its implications for social science we must examine the premises and conventions of social research. Views of subject and researcher that are encoded in traditional social research have their roots in historical and metatheoretical considerations. The way they have been conceptualized and reported owes more to the glamorous example of nineteenth-century physics than to the empirical lessons of research. In order to understand the "domain assumptions" of today's mainstream social science, we must briefly examine this legacy.[2] For the several components of "objectivity" in today's social science—control, impersonality, "value freedom"—derive from early readings of this model. Unilateral control and unidirectional observation are hallmarks of research in physics (Devereux 1968, 20). The attempt to follow this model in social research results in certain identifiable contradictions.

The twin imperatives of impersonality and value freedom give rise to value phobia in social science. Value becomes synonymous with bias; the disembodied scientist becomes the ideal. The controlled experiment exemplifies the standard of "scientific" social science.[3] In experimental research, the researcher controls the definition of the situation and determination of what occurs. He can isolate the subject from her usual social and physical context and radically restrict what can occur in the research situation. The subject's behavior is controlled by the way the research situation is structured and by means of instructions. Control is unilateral; reciprocity is negated. This nonreciprocality is, in large part, the basis for any reputation as an objective science.

Conventions of social science methodology equating control and distance with objectivity are translated into role prescriptions for the social researcher. The researcher is held personally and stringently responsible for objectivity. In attempting to comply he tries to purge himself of all personal attributes—his biography, his psychological functioning, his reactions to the process and subject matter of research, his affinities and commitments. All human qualities of the researcher are seen as irrational and a threat to scientific objectivity.[4]

Valorizing rationality and objectivity leads to rejection of subjectivity, that of the subject as well as that of the researcher. "Value-freedom" defends the researcher against being touched by the subject and functions as a barrier to intersubjectivity. This thinking results in a double disavowal that becomes normal practice, defining both the researcher and his subject. The first disavowal involves the researcher's attempt to control the subject—specifically, his subjectivity.[5] Attempts to reduce the subject's scope may help to obscure the connection between subject and narrator. But the human subject refuses to be confined; in the social world that which is observed can also observe, and the subject talks back. Extensive research on the social psychology of the social psychological experiment highlights the inapplicability of the principles of physics. It is nearly impossible to "control" the active, problem-solving orientation of the human being.[6] Unlike mice, human subjects actively engage the experimenter in symbolic acts of cognitive mastery. In social situations (including research) humans seek information about what is required; they try out different responses and keenly scrutinize the reinforcement contingencies. Wherever possible, they consult their peers and engage in social comparison. Much work in social science misrepresents this active, problem-solving subject, much as it misrepresents the equally human researcher.

A second disavowal occurs when the researcher tries to achieve distance and neutrality by rhetorical means—that is, by merely using concealing language. He goes into hiding by purging the self from his text, "removing" himself from his time and place. The second disavowal requires an invention that plagues social science : the third-person voice. This new fiction conveys a spurious facticity to accounts from which the researcher has only been rendered invisible, not truly subtracted.[7] This convention encourages reporting from within the invisible cloud. Ironically, the objectivity that is the researcher's goal is threatened by disavowal. For in donning the mask of objectivity the researcher conceals his motivations even from himself and falls prey to mystification. When the disembodied scientist prevails over the biographically real researcher he helps to create an artifactual body of knowledge based on counterfactual premises. The disavowal of his personhood is more than a pose, for it is constitutive of the researcher's personal and professional reality. He actually believes that he has made himself invisible by closing his eyes. The researcher presents himself in print as detached and disinterested. The effect of this distortion is multiplied when his professional peers accept the published account. The collusion of writer and reader has negative implications for the validity of the research enterprise as a whole.[8] The culture of science exerts pressures on its practitioners in the direction of cumulative distortion. Fallout from the invisible cloud of disavowed researchers includes serious falsification in the database of the discipline, and in knowledge claims based on it. In many instances the researcher's own sex, class, or race, unacknowledged in the text, has made the subject "unintelligible" or led to faulty interpretation.

Objectivity in the sense of detachment and neutrality may be impossible when the researcher confronts a member of her own species.[9] Research on humans by humans is inevitably anxiety-producing. The narrator experiences the otherness of the subject as overwhelming and unmanageable. A researcher in the grip of an anxiety that he cannot admit may employ repression or denial, and thereby introduce a distortion in the image of the subject matter he produces. Vincent Crapanzano, an anthropologist, is concerned about this effect.

> The ethnographer's entry into the field is always a separation from his world of primary reference—the world through which he obtains, and maintains, his sense of self and his sense of reality. He is suddenly confronted with the possibility of Otherness, and his immediate response to this Otherness is to seek both the security of the similar and the distance and objectivity of the dissimilar . . . he vacillates between an overemphasis on the similarity or on the dissimilarity; at times, especially under stress, he freezes his relationship with—his understanding of—this Otherness. He may become rigid, and *his rigidity may determine the "texts" he elicits and the form he gives them.*   (Crapanzano 1980, 137; italics mine)

The most rational response would be to subject the researcher's feelings to analysis, as we would do with any other aspect of the research situation. Instead, a phobic response gives rise to defensive epistemologies and dissociative methods. Methodologies that attempt to control the anxiety cannot dissipate or neutralize this distortion, but only compound it. When "normal science" is based on denial, research routines are designed to protect the researcher from the rigors of a full-blown I/thou encounter.[10] The denial of the researcher's subjectivity is a major source of distortion in ethnographic accounts. The fiction of objectivity is operationalized by writing as though the ethnographer had not participated in a relationship.

Crapanzano places the problematic relationship between the subject and the researcher at the center of the field of ethnography and warns of distortions produced by disavowal.

> By eliminating himself from the ethnographic encounter, the anthropologist can deny the essential dynamics of the encounter and end up producing a static picture of the people he has studied and their ways. It is this *picture,* frozen within the ethnographic text, that becomes the "culture" of the people.   (Crapanzano 1980, ix; italics in original)

Concern with cumulative invalidity has prompted a number of social scientists to critique conventional methods and epistemology (Devereux 1968; Oakley 1981; Reinharz 1985b; Eisenstein 1983; Freeman and Krantz 1980). Scholars are concerned about the quality of a social science based on the concealment of the researcher's subjectivity, and about the cumulative effect of the neglect of researcher factors. They are critical of the flawed social science produced as a result of these omissions. The disappointing achievements of life history research may be the direct result of the neglect of the narrator and her relationship with the subject.

Orthodox methods operate routinely to increase the distance between subject and researcher.[11] Methodologies that attempt to deny connection cannot dissipate or neutralize distortion, but only compound it. For this reason Georges Devereux (1968) condemns "isolative" methods, observing that a methodology based on ego defense mechanisms makes for a crude sociology that has little potential for making valid contributions to knowledge. Methods founded on denial cannot generate reliable observations; on the contrary, they give rise to uncontrolled error. In short, methods that suppress the narrator from social research are incapable of correcting bias and instead increase the cumulative invalidity of social science knowledge.

The ideal of "value-freedom" is, as we have seen, mired in contradictions.[12] The fetishization of value-freedom—requiring disavowal of subjectivity—leads also to "methodolatry" (Daly 1973), when researchers begin to think that methods are more important than questions. Methodolatry can arise when social scientists seek a neutrality that method seems to embody. Reliance on methods, and the effort to perfect the instruments of research, are appealing when they seem to promise an antidote to subjectivity and variability. Focussing on method allows the complexities of subjectivity to recede. But method embodies its own implicit agenda. As a vocabulary for classifying research projects, it has a totalizing effect. When methodology embodies premises that exclude major portions of the subject matter, invalidity is inevitable.

The culture of science, emphasizing detachment, combines with a gendered culture of society to intensify the tendency to disembodiment. The culture of social research itself embodies a significant, unproblematized dilemma of gender.

The Researcher's Dilemma of Gender

The professional ideal of disembodiment closely follows the contours of unacknowledged sexual scripts, and reinforces the rigorously enforced socialization of boy children. Thus when the social scientist withholds himself from the relationship with the subject, or purges his biographical presence from his report, he is following a repeating cycle of separation and renunciation that Western cultures have required of men. Male sex role socialization enforces a sense of self built on separation and repudiation of parts of the self. Making oneself open to another's reality has the significance, for many men, of making oneself vulnerable to attack or annihilation (C. Keller 1986). The "separative self" conceives relationship in terms of a dichotomy between incorporating the other and being annihilated by him. The reliance on dualistic thinking seems to offer only these desperately self-defeating alternatives.

In a detailed and moving account of the dilemmas of ethnographic fieldwork, Vincent Crapanzano illuminates the limits imposed by the researcher's socialization for masculinity. In attempting to put aside the mask of objectivity, Crapanzano begins to contradict the masculine script—a beginning that is frustrated by his failure to analyze and to transcend the strictures of gender. In Crapanzano the pains of the separative self are projected onto the research relationship. He emphasizes (and incidentally universalizes) separation and vulnerability in speaking of his field experience. In his discussion, the uprooted field worker, jolted by the confrontation with otherness, alternates between a desire for fusion and a desire for distance, as mentioned earlier. Crapanzano cannot conceive of a way of deep knowing that preserves difference. He has no language for describing a way of knowing the other that does not despoil, no way of participating in another's experience that does not threaten to annihilate one or the other. These conflicts give rise to a sense of pessimism in Crapanzano's work.[13] Crapanzano's difficulty with intersubjectivity relates to his subject positioning as a male.

Ideologies of objectivity and gender combine to deform the researcher's role in a second way. One aspect of the required disavowal is resistance to self-disclosure. Research reveals that men regard self-disclosure as a sign of weakness, and feel bad after they reveal themselves.[14] This sexual script is congruent with the researcher's yearning for control and neutrality, but it constitutes a significant obstacle to empathy.

Dilemmas such as these emphasize the central part played by the relationship between subject and narrator in social research. Rather than disavowing this connection and suppressing evidence of its existence, we should move toward examining the relationship between narrator and subject.

The Subject/Narrator Relationship in Social Science

The nature of the relationship between the subject and narrator remains a major problematic for social science. When the relationship is defined, following the model of physics, in terms of asymmetrical exchange and control, it is often troubled by interpersonal and structural issues such as power and proprietorship, reciprocity, termination, dialogic contestation, and responsibility. As we have seen, traditional definitions of subject and researcher roles maximize social distance and minimize connection.

Formulations such as Crapanzano's highlight the problematic of how the researcher is conceived. Lacking the concept of intersubjectivity, with its emphasis on both/and, Crapanzano operates with an either/or framework. He conceives polarized alternatives: the researcher can incorporate the other or be swallowed up. A very different relationship between subject and narrator can be conceptualized on the basis of intersubjectivity. For example, rather than the rigid division and dominance of the separative self, we can conceive a narrator whose boundaries are not so rigid as to rule out role-taking, or the imaginative participation in the other's social or experiential world. We can challenge the distance-equals-objectivity equation. The analyst must become an integral part of the subject's psychological field, and experience it fully, without either resisting it or being damaged by its tensions. The analyst must be able to tolerate a lack of control (Loewenberg 1969).

By expressing the relationship between subject and narrator in spatial metaphors we can avoid the fixity of a subject/object duality. We can postulate a "partition" between subject and narrator that is mobile, temporary, and bilaterally determined (Devereux 1968). In a recent account of fieldwork Nancy Naples (1996) reveals that the researcher's perceptions of "insiderness" and "outsiderness" are changing rather than fixed.

The Problem of the Text

The text is a site where the contradictions in social science are made concrete. Traditional scientific writing obscures the relationship between subject and narrator, much as the ideal of the disembodied scientist denies it.[15] Conventions of social science writing militate toward the effacement of both relationship and narrator; virtually all traditional forms of reporting obliterate the interpersonal frame. Accounts of fieldwork or oral history contain subtexts concerning the protocol and politics of face-to-face encounter.[16] Even these tend to be obscured by the convention of disembodiment.

Ostensible first-person accounts such as we find in oral history and ostensible third-person accounts are both severed from their origin in discourse. The subtraction of the narrator materially transforms and negates the specific context of the account. In fact, the "problem of the text" emerges with the disappearance of the second person.

Decisive changes accompany the transformation of discourse into written text. Writing arrests the inevitable disappearance of discourse; it fixes meaning (Ricoeur 1984). Relations among subject, narrator, and reader are altered with the production of a stand-alone text. For once written, the text escapes the horizon of its subject, facing toward an audience that has never been face-to-face with the subject, and may not include her. Particularly when the narrator absents herself, the interpretation of the text is determined more by the reader's preunderstandings than by the author's intentions.[17] A "dialogue" created by reading is never fully equivalent to the dialogue between the narrator and the subject face-to-face.

For social research, the momentum toward falsification and distortion accelerates at the moment of writing. Texts symbolize their authors' escape from the face to face, and from the control of its protocol and politics.[18]

> The ethnography . . . is an attempt to put a full stop to an encounter that is necessarily disorienting. The same may be said of the portrait, the case history, the biography, and even the autobiography. In their own ways they all demand a cessation of time—a complete departure from the encounter.
>
> (Crapanzano 1980, 140)

The text purged of the author bulges with discontinuities and eruptions that mark the operation of repression, where something or someone has been made invisible.[19] The practice of hiding the researcher's sex, class, or race makes the subject "unintelligible" or confuses interpretation. Conversely, when narrators attempt to remain visible in their writing they produce innovative social science texts.

Problems in the researcher/subject relationship and in the creation of texts are not inevitable. There are some signs that the monolith of sex-cum-science is breaking up. In a consciously self-critical "reflexive sociology" sociologists would interrogate their beliefs and presumably their relationship to their social location.[20] This prophetic idea prefigures Reinharz's "experiential sociology" in which narratorial subjectivity is viewed as instrumental to social research (1984a). In some work the second person remains visible, as where the narrator believes that the subject's reflexivity is facilitated by the presence of the second person.[21] When the narrator serves as a mirror before which his subjects puzzle over their lives, they use it as a means for setting the record straight and making their life permanent (Kotre 1984). In this approach the narrator is not reflexive; the researcher's psychological processes are kept out of the account. Other theorists believe that the psychological processes of the researcher inevitably affect the portrait of the subject, and are thus valid components of the text (Loewenberg 1969). The valuable concept of countertransference allows the narrator to make use of his own subjectivity as an instrumentality in research. The observer perceives the unconscious of the subject via her own unconscious (Loewenberg 1969, 4).[22]

The perennial challenges of social research call for an emphasis on connection rather than distance, requiring no less than a radical reorientation of social science. This involves bringing the second person back in and redefining the researcher as narrator. It means including the subject/narrator relationship as part of what is studied and reported. It means taking intersubjectivity as the fundamental ground and condition of social research, and exploring the implications of this for research methods.

Intersubjectivity as the Fundamental Ground and Subject-Matter of Social Science

The ethnographer's goal of "knowing another's reality" requires a sphere of shared meanings and a means of communicating about them. For the duration of the research encounter, subject and narrator share a common material and social world that is the irreducible frame and context for their exchange. "The reality" itself is negotiated, in a back and forth process that modifies each party's understanding, as long as the face-to-face relationship persists. The negotiated reality is a social emergent; it is neither the reality of the subject nor that of the narrator. It comes into being because of the relationship and "belongs" to the relationship rather than to either of the parties. This intersubjective reality is also the ground in which the text develops; in which, in fact, social science exists. The second person is ineradicably part of social research: we are dependent on face-to-face relationships to generate the data on which the social sciences are based.

Given the nature of social research, if intersubjectivity did not exist we would have to invent it. The material conditions of social research call for a narrator defined in terms of intersubjectivity. Unlike physicists, social scientists are interested in phenomena that often cannot be experimentally manipulated, that we are obliged to study *in vivo*. Fortunately, the urgent force of relationship is continually undermining the ideal of the disembodied researcher and countering the powerful pressures toward disavowal. Face-to-face encounters such as interviews tend to subvert "control" and "impersonality"; it is almost impossible to purge elements of parity and reciprocity from the interaction of two subjectivities. Nor can the second person be invisible: the nature of social research requires us to be physically present. Our visible presence, in turn, requires us to have some intelligible social identity. We must fit in somewhere; and any social location involves interactions with others whose social identities articulate with our own.

Intersubjectivity defines fundamental subject matter for all of the social sciences. It is the practical basis for every kind of social solidarity, including tribalism, nationalism, class consciousness, and ethnicity (Frank 1979). The phenomena of intersubjectivity comprise the subject matter of social psychology and sociology: persuasion and influence, group dynamics, identification, role modeling, transference, reflexivity, affinity, and social comparison. Effective participation in any organized social activity requires cognitive activity that is based upon intersubjectivity.

Intersubjectivity provides a framework that can accommodate both subject and narrator, and potentially provide language for studying their relationship and interaction. Among forms of connection subsumed under the general rubric of intersubjectivity, empathy has emerged as a concept with potential for developing a method for studying lives. Yet paradoxically, the development of concepts and language to describe interpersonal events is underdeveloped. Systematic training in empathy remains completely undeveloped.

If intersubjectivity is indeed the foundation of our ability to do social science, the deliberate cultivation of empathy will be central to valid intellectual work. Focussing on empathy as a method of research requires us to think in terms of the skills involved, and the training required to produce those skills.[23] Empathic intention is a skill that can be taught and learned; acquiring, sharpening, and maintaining this skill requires discipline.[24] Nor is empathy to be viewed as a tool, to be picked up and put down again. We would do better to think of method as more like the hand and wrist of the researcher. Beyond this, empathy is embedded in a particular sense, for unlike one's hand, empathy is not entirely under one's own control. It is implicated in a dynamic ebb and flow involving the subject. Rather than being an introjected part of a defended self, a "personality attribute," or any other reified construct, empathy occupies a "space between" subject and narrator. It is not located in the narrator; empathy dwells in relationship.

Implications for Graduate Training

Revisioning social research in terms of intersubjectivity has startling implications for graduate education. It means discontinuing established practices and initiating new ones. It means recognizing that the research encounter fits the model of exchange better than the model of scientific control. A cultural norm of reciprocity links the expectation of exchange with feelings of equity, trust, and cooperation (Gouldner 1960).[25] An embodied, biographically present narrator is a constant reminder that research is relationship.[26] Replacing the unidirectional language of "data collection" with a reciprocal process of understanding and communicating signals a relationship of parity. Keeping this relationship in focus has significant implications for graduate training and professional ethics.[27] Such changes may help to circumvent perennial problems of the text.

Of course, the narrator is central to this new vision. Empathic intention must be developed as a basis for research practice, emphasizing consciously applied cognitive activity in pursuit of understanding. Professional socialization must develop skill in understanding complex and enduring states of being in other people. The narrator's task requires intersubjectivity directed outward, involving the joining of thinking and feeling, in the context of intention and effort.

An example from feminist biography provides practical guidelines for developing an instrumental empathy. In the postscript to her biography of Susan B. Anthony, Kathleen Barry describes a method that begins with cognition and moves through identification to insight. She began by recreating the objective conditions of her subject's life, closely observing the events and routines of daily life—from the outside. She constructed a picture of Anthony's subjectivity by examining her personal accounts and communication directed at her. Barry next moved into the realm of her subject's mind, reading her favorite novels and other reading materials. By this time the narrator knew her subject in her reflexive, inner mode, and could identify what in these sources inspired the subject, what defined her to herself (1988, 362).

The narrator continued to keep her subject in context, by placing herself in the locales Anthony had frequented and taking the walks she took. She records that on occasion she stood at a lectern as Anthony so often did, and spoke her words aloud. In all of this Barry used her own subjectivity to tune in on that of her subject. She allowed her imagination to be fired by the conditions of her subject's life, the places and papers she frequented, the thoughts she wrote, the ideas she read. This is subject-to-subject knowing (1988, 364).

Analyzing the Subject/Narrator Relationship

Exclusive focus on the subject has meant that the narrator has traditionally escaped analysis. It is necessary to change this practice and examine the subject/narrator relationship within a framework of intersubjectivity. In a revisioned social science, the narrator and the relationship between subject and object will both be objects of study as well as causes of action. One starting point is the "invaluable upset" in the researcher's response to his subject. Far from treating the relationship as "noise" to be eliminated, the perturbations produced by the researcher could be the most significant and characteristic data of behavioral research. Treated as data, the researcher's reactions are more productive of insight than any other kind of data we create. Developing awareness of narrator factors is an essential corrective for invalidity resulting from the "invisible cloud" of observers. The subjectivity inherent in all observation could be used as the royal road to an authentic, rather than fictitious, objectivity (Devereux 1968, xvii). The researcher's emotional and subjective resonance with her subject's life, far from confounding the work, contributes depth and conviction (Loewenberg 1969).

Disruptions produced by the observer's activities and anxieties are integral to our subject matter and our 'instrumentation' in social science, and to the relationship between the two. This need not be a source of invalidity. Instead, the inescapable subjectivity of the social scientist can be turned into an asset. Anxiety is a valuable signpost for the researcher, who can allow it to guide her in self-analysis. The narrator must follow the anxiety to its source in her self and the relationship with the subject, and incorporate the resulting insight into her understanding.

It is not the researcher's "option" to include (or exclude) the subjective; the only question is, given its unavoidable presence, whether it shall be formed into a tool useful in the work or remain an unacknowledged impediment. There is thus no substitute for self-analysis, for the surfacing and analysis of one's countertransference. To quote Loewenberg:

> Distortion arises from the failure to account for the observer *in each act of knowledge.*   (1969, 12; italics mine).

In addition to studying the narrator /subject relationship there are strong arguments for including it as part of the text. Since the process of taking a life history is an integral part of that history, it should not be excised from the published account. The relationship is not a mere methodological scaffolding to be discarded when the final result is achieved (Freeman and Krantz 1980, 9). It is constitutive of the phenomena we study.

The New Objectivity

Social science conceived in terms of connection rather than separation requires a decisive departure from the invalidity spawned by dissociation. Real objectivity decreases the psycho-social distance between the observer and the observed. The new objectivity begins, therefore, with the narrator's movement away from defensive methodologies, the commitment to unilateral control, and the taboo on self-disclosure. Objectivity in social science can only be achieved through "the creative control of consciously recognized irrational reactions, without loss of affect" (Devereux 1968, 101–2). This defines a new objectivity that incorporates subjectivity.[28]

The change from disembodied scientist to narrator is fundamental to the new objectivity. This direction will take the narrator toward connectivity and the capacity for emotion work. Narratorial reflexivity is an essential element of the new objectivity. That reflexivity must recognize affect as well as cognition, feelings as well as thinking. The new objectivity calls for control with feeling, not control of feeling. The conscious recognition of subjectivity is the necessary first step toward control.

To be sure, revisioning the social researcher as narrator means being conscious of gender (among other dimensions of identity). The imperatives of the new objectivity bring the narrator into conflict with sociological custom, and indeed with masculine sexual scripts. A "problem of intersubjectivity" in social science results in part from the taboo on avowal and self-disclosure on the part of the narrator.[29] In addition, we can predict that the new objectivity will challenge women and men in different ways.[30] The dimensions of intersubjectivity are conditioned by one's gender positioning. The separative self and the connective self make for dramatically different narratorial styles.

Taking intersubjectivity as the essential ground of social research imparts a new vision of the research process, its methods and epistemology. Inevitably, subject, narrator, and text are transformed. The second person is resurrected and resumes the interrupted dialogue with the subject. The subject, freed of control, becomes more challenging and demanding toward the researcher. The researcher reveals herself as a narrator, whose voice is heard in the text. Methods emphasize association rather than dissociation. Research practice becomes more interactive and more open-ended, and texts reflect this character. The requirement of intersubjectivity extends beyond method to epistemology—to theories of known and knower, subject and narrator.

6

Sociological Life History

> To experience the Other as a subject through the full range of his emotions, Sartre . . . observes, is not an act of passive cognition. It is an active granting of importance—importance for oneself—to the Other's subjectivity. The Other must matter in one's own self-constitution; he must not simply be an object of scientific or quasi-scientific scrutiny. To understand the Other, the ethnographer must come to participate as best he can in the Other's reality.
>
> —Vincent Crapanzano (1980, 141)

In the last chapter I argued for a transformation of the way we think about social researchers and social research, replacing the researcher with a narrator. I proposed life-telling with a narrator who is sociologically situated, and suggested a way of reading texts that acknowledges the narrator's location in hierarchies of social class, gender, age, and race. The tradition of sociological life history offers a strategic site for the contestation between old and new philosophies of sociological research. Life history tells uniquely on issues of subjectivity and objectivity in life-telling. Moreover, in life history the narrator is an important and equivocal focus of the tradition.

Life history is comparable in certain ways with the literary tradition of autobiography. Life history is the narrative of an individual life, and aims to convey the subject's personal experience; narrative in form, subjective in focus, it speaks in the first person. But even when presented in the first person, the life history differs in significant ways from autobiography. The life history cannot be read as the subject's conversation with herself, nor taken as an expression of unimpeded subjectivity. For life histories originate reactively rather than spontaneously. They are first-person accounts that are shaped by the requests of the narrator; these in turn are shaped by the traditions of social science. The subject is knowingly involved in a face-to-face relationship with a narrator, but also has a relationship with an unseen and exacting audience that she will never know. The narrator is involved in a temporally limited relationship with the subject, and is simultaneously involved in a more lasting relationship with the audience of his professional peers.

So in life history the researcher's sociological agenda is intertwined with the subject's personal narrative. The narratorial role claimed by sociologists has traditionally been a dominant one. In the most famous American life history, sociologists W. I. Thomas and Florian Znaniecki selected Wladek Wisniewski as a personification of processes of social change they wanted to study. In the life history their narratorial voice introduces, surrounds, and even contradicts the subject's account. The narrator's heavy hand can also be detected in the chronicles of juveniles and felons by the Chicago sociologists of the succeeding generation, who sought to typify in individual lives a particular social milieu and "delinquent career." The social scientist has a proprietary interest in and influence on the life history:

> The life history is more down to earth, more devoted to *our purposes* than those of the author, less concerned with artistic values than with a faithful rendering of the subject's experience and interpretation of the world he lives in.   (Becker 1966, vi; italics mine)

It is the narrator, as a social scientist, who has the last word. Becker continues:

> The sociologist keeps the subject oriented to the questions *sociology* is interested in, asks him about events that require amplification, tries to make the story told jibe with matters of official record and with material furnished by others familiar with the person, event, or place being described. He keeps the game honest *for us*.   (1966, vi; italics mine)

Since the first-person narrative of life history is definitively shaped by the unseen narrator, clearly it matters who the narrator is and what his/her attributes and motivation are. The relationship between subject and narrator is also affected by gender, race, and class. Issues of authorship and authority are brought into particular focus in life histories with women subjects.

The long tradition of sociological life history is known for classics of male lives; women's lives are notably absent from the canon. In this chapter I seek to rebalance the tradition by focussing on three rare classic life histories of women. These are particularly valuable when the subject's voice reaches us unimpeded by narratorial framing, as in the cases of Bertha Thompson in *Boxcar Bertha* and "Janet Chase" in *The Fantastic Lodge*. They are of intrinsic interest in providing a needed picture of women's involvement in work and social institutions. Women's narratives also cast new light on what I see as perennial dilemmas in the life history tradition: sociological ambivalence, conflicts over authority and authorship, and gender blindness. Thus in addition to the intrinsic interest of their stories, the particular female subjects who appear in this chapter confront their particular narrators with contradictions and challenges that have the potential to expand the life history tradition.

Boxcar Bertha: *A Female Subject*

Boxcar Bertha is the life history of a woman hobo, one of an estimated half a million to two million hoboes in the U.S. in the 1930s,[1] a tenth of whom were women (Acker 1988). The subject of *Boxcar Bertha* claims a position of stark individualism, positioning herself outside the familiar institutions of civil society. The railroad, an instrumentality for travel, is a trope for freedom, and the rejection of conventional identities. In gender terms Bertha is an anomalous subject. She eschews the feminine narrative strategy of telling her life in terms of relationships (although relationships occur). Rather than placing herself in a patriarchal genealogy, Bertha claims a symbolic community, a female and unconventional one. Bertha begins:

> I am thirty years old as I write this, and have been a hobo for fifteen years, a sister of the road, one of that strange and motley sorority which has increased its membership so greatly during the depression. I have always known strange people, vagrants, hoboes, both males and females. I don't remember when I didn't know about wanderers, prostitutes, revolutionists. My first playhouse was a box car. Conductors in freight yards used to let me ride in their caboose. Before I was twelve I had ridden in a box car to the next division and back. (Reitman 1988, 7)

Her role models for this kind of unfettered life are significant. Of the few women who passed through, one made a particular impression on Bertha. Bertha remembers that she traveled with a book; she had a child in Memphis; and she was on her way to the coast to speak at an Industrial Workers of the World meeting.

> The look on her face as she talked about going on west, and the sureness with which she swung under the freight car, set my childish mind in a fever. The world was easy, like that. Even to women. It had never occurred to me before. (Reitman 1988, 14)

This narrative by a woman contradicts many narratives about women. Bertha subverts the conventions of childhood as a protected and bounded zone, where the young person is defined by her parentage. She continually inverts the judgments and perceptions of that limited zone, defining herself as a citizen of a much wider world. The constructed character of "childhood innocence" is revealed as Bertha draws on the example of her mother, impervious to disgrace and hard luck because she did not construe experience in these terms. When they lived in a commune near Little Rock, Bertha and her siblings were left in the care of the community when their mother followed her political convictions and went on the road. Bertha's account of these events contains no sense of abandonment or frustrated entitlement. Bertha's "natural attitude" was the legacy of her mother, "to whom nothing was ever terrible, vulgar, or nasty" (Reitman 1988, 7).

> My mother wasn't what the world would call a good woman. She never said she was. And many people, including the police, said she was a bad woman. But she never agreed with them, and she had a way of lifting up her head when she talked back to them that made me know she was right. I loved her deeply from the first day I can remember until she died. I love to think of her. Her example and influence and sacrifice (she always denied that she ever made sacrifices for her children) proved that she loved us and that she was a woman of rare courage and of fine principles all her own.
> (Reitman 1988, 8)

When her mother returned the children joined her and her current lover on the road, settling next in Seattle. Bertha's mother was a good provider, working in restaurants and making her clothes that were the envy of schoolmates. To Bertha, school never seemed important, and her pronounced intellectual interests were fed by extracurricular projects such as the Hobo colleges with which she was involved as an adult.

Bertha's sexual initiation came when she was sixteen: the man who was her mother's current lover, a university instructor, became her lover as well. Later that year Bertha became restless and, with her fourteen-year-old sister Ena, went on the road. In her farewell Bertha's mother said:

> I knew you were getting ready to leave me. I want to tell you something before you go. I've always been a rough-neck. I never had any morals, nor did I ever teach you any, but I've been a happy mother. I'm proud of both of you. Remember that I never made any sacrifices for you, nor did I give up any pleasure or good times for you. I never did anything different because I had children. And so don't either of you ever do anything for me that isn't easy and natural for you to do. I haven't any advice to give you. You both know plenty now. Just remember one thing, however—a woman's character, her value to the world, and her love for man is not in her hips, but in her heart and head. (Reitman 1988, 31)

In San Francisco, the sisters found jobs and began attending public lectures. Bertha fell in love with an anarchist orator, and took up riding the rails to follow him to New Orleans. An experienced hobo offered to be their guide, and later they traveled with other women hoboes. These travels provide not only a gallery of individual portraits, but also an account of the institutions and infrastructure of hobo life. *Boxcar Bertha* provides a record of the intellectual networks that flourished in the hobo milieu. Reporters and professors, actors and activists populate her pages, which document the activities and procedures of a social movement. The tide of hoboes flowed from city to city along the infrastructure provided by the railroads. A network of hobo colleges, unemployed councils and radical forums provided services and information, or access to them. Bertha circulated among these, seeking and meeting mentors and lovers. While working for a labor activist and lawyer in St. Louis, Bertha met General Jacob S. Coxey. The march of Coxey's army on Washington was designed as a demonstration to raise support for his plan to employ the unemployed in public works. Bertha also met Dr. James Eads How, the "millionaire hobo" who had organized the hobo colleges. By providing radical speakers for audiences of homeless and unemployed people, he gave the unemployed a forum (Reitman 1988, 51).

During her travels Bertha collected the stories of women hoboes.[2] Her narrative is packed with thumbnail sketches of hobo women and their life stories. Some of them she clearly admired, including a number of women who vied for the title "Queen of the Hoboes." Among these were two elderly widows of the Haymarket anarchists, who were soap-box orators. The most famous queen of the hoboes was "Red Martha," who ran a boarding house through which passed most of the intellectually oriented hoboes of the time. Hobo girls who were broke or hungry could get a meal and a bed there, no questions asked (Reitman 1988, 60). Lizzie, another of the hobo queens, reminded Bertha of "a large turbine engine, throbbing away" (Reitman 1988, 63). Bertha characterizes Lizzie as "a genius": she was into every kind of perversion and criminal activity, a voracious gossip and inspired listener. She loved literature and psychological research and anything sordid. Her son and the dreams she had for a life with him were a long-running counterpoint to her criminal history. Bertha records that Lizzie had many claims to fame:

> She was not like many women on the road whose place in the sun depends upon the fame of their lovers. And she has a group of sweethearts, as fine a group of men as ever went unhung. (Reitman 1988, 62)

Bertha does not stereotype or typify these women; her portraits are multidimensional. Lizzie, for example, had stenographic and typing skills in addition to shoplifting and panhandling abilities. As Bertha says,

> She was the fourth generation of hard-working American women, and she worked when she wanted to. (Reitman 1988, 65)

Bertha had an eminently sociological perspective, which adds considerably to the value of her observations. In studying the survival strategies of "sisters of the road" Bertha Thompson anatomizes social agencies that filtered resources to the poor, and the stratagems developed by their clients. Sitting around the campfire at "Camp Busted," Bertha learned more about using the welfare system.[3] Other women, however, warned against going to a charity or the police, who were anti-poor and might take their children away.

As a subject operating without a narratorial censor, Bertha is free to exercise her sociological imagination. When she becomes involved with a criminal gang she justifies her excursions into anti-social behavior in terms of an eminently sociological curiosity:

> I had wanted to learn the intimate details of the lives of crooks and now I knew. . . . When Lucille first introduced me to her friends and later to any of her friends' friends who were in the racket I was thrilled, and made up

my mind to learn all I could about this group. My first reaction was one of astonishment. They looked and they dressed like respectable men and women. (Reitman 1988, 111)

After parting from Big Otto and the gang Bertha traveled to New York and confronted the father she had never met. He was living in a basement apartment that also housed the radical bookstore he operated. Bertha found that he was living with two other men, in "a sombre, intellectual, honest, thoughtful and non-earthly atmosphere." These men were bachelors and bibliophiles. On Sunday mornings a woman joined them for breakfast, as she had been doing for twenty years; for twenty years she had maintained a sexual relationship with two of them.

Bertha's indignation about her fatherless childhood found no satisfaction, but in taxing her father about his lack of attention she records his philosophy. His concern was the world's children, he said; the small scope of family life was not his calling. A number of the men to whom Bertha was most passionately attached had a similar philosophy: when their focus was on world conditions and revolution, they had no time for love and dalliance. Bertha came to understand and accept this perspective, though it did not keep her from pinning her own desires for home and family on such men.

Bertha settled into work with Andrew Nelson at the Research Council, involved with a whole range of activities and research focussing on transients. She continued to travel and investigate facilities for the homeless, sometimes undercover, and persuaded some wealthy benefactors to underwrite the Female Hobo College. When her mother died in the aftermath of a fire, Bertha's eight-year-old child was sent to her. She concludes her narrative with the resolution to redirect her sense of a mothering responsibility from the universe to her own particular child.

The ending of Bertha Thompson's extraordinary narrative is an apparent contradiction to her philosophy, seeming to reverse her priorities for public and private life. History is silent concerning her later life. But this is only part of the mystery; the text itself contains enigmas. In contrast to the classic male life histories, Bertha's story appears to owe nothing to narratorial framing or theoretical interpretation. Bertha's forceful first-person account is nevertheless one that has passed through the hands of an invisible narrator. It was originally published in 1937 under the title

Sister of the Road, "as told to" Dr. Ben Reitman.[4] A new edition was copyrighted in 1988 by Dorothy Reitman and Amok Press. In an afterword, Roger A. Bruns places Ben Reitman in the frame of Bertha's account, referring to him as Bertha's "scribe."

Another puzzle lies in the obscurity in which this lively life story has languished. Despite a voice that has an immediacy and iconoclasm that belie the 1930s origin of the account, its contributions to the understanding of urbanization, criminology, poverty, and life on the margins have been largely overlooked. Like so many female narratives, *Boxcar Bertha* documents the participation of women in a social movement whose official history has come to exclude them. It is particularly notable for its portraits of women living independent of men. In her introduction to the 1988 edition, Kathy Acker historicizes Bertha's narrative, placing it in the context of the march of Coxey's Army of the homeless into the capital in 1894, and the hobo colleges formed at the turn of the century. She reads *Bertha* in terms of structures of patriarchy that shape the lives of daughter (the subject) and mother.

Bertha Thompson is particularly memorable for the way she positions herself as subject. She asserts herself, claiming an authorial stance that repudiates feminine roles and conventional ties. From the beginning of her narrative Bertha positions herself—writing as a young woman of fifteen—as a political actor. She was nurtured in a family notable for abolitionist, anarchist, and free love philosophies, and claims this familial inheritance.[5] She articulates the Outsider's perspective on the institutions of her society, particularly as these reflect economic inequalities. The work is of particular interest in the context of today's economic dislocations, which parallel those of Bertha's lifetime. In reciprocal relationship to this formidable subject the narrator in *Boxcar Bertha* is invisible and inaudible, making no claim on the text or the subject. The lack of narratorial presence gives credibility to the subject's strong first-person voice, enabling both authorship and authority.

Sociological Ambivalence in Letters from Jenny

In contrast with *Boxcar Bertha,* a second classic female life history features a palpable narratorial presence and is colored by his sociological ambivalence. *Letters from Jenny* is an unusual life history in that it involved no face-to-face relationship or direct connection between narrator and subject. Gordon Allport, a Harvard professor, constructed a life history from human documents created by a subject he never met.[6] He assumed a biographer's power in constructing the text (and the relationship).

Jenny's letters contain two intertwined narratives. Allport's analysis—and consequently the attention of his audience—is limited to only one of these, the painful story of conflict and alienation between a mother and son. A second, equally compelling narrative of Jenny's gallant struggle to preserve her economic independence is completely overlooked. Allport is exclusively preoccupied with the mother-son conflict in *Letters from Jenny*. He universalizes this dynamic, characterizing all readers as sons or mothers (1965, vi). In this "universal" dilemma, Allport sympathizes with the son's position rather than that of his subject. This identification signals an eruption of the narrator's biography into the life history.

Here is the story that Allport read: Jenny Gove Masterson was a hardworking widow with a single son when in 1926 a crisis in the relationship between the two caused Jenny to begin a series of 301 letters to two friends of her son Ross, Isabel and Glenn.[7] After she died in 1937 the letters came into the possession of Gordon Allport, who edited out two-thirds of them, and shaped the remainder into a chronological account (1965, 24).

Jenny was the first-born of seven children of Scotch-English parentage. Her mother was a school principal and her father the chief caretaker on a large estate. She was born in Ireland in 1868; her family migrated to Canada in 1873. Her father died when Jenny was eighteen, and she worked to support the family until she was twenty-seven. She reports herself rebellious, solitary, intellectual, and at odds with her siblings—an account confirmed by the sister who figures in her letters.

At twenty-seven Jenny married an American railway inspector and, because he was divorced, she was shunned by her family.[8] Jenny broke contact with them for a period of seven years, and moved to Chicago with her husband. She wanted to work but her husband would not hear of it. This conflict was eliminated when Jenny's husband died in 1897, when she was twenty-nine. Her son was born the same year, and Jenny had to work. She devoted her life to earning for her son. Jenny had independence in her job as a telegrapher, and could keep her son close by. They were a self-contained unit, and one that appears to have satisfied

Jenny. In this period Jenny refused several offers of marriage. Mother and son were the closest of companions until Ross went off to Princeton at seventeen. He enlisted in the ambulance corps in 1917, and seemed disoriented when he returned. Jenny supported him while he floundered.

During Ross's childhood Jenny developed a pattern of denying herself so as to provide Ross with luxuries. When he was young Jenny assured him that he had no obligation to her; rather it was her duty to care for him. In later life, however, Jenny was embittered because Ross did not take responsibility for her, and this conflict is a major theme of the letters. A second theme was Jenny's enmity toward Ross's girlfriends, which was a continual source of the conflict that fires the letters.

After the war, Jenny moved from Chicago to New York at Ross's suggestion, and was the economic mainstay while Ross worked intermittently. Their life in New York was punctuated by fights over girlfriends. Ross married secretly in 1923. When she discovered it Jenny violently broke off her relationship with Ross, denouncing him as "a cur" and declaring him dead to her. It was at this time that Jenny established the epistolary lifeline with Glenn, Ross's college roommate, that produced *Letters from Jenny.*

The letters trace a repeating euphoria-betrayal sequence in Jenny's relationship with her son. The narrative resembles a soap opera, with an intensity that is more usual in the story of a woman and her lover. After a rapprochement is arranged through the mediation of Glenn, the final idyll in the relationship between mother and son begins. Early on, the letters are full of Jenny's protestations that their new relationship takes the form of a disinterested friendship:

> Our arrangement is quite satisfactory to each of us—we each run our own show. . . .He drops in every evening to say "good-night." . . . We have no confidences, no explanations, no promises. . . . I expect nothing, and it is not in his power to disappoint, or hurt me—ever again.   (Allport 1965, 46)

But by August Jenny confides:

> I am again in the Slough of despond, and am quite undecided what to do. It has been a question with me for months whether it was the decent thing to speak about it, even to you, but at a crisis in my affairs, if I do not turn to you, then to whom can I turn? One cannot stand alone always. It seemed for a while that as long as I eat Ross's bread, I should keep my mouth shut, but—But it isn't money that stands between Ross and me—not by any means—it's *women*—more women. (My writing is awful—I'm all nerves.)

Sometimes I wonder if Ross is a trifle off balance—sex mad. At first he talked lovely about saving money, building up a character in business and that sort of thing, and I was in 7th heaven. He *has* saved money, it's in our joint names in a bank, several hundred dollars. That's why I skimped so. But all the time he was carrying on an affair with a woman, a Russian Jewess, a very bad affair, and before he got out of it, he wasn't so far from the Pen. I helped him out of that
. . . But the climax came Sunday before last, and Ross and I had a storm.
. . . Ross and I had a scrap—I refuse to do it. Marie will never again enter any house that I am in.

Now, my dear ones, I do not want you to misunderstand. I *do not* object to Ross's marrying, and said so, he is so made sexually that he *ought* to marry. But I won't be party to a *lie*. Ross is the *greatest liar* I have ever known.

I did not intend to say so much, but I'm heartsore, and sick, and truly discouraged. Ross cares absolutely *nothing at all* for me—I am a great drawback and burden to him.   (Allport 1965, 53; italics in original)

Two days later the skies have cleared:

You will be glad to hear that my little cyclone has, I believe, blown over, for the time being anyway.   (Allport 1965, 53)

But they cloud over again:

Ross cares as much for me as he cares for a dead dog, and right well I know it. That I am a burden to him is beyond a doubt, but what can I do? It is rather a disgrace for him to say that he has a mother living but that he cannot get along with her, and that she despises him.   (Allport 1965, 55)

Intervening letters reveal she has been "investigating" Ross's correspondence, among other things. Another girlfriend is on the scene, and Jenny changes from an initially favorable impression to a sarcastic and disparaging one. She refers bitterly to him and Vivian, and in April 1929 she writes:

The chances are that Ross and I are again near the parting of the ways. He has never cared anything at all for me since he adopted, and was adopted by, the old philanderer [his professor's wife in college]. It is as well for him to try his luck again at matrimony—he can then take his other wife to visit his "Beloved Mother" his "B. M." as he did the first one, and they can all be happy together.   (Allport 1965, 62)

Jenny alternates between sarcastically disparaging Ross and hoping he will "settle down."

Allport's text contains a letter from Ross to Glenn (July 1929) that portrays a situation of constant warfare between mother and son. In August Ross loses his job, and Jenny writes Isabel in a desperate frame of mind:

> I am getting up at *4 am* staring like a fool at the "roseate hues of early dawn" creeping in between the great buildings—I am often out for a walk at 6. Something must happen. Someone will put a bullet in Ross, or he will murder the chip, or she will murder him, it is all so wicked and wrong. *Why* does he do it? (Allport 1965, 68; italics in original)

To the last Jenny is scheming how to "save" Ross. However, Ross contracts an ear infection, suffers a relapse after surgery, and dies suddenly in November 1929. Vivian, with whom Ross has been living, makes claims on his estate, and Jenny throws herself into the legal contest with a vengeance. She avers that Vivian killed Ross. Once his ashes are in her custody she can say "Ross is all mine now" (Allport 1965, 85). Now Ross is "safe with his mother again—nothing can separate us now—Ross is safe."

Intertwined with this agonizing account is the second narrative, which recounts Jenny's day-to-day struggles to provide for herself and to safeguard her personal dignity. Jenny's letters reveal her to be an active, planful individual. She is adamantly self-sufficient and self-contained. Jenny never accepts help when she has any money; she sometimes returns the amounts that Glenn sends her from time to time.

Jenny always has a strategy for finding work. Her accounts of job advertisements and interviews are meant to amuse her correspondents. However, as the years pass, her job searches are shadowed by age discrimination. The rigors of being continually in the job market begin to tell on Jenny. In August 1927 she writes to Isabel:

> In the first place a sort of terror seizes me when I think of going into a new job; an unaccountable, but very real *fear*. I've lost my grip. In the next place I am not physically fit—my sight became so bad, in the Hospital, that I could hardly see objects in front of me. My heart literally 'quivers'—I feel it quiver. If I attempt hard work and drop dead, it would be fine, but— would I drop dead? What would happen if I merely became ill, paralysed, or some fool thing? (Allport 1965, 44)

Jenny's work history is one of persistent effort and downward mobility. At a certain point Jenny becomes willing to take service jobs. One of the most memorable is at an institution for children:

My dear, if you ever have a child and are so unhappy as not to be in a position to personally take care of it, I beg you *never* to place it in such an Inst'n as this; if there is no other course open to you, then take the child to the sea and shove him in. . . .

I would rather be dead than remain in this place. I am just only a whipper, a common spanker of little children, a beast, a cur, for $50 a month. The children are as young as 3 years—think of it! *3 years*. There's a little fellow of 3, pink all over, and bright sunny hair like a sunbeam. I told him (when I came first—*now* I'm just a beast) that he was my Sunbeam, and that brought him more than one spanking and pretty near cost me my $50. God! how I despise myself for accepting money for spanking babies. There's a tiny child, white all over, her hair cream, her little body pure white, I called her my snow Flower, and that was pretty near being my Waterloo. (Allport 1965, 32; italics in original)

Jenny develops extreme physical symptoms associated with this distress, and tenders her resignation.

I am in the Nursery Dept. There is a Supervisor, a 1st Asst. and 2nd Asst. I am the latter. That means 2 bosses. The supervisor is practically new—only here 2 mos. The 1st Asst. has been here a couple of years, so you see that the Supervisor is very much dependent on her. She is a Devil if ever there was one; she has a little thin squeaky voice, a sort of whine, and thin cruel lips. She dislikes me, has from the first moment. If the first 10 days it was common to hear one of those women (Beasts) say as they spanked the babies, "Now just see Mrs. Masterson squirm"—and sure enough, she did squirm, all the blood in her body rushed to her head, and she wanted to go screaming mad. The children are not marked—haven't a scar on them—it is all done on the legs, their little bumty-bum, and arms. They are taught simply nothing at all by us—except to hate humanity. Not a story—not a game—They go to Kindergarten morning and afternoon, and I believe they are happy there, but we see only to their physical needs. We bathe them *twice* a week—mend clothing (think of the pile of darning), polish their shoes every morning—spank them to bed—spank them out of bed—never a kind word. . . . It's a shameful thing to accept money for spanking little children—their little faces will haunt me as long as I live. (Allport 1965, 33; italics in original)

This narrative continues in the next letter, originated in "Hell," February 20/27:

Oh, you should see little Eddie—the darling, lovely boy of 3. Soon as those Devils find out that I particularly love one child they make a point of beating him. One evening he came up to me and held up his beautiful little face,

he said "I can't *always* be a good boy because I am only a *little* boy." . . .
My little Sun-beam boy is not allowed to speak to me—I cannot even bathe
him—and he did so love to be a "fish" in the tub. You should see the woe-
begone looks he gives me; he, too, is 3. . . .

"Mrs. Masterson (strong emphasis on the Mrs.) will you please remember that you are in an Institution, and *not* receiving $100 a month for
giving individual attention to the children"—I hear that every day.

But yesterday! Saturday—that was the straw that broke the camel's
back. There is no school on Saturday, and that means the Nursery *all day*
for the children. After breakfast we polished the shoes—40 pair—the children were ordered to sit still and not speak or move. The noise was not
great, but Devil No. 1 got mad and ordered them all to stand, close their
eyes, and place their hands on the top of their heads.

As sure as there is a God in heaven (if there be) they stood that way for
one hour and 20 minutes.

I could have screamed (I was mending). If the children moved they got
whacked across the legs, and they got whacked to stop crying. (remember
the babies of 3—1 hour and 20 minutes). finally they were ordered to sit
down, but *not a word*! They sat down and there we heard baby talking,
and then to my unspeakable horror I saw that infernal Devil (my Boss) get
a big sheet of sticking plaster—cut it into strips—and *paste the babies lips
together*. It was put on star-wise. I nearly went mad. You should see the expression of those children's eyes. . . . But when dinner-time came, we could-
n't get the plaster off. I don't know how those Fiends managed it, but when
I came to wash them, the marks *would* not come off with soap and water.
I think those Hell-hounds were scared, for they whispered together and
kept looking at me. I saw myself in a glass and I looked like a dead woman.

At 3 o'clock, when off for an hour, I went straight to my room, and
wrote my resignation, and placed it on the matron's desk.

(Allport 1965, 34–35; italics in original)

Physical problems also play a role in Jenny's account. In Jenny a
physical hardiness was combined with frequent illness and the need to
sleep for twelve or more hours. Physical crises often corresponded with
crises on the job. Her heart condition was also a chronic source of anxiety. Jenny had a dramatic vision of herself falling dead on the street,
lying unidentified, and being buried in Potter's Field, with no-one to
claim her bank account. Throughout the period covered by the letters
Jenny is planning for her old age and trying to provide for her burial.
By 1931, feeling she is at the end of her working life and lacking any
family, Jenny considers moving to a Home. Her letters contain humor-

ous accounts of her investigations into available alternatives. By May she has located a suitable Home, been interviewed by the Board, and admitted. Initially Jenny enjoys and approves of every aspect of her new home. Soon, however, the staff become inimical. Jenny runs away but is involuntarily returned after misadventures. In October she writes:

> I have now no hope of getting out of here, and so accept my fate in a stupid, stolid manner as one would if at the bottom of a well. . . . Often I do not speak one word for weeks at one time—it is hard to be alone.
>
> (Allport 1965, 127)

With age Jenny's independence is eaten away. The letters record dental extractions, broken bones, numbness, and humiliating experiences as a charity patient at the hospital. In May she reports that she hasn't been eating enough and is weak. She begins in earnest to give Glenn instructions about arrangements for her obsequies. In August she reports reading the newspapers with keen interest, and trying to build up her strength to "walk to the Bridge."[9] Often she quotes favorite lines from Swinburne: "even the weariest river Flows, somewhere, safe to Sea."

She writes Glenn in September:

> My dear, no matter how crowded you may be with duties and work, never let me slip entirely out of your life and interests. You have been wonderful to me—I wish I could express how greatly I appreciate it all, and how grateful I am to you. Without you I would be lost and indeed alone. I will try not to bother you too terribly with my little woes, but you are always with me, and I 'talk' to you by the hour. (Allport 1965, 144)

In a brief note Jenny congratulates Isabel on her new house, and repeats her warning about the mail to "The Prison" being tampered with. Three weeks later she is dead.

Gender Stereotyping and the Invisibility of Women

The neglect of women's life histories has left a gap in sociological knowledge about women's place the economic sphere and macrosociological trends. Equally serious is the tendency to reject women as full and representative social actors whose experiences can tell on social arrangements of their society.[10] This bias continues to produce an androcentric social science. In their search for instantiation of their theoretical interest in modernization and dislocation, Thomas and Znaniecki selected a male protagonist to produce the most famous life history in American sociology.[11]

In *Letters from Jenny* Gordon Allport overlooks a valuable narrative whose central concerns would command the attention of present-day sociologists: female employment, the female-headed household, aging and disability, women in poverty. In neglecting Jenny's work narrative Allport fails to recognize her sociological significance. Jenny's life is presented to the reader without sociological context or theoretical lineage. Anomalously, the narrator does not position Jenny to represent any social position or life trajectory. Equally curious, the book's limited sociological readership has also overlooked Jenny's sustained commentary on the structure of the labor market.[12] The life history of Janet Chase, the subject of *The Fantastic Lodge,* suffered a parallel neglect—although those who knew her agree that she was hard to ignore. The neglect in which she languishes is not "benign," but results from a more active process of suppression. And Bertha Thompson's account, out of print for many years, is unknown to most sociologists today.

Letters from Jenny involves a particularly interesting relationship of subject and narrator. Despite the lack of a face-to-face encounter, it is clear that a relationship came into being. Allport's account of the connection between Jenny and himself is colored by a sense of contest. He experiences his subject as confrontive. He reports feeling "pinned down" by Jenny's challenge to produce an authoritative interpretation of her life.[13] This is no mere intellectual challenge. The power that Allport tries to resist is the force of Jenny's subjectivity. Jenny's emotionality and the tragedy of her life make demands on Allport. Hers is a wrenching life and a compelling voice. Allport responds to both, his response full of contradictions. The contest with Jenny arouses a deep ambivalence toward his subject.

Allport's first response is to structure the situation by defining the roles of narrator and subject, positioning his conception of the narrator's function in opposition to Jenny's subjectivity. As narrator of this life history, Allport relies upon the tradition of the disembodied scientist, amended by the division of labor. Allport reports how Jenny seeks to engage him, but he does not respond in kind. He adopts a distancing response, defining himself as an objective scientist, and denying his own subjectivity. He identifies himself as a reader whose intention is to analyze and interpret.

Gender Blindness in *Letters from Jenny*

Allport is explicit about his role as narrator, but he fails to articulate his subject-positioning with respect to gender. This causes difficulty in his interpretive task. Gender influences Allport's response in two ways: his evaluations are affected both by gender expectations and by his subject-positioning as a male. Unexamined gender scripts confound his response to Jenny: he admires but cannot accept her strengths when they contradict gender stereotypes; and he can accept but not admire feminine weaknesses. Allport finds Jenny "extraordinarily expressive," with a "naturally brilliant literary style" (1965, viii). He reads masculine virtues in Jenny's handwriting, which "seems to confirm the impression of fluency, clarity and forcefulness that mark her entire personality" (1965, ix). Allport balks at describing her character in these terms, however. He distances himself from the disruptive spectacle of an androgynous subject by recognizing only her feminine qualities. Allport chooses to describe the "entire personality" in a stereotyped vocabulary of female psychopathology.[14] In an odd rhetorical invention, Allport distances himself still further by hiding behind a hypothetical assessor who "might label her as hysterical, overprotective, aggressive, asocial, extropunitive, and isolate, paranoid, having a character disorder" (1965, viii). This is the only place in his account where Allport employs the rhetorical device of a hypothetical hatchet man.

Since the norm of disavowal is strong in sociology, it is rare to find direct reference to the narrator's struggle against his own subjectivity. But Allport reveals much about himself in writing about his subject, and allows the reader to see how much the text is colored by the narrator's view of the subject. Allport provides us with a lesson in narratorial ambivalence, as respectable objectivity wars with disreputable subjectivity within him. The narrator's training as social scientist enables him to suppress his own subjectivity, but this control is threatened by untrammeled self-expression on the part of the subject.[15] In his introduction to *Letters from Jenny* the narrator ambivalently comments on Jenny's expressivity, noting her fluency and "naturally brilliant literary style," and at the same time her "uninhibited expression" (1965, viii). In his judgments of Jenny Allport manifests both attraction and rejection; moreover, he responds selectively to her characteristics.

This narrator is affected by the troublesome opposition between his own objectivity and the subjectivity of the respondent. The concomitant suppression of his own subjectivity, however, blocks Allport's empathy and impedes his ability to understand Jenny's life.[16] His preoccupation with the mother-son conflict leads Allport to universalize the mother-son dynamic, characterizing all readers as sons or mothers (1965, vi). In this "universal" dilemma, Allport sympathizes with the son's position rather than that of his subject. This identification signals an eruption of the narrator's biography into the life history.

The Unruly Subject in The Fantastic Lodge

As a subject of sociological life history, the pseudonymous "Janet Chase" comes across as a flamboyant challenge to the tradition. One imagines potential narrators fleeing in terror. Very few narrators following the traditional scientist script could have succeeded in a relationship with Janet. And indeed, the relationship between this subject and her narrator was decisively different from the conventional pattern.[17]

"Janet Chase" was a young white female addict living in Chicago in the 1950s, who said using heroin made her feel like the member of "a fantastic lodge."[18] Janet's story begins:

> I was born in 1929, something like that, and my mother and father had been married for some time, and had had no children by this time and had not wanted any, really, as far as I can tell. (Hughes 1961, 1)

This identity as the unwanted being was confirmed when Janet learned she had been born as the result of a failed abortion. Her mother worked as a nurse, supporting a household that included Janet's father, grandfather, aunt, uncle and cousin, and a baby-sitter. Her father treated her like a toy, and terrorized her on their occasional outings; her mother had a violent temper and beat her severely from infancy. After her parents divorced, Janet acquired the habit of hiding in her bed until her mother returned from eighteen-hour shifts and she could feel safe.

> It was as though I had to hibernate in a cocoon of complete misery, and could only be safe when I heard the door open and I knew she was back. (Hughes 1961, 5)

Subsequently Janet was sent to live with the aunt and uncle in another city, traveling back and forth on the train at the age of five and garnering

compliments about how self-sufficient she was. A memory of being mo-
lested by an old man on the train echoes Janet's suspicion of the "love
play" her father would initiate. In the aunt's household a comparison between Janet's cousin May ("a beautiful child") and herself ("a bright
girl") took hold. She also learned that sex was what made everything all
right between adults after a frantic fight and severe beating. Growing up
in this household, Janet entered school.

> The teachers were always my first love. I would impress upon them that I
> could be a very brilliant child if they would take me right. . . .
>   When I first learned how to read, I began to see that there was a whole
> new world of possibilities, and from that time on I was a complete and
> utter bookworm.   (Hughes 1961, 12–13)

Janet's father was known to her only through clichés written on
postcards, but his unexpected death hit her hard. She grieved fiercely,
denied that he was dead, and tried to "pray him" alive again. Adults'
attempts to comfort her instilled a deep mistrust and sense of conspir-
acy, a conviction that "they" had done this deliberately. She became
alienated from the normal world, feeling that only she had any real
conception of tragedy. She campaigned successfully to return to live
with her mother:

> I felt that this was the answer to all my dreams; that now, at last, all the
> suffering, everything I'd felt, all the loneliness, all the anxieties would just
> be wiped away . . . . But I had some sort of idea that I would be with her
> all the time or a great deal of the time, that we would be buddies—she liked
> that idea rather than the mother and daughter idea, incidentally—that we
> would be sharing everything together.   (Hughes 1961, 24)

In this volatile household Janet continued to develop. She characterizes herself as a tomboy, and a particularly competitive one:

> I wasn't even content to be known as just one of the boys but I had to be
> *the* boy in the group.   (Hughes 1961, 19; italics in original)

Janet's adventures with intoxicants began with a teenage party she at-
tended, as a nine-year-old. Participating in a precocious orgy of drunk-
enness and sexual experimentation aroused memories of the old man in
the train, and caused Janet to flee. When she was about ten she attracted
a seventeen-year-old boyfriend; although she was oblivious to his interest the aunt talked her into a dating relationship with him. Female relatives encouraged Janet to begin to pay attention to boys. Experimenting,

she peroxided her hair, shaved and redrew her eyebrows, and acquired a series of gaudy dresses. She threw parties for an all-male guest list while her mother was at work.

Unpleasant sexual experiences in this period made Janet conclude that men were filthy, abominable animals and she would never have anything to do with them. Her sexual initiation did not fulfil her romantic expectations. When her "steady" stayed overnight in her bed, their relationship was ignored by Janet's mother. Bored with this boyfriend, Janet began a flirtation with an older man from night school. As she sought excuses to break off with Jimmy, Janet found she was pregnant. Following her mother's example,

> I think I knew from the first time, really, somehow, that I was pregnant, but in another sense I was never aware of it. It simply wasn't going to be, that's all.
> (Hughes 1961, 43)

Attempts to find an abortionist or precipitate a miscarriage failed; Janet gave birth and released the baby for adoption. The following six months were "nightmarish," and Janet cried all the time. Afterwards she felt changed in a thousand ways, and everything appeared changed to her. She began to write poetry. She wrote of this period:

> Then they dragged me back home. This was my first experience with imprisonment. I was told to stay in the house. I could not answer the phone, I could not go out. I didn't go out for weeks, not even out at night. Not even out of the door, out on the back porch, because of the public. I began to get the idea that all society was out to kill me, just because I had a child. . . . I had to do something, so I scrubbed. I scrubbed everything I could get my hands on in the house. . . . I'd cook piles and piles of food, you know, until the icebox was just full of old leftovers of all kinds. And I'd read. The reading wasn't very safe because that was something that had to do with thinking and that was what I couldn't afford to do at this point.
> (Hughes 1961, 53)

Janet began spending her evenings bar-hopping with a girlfriend. She began to play the "fascinating role" of the musician's chick and to smoke marijuana. Janet recounts the story of her meeting with Bob, who was to become her second husband (Hughes 1961, 103ff.):

> For the first time in my life I was really moved sexually by a man. . . . the feeling, the emotions he was able to arouse in me. They frightened me, they really did, they were so strong. I didn't know what the hell was happening,

and I used to stay really high then a lot on pot and lush and things like that, anything because I didn't want to realize all these feelings. . . .

Every time I think of that week now, it's just probably the only real happiness that I can really think of, that gasses me, that I don't regret, that I don't feel sorry about in any way. (Hughes 1961, 106)

One fascination in Janet's account is the way she precisely and poetically anatomizes the experiences that characterize different drugs.[19]

Most people tend to group narcotics all in one bunch; you know, "dope." But they're so entirely different, each one is an entirely different kick. Pot, pot is a young high, I think. It's for the time when you're in your teens and twenties and when you're operating a lot, making it to parties and bars and places like that because it's an all-inclusive high and a very social high. . . .

At first, when I started smoking it, I couldn't do anything on it. I just had to sit somewhere and dig or else giggle helplessly. . . . but it got so I'd be smoking it day and night, you know I got on a kick, I remember, for awhile. I would get high and it would just gas me to make phone calls because they always turned out completely strange, each one was an entirely new adventure, you know, without moving. And what was even better was getting a phone call, because this was an entirely different thing. Everything has worlds and worlds of meaning with pot.

(Hughes 1961, 72)

I was at a stage where in order to run for myself I had to be very social, you know, fill myself up with people, lots of them—and I've always had difficulty doing that. Pot made it possible. (Hughes 1961, 78)

I used to be almost an alcoholic at that time. It was before I discovered the rest of this junk. . . . I would just drink and drink until there was nothing, until I was in a state of being permanently numb. . . .

. . . lush has very unsatisfactory holding powers with me. . . . And second of all, it's an undependable high. And I've never liked lushes. . . . people who make lush really lose their inhibitions much more so than, say, a cat who's making heroin. You get a clumsy high on lush. Embarrassed high and painful high. (Hughes 1961, 99)

When you're not hooked you feel, first of all, there's a definite body sensation with horse, with the high that you get from horse, with being stoned. In fact, I can always measure whether I'm coming up or down by exactly how much of that feeling I have. . . . it's like having warm milk flowing through your veins, instead of blood. (Hughes 1961, 112)

After you make it, first there's a flash. That's the sudden onrush of the horse feeling. It starts usually in about the third time you jag it off. . . . it's a feeling as though, all of a sudden, something good and easy and fine has happened. (Hughes 1961, 113)

And one of the biggest effects of horse is that you simply do not worry about things you worried about before. You look at them in a different way. You still think about them. I mean horse is a thinking cop. You know, making all things possible and changing the entire outlook on all of your problems. Everything is always cool, everything is all right. It makes you feel like not fighting the world. (Hughes 1961, 114)

I didn't know much about heroin in those days. I knew everybody was doing it and it was just a socially accepted thing. More than that, you just *had* to. It was just the next most natural step for anyone to take, after joining that group. . . . So Bob didn't stop and I found out that the one time I felt apart from him was when he made it, you know. . . . And at first I couldn't understand it and that, I saw, was because he was in an entirely different world, and I just wasn't there.

(Hughes 1961, 109)

And one night I told him to turn me on. Well, we both lied to one another. I told him I'd made it before. And he said "Yes," knowing that I hadn't, "So, solid! I'm not really turning you on for the first time"—that sort of thing, both absolving one another. (Hughes 1961, 110)

Janet and Bob began to deal drugs as a way of insuring their own supply. Their history came to include arrests, incarceration, and drug detoxification programs. Janet's narrative ends as she contemplates a return to the federal facility at Lexington, skeptical about whether it can make a difference. She is twenty-three years old.

Like *Letters from Jenny*, *The Fantastic Lodge* brings the reader a second narrative as a bonus. This story concerns the "politics of autobiography" (Bennett 1987) that directly affected the reader's access to this life. The history of *The Fantastic Lodge* can be read as a narrative of gender politics. For in seeking to retain ownership of her life story, Janet challenged the authority of the male research establishment. She failed to respect the narrator's monopoly on writing and publishing. She wanted to own her book, and she wanted to profit from it. Janet hoped to use the proceeds to support her psychotherapy. The book was her ticket to a life beyond addiction, a life that was under her control.

The opposition to *Lodge* resulted in a long delay in its publication. In the meantime the clock ran out on Janet: she died of an overdose in 1959.

The Fantastic Lodge and the Conflict over Authority and Authorship

The first-person sociology of life history challenges the conventions of social research, with its narrator's monopoly on authority and authorship. Articulating the link between the individual and society is traditionally sociologist's work. But an emphasis on subjective accounts and the subject's "own story" dictates a larger narrative role for the subject and a correspondingly less dominant role for the narrator, giving rise to a potential conflict over the power of naming. In the classic male life histories, subject and narrator appear at times to be competing for authorship. One way to resolve the authorship/authority conflict is through a division of labor where the subject provides (only) raw material and the narrator provides interpretation.

The subject of *The Fantastic Lodge* did not adopt this solution. Janet refused to disappear into obscurity after being interviewed, and resisted abdicating her authorship. At the point where the subject ordinarily loses control over her narrative, Janet claimed hers. For Janet wanted to be a writer. Indeed, Janet was always writing.[20] As a child, she says,

> And I would write papers, thousands and thousands of papers about everything I saw and did, and how it affected me and what it meant to me and so forth. (Hughes 1961, 16)

Once her utterances were transcribed and the text was in hand, Janet took herself seriously as the author of a book. Janet's text had instrumental value for her; it represented an alternative future.

The Wrongly Authored Text

Janet's narrative ranks with the famous life histories of delinquents such as *The Jack-Roller* and *The Professional Thief*. It comes, like them, from the Chicago tradition of life history research. However, the fate of this female subject and her narrative was profoundly discontinuous; she was ultimately impossible to assimilate to the tradition of the Chicago life history.

One explanation could lie in an excess of subjectivity. Even more than

Wladeck, even more than Jenny, Janet's dominant subjectivity created problems. By virtue of her personal attributes, her attitude, and the way she related to the narrative itself, Janet exceeded the usual limits on the role of the subject. Janet was different from the typical subject of Chicago life history. At twenty-one, she was older than some of the other subjects of Chicago life history. She was a cosmopolitan; she had lived in a number of places and had been in boarding school. She was familiar with the university neighborhood of Hyde Park, and was comfortable in the homes of professors and graduate students. She was highly articulate, even voluble.[21] Compared with the subjects of other life histories, Janet came from a more middle-class background.[22] She was less easily controlled than the typical subject of life history (Bennett 1987). As a subject, she could not be contained via the stigma of delinquency nor her life defined by her arrest record. The social scientist/authority could not fix or situate Janet as readily as he could a youth from a bounded ethnic neighborhood.

Janet also ran afoul of gender expectations. She did not recognizably embody any feminine virtues; she was neither silent nor demure. She had a voice that was sardonic, profane, anti-establishment.[23] She did not position herself as a victim nor accept stigma for her antisocial behavior; on the contrary, she was merciless in her criticism of the criminal justice system and its posture of rehabilitation.

Besides flouting the sex role expectations for a good woman, Janet contested the accustomed relations of authority and authorship between subject and narrator. Her voice dominates the text. An authoritative narrator would have been superfluous in Janet's text; the subject provides her own narratorial comment, alternating descriptions of experiences and feelings with observations and reflections (Bennett 1987, 231). Her account of the development of a moral career as a dope addict is the equal of anything in the literature.[24] Like Jenny, Janet had an intelligence and an eloquence that put pressure on those who were accustomed to the roles of narrator and gatekeeper. The conflict over authorship and authority that erupted in the case of *The Fantastic Lodge* pitted the subject and narrator against the gatekeepers of publication.

Howard Becker, who was affiliated both with the Institute for Juvenile Research and the University of Chicago Press, tried to bring them together to effect publication of Janet's text as a book. He ran into enormous resistance from Clifford Shaw, the father of Chicago life history (and the narrator of *The Jack-Roller*). James Bennett (1987) has chronicled the maneuvers Shaw used to block the publication of Janet's text. The course of the negotiations provides a history of attempts to limit, contain, or neutralize the threat posed by Janet's differentness.[25] The defense of atypicality was central in Clifford Shaw's campaign to block the publication of *Lodge*. Shaw's counter-proposal was four other life histories (all male) that, in his opinion, illuminated addiction better than did Janet's. At the same time he sought to reassert an agenda for IJR's publication series and research that marginalized Janet and defined her experience as falling outside the focus and mandate of the institute.

Throughout the 1950s, Bennett records, Janet carried the type-script around with her in a shopping bag. Even after Becker retired from his role as advocate for Janet and her text, she persisted in seeking publication. She engaged in active negotiation with Clifford Shaw concerning the conditions under which he would permit the publication of the text. The manuscript still seemed "a hot potato," and various parties at IJR considered cannibalizing Janet's text and using dismembered parts in a publication on the larger drug study. It was proposed that Janet be allowed to use the rest as she wished. Subsequently, in the interests of protecting the institution against various dangers, they decided to deny her all rights to the transcript (Bennett 1987, 222).

Later Shaw became convinced of the scholarly merit of the manuscript, and seemed ready to accept its publication as long as IJR and the Chicago Project were divorced from it (Bennett 1987, 221). Janet increased the pressure by negotiating with Shaw face-to-face in 1954. Everett and Helen MacGill Hughes undertook a sponsorship role in 1955, and Shaw expressed a willingness for the rights to the material to revert to Janet. By this time, however, the fear of "nuisance" lawsuits had spread to the University of Chicago Press and their interest in the project faded.

In transgressively claiming the power of the narratorial voice, Janet highlights the constraints on the subject that had been established in this tradition. Janet Chase was a victim not only of a particular gate-keeper but of the conventions of life history. By exceeding the subject role she put intolerable pressure on the narrator role and the research orthodoxy that buttressed it. Shaw responded with a series of moves that seemed designed to reduce Janet's claims and put distance between them. In addition to his steadfast resistance to the publication of the text, Shaw also invented a number of other procedures for "handling" Janet, which were unprecedented in the Chicago life history tradition.[26]

The institutional forces of repression had human consequences. The suppression of Janet's text meant the denial of her hopes of escaping her circumstances. Ultimately the publication of *The Fantastic Lodge* would be delayed until after the death of Clifford Shaw—and of "Janet Chase." Clifford Shaw died in 1957, "Janet Chase" in 1959. Helen MacGill Hughes edited the ill-fated manuscript. Finally, through the intervention of David Riesman, the text was published in 1961.

New Configurations of Subject/Narrator/Reader/Text

A reading of *The Fantastic Lodge* illustrates some of the fundamental dynamics involved in relationships among subject, narrator, and text. *Lodge* highlights the potentially powerful role of the subject in life history, a power revealed only because the narrator accepted a smaller role. Howard Becker, an unconventional narrator, resisted dominating his subject and her text. In so doing he changes the subject/reader relationship. Becker's narratorial silence provides the reader with an unobstructed view of a vivid subjectivity that overflows the limits of conventions defining the female and the life history subject. However, without the narrator's voice to overrule her, his subject incurred the full weight of sanction controlled by the social science establishment. The controversy that surrounded her and her text sheds light on the authorship/authority conflict as inflected by the politics of gender.

Like today's feminist narrators, Howard Becker was an advocate for his subject and attempted to sponsor Janet and her text vis-à-vis the class of professional/critical readers.[27]

Conclusion

Traditional practitioners of life history research have valorized subjectivity while maintaining a scientific posture that insists on control. It is strikingly apparent that when the researcher lays down his scientist's insistence on distance and denial, new configurations of subject, narrator, reader, and text become possible. *The Fantastic Lodge* reflects a relationship of some parity and intimacy, even though the narrator remains invisible. In contemporary life histories the second person is often present in the text, in dialogue with the subject. In such texts the narrator reveals herself to a much greater degree.

Altering the subject/researcher dynamic expands the subject's scope. Such a subject remains subject, retains agency in the course of collaborating in research, and engages in sustained dialogue with an embodied second person. The principle of dual authorship is actualized in texts that contain multiple, sometimes contradictory, accounts. In more recent texts the subject talks back. We hear directly from the subject as she/he contests the narrator over issues of interpretation (see Borland 1991; Mbilinyi 1989). Such exchanges lead narrators to extend their thinking about issues of authorship and to problematize the form in which the text will appear.

Current work in sociological autobiography illustrates some of the directions that life history is taking.[28] Two recent collections of brief autobiographies of women sociologists exemplify the rapprochement of narrator and subject. Researchers who explicitly share the identities of their subjects undertake a collective portrait of significant experiences in *Gender and the Academic Experience* (Orlans and Wallace 1994) and in *Individual Voices, Collective Visions* (Goetting and Fenstermaker 1995). These editors position themselves in the experiential field, not apart from it. They seek a multiplicity of accounts and refrain from aggregating, averaging, summarizing, or comparing-and-contrasting individuals' experience. The editors expect and rely on their subjects' ability to share the function of interpretation. The tension between authority and authorship has abated, with no abandonment of the interpretive function.

The expansion of narratorial functions can be seen in the way Goetting inscribes her subjectivity in her text. In her reflections upon her editorial/narratorial task, the feminine theme of connection appears both as a motive and as a method. Goetting's motivation for initiating this project stemmed from her increasing recognition of the importance of a past relationship with a mentor and role model. Giving public recognition to this connection is a filial act for Goetting—and also a maternal one. In creating a resource for future readers Goetting emphasizes reciprocity, linking the inspiration she received from a young female mentor with her gift to the next generation of women sociologists. Goetting reflects also upon the relationship that developed between herself as editor and the contributors she had never seen. As editor, she became in a sense the agent of the life that was to be newly presented in public: its midwife. Her formulation of the ensuing commitment is unique in the sociological literature.

Contributions from feminist methodology and gains in the analysis of gender have enriched contemporary sociological life history. In turn, life history holds extraordinary promise for social science. Sociology as a whole benefits from a developing life history literature that reflects a sentient and situated narrator. The transformation, manifestly, is incomplete; the emergence of the narrator is only a first step. The next step, the exploration and development of the narrator's subjectivity, remains to be achieved.

7

Feminist Biography

If certain lives have the power to touch or to transform our own . . .
to exalt or terrify us, then we, with the biographer as our representative, have the right to make sense of those lives, to their innermost
nature.

—Marc Pachter (1979, 6)

In the life history tradition, failure to come to terms with un-
resolved issues in the relationship between subject and narrator created
persistent contradictions. That relationship, more thoroughly examined
in the literature on biography, is the starting point of this chapter. Biographers seek to grasp and communicate the subjectivity of the subject
and, often, their own as well. In biography the neglected second person
is often visible—and audible. The subject "speaks to" the narrator—and
the narrator, more often than not, replies. Sometimes the narrator speaks
directly to the reader.

With biography defined as the intersection between the personality of
the subject and that of the biographer, two subjectivities are recognized
(Clifford 1970, 12). Biographers take for granted the existence and vi-
tality of a relationship between the subject and narrator; life-telling is
seen as an intimate act (Pachter 1979, 14). Feeling is not disavowed and
the language of emotion is prevalent. Loewenberg's "countertransference" reappears in the biographer's avowed responsiveness to the subject. The biographical act results from the narrator's response to the
subject and the commitments that she makes. Biographers, refreshingly,
have owned their narratorial agency, and in doing so open up a discussion that is lacking from social science discourses. Studying what biographers say about their work extends our understanding of the possibilities of the narrator's role. Feminist biographers in particular have introduced unabashed exploration of the narrator's relationship with the

subject, a more visible (and vocal) narrator, and texts transformed by these inclusions. These advances demand a more complex reading of biography, leading the way to a renewed focus on the problematics of interpretation.

Gender pervades the definition of biography's traditional dilemmas. Many of these center on the relationship between narrator and subject— in fact, on issues of closeness and distance. Problematics of identification and advocacy rest upon the biographer's feelings about closeness and distance. Other enduring dilemmas of biography deal with the narrator's rights and responsibilities in his relationship with the subject: dilemmas of revelation and concealment, advocacy and interpretation, power and responsibility. These too are gendered.

A narratorial distrust of the subject often surfaces when biographers discuss issues relating to power and responsibility. Distrust of the subject often mirrors mistrust of one's own subjectivity, as where the narrator tries to stifle his values or commitments or affinities (Chevigny 1983; Edel 1979; Maurois 1929). The masculine prohibition against the avowal of feeling makes the biographer doubt his work, even perhaps to redefine it as autobiography disguised as biography (Maurois 1929, 285). In searching for the truth in a life, the biographer encounters a fundamental dilemma in deciding how much to reveal or conceal his subject's secrets. Scenarios of power, rights, and responsibilities are played out in conjunction with stratagems for wresting information from an unwilling source. If the task of biography is exploration of the subject's personal mythology, then material that the subject customarily conceals yields the greatest insights (Rose 1985). Probing beneath the "revealing mask" increases the biographer's power and also his existential responsibility. One school of thought holds that the biographer should disregard limits the subject places on revelation.[1] In pursuit of this goal biographers may adopt a predatory stance vis-à-vis their subject.[2] The biographer can become an inquisitor or antagonist to the subject.[3]

The classic dilemmas of biography raise issues about the location and prerogatives of subject and narrator vis-à-vis each other. Feminist biographers have a commitment to parity that influences the way they deal with the dilemmas of biography. They tend to accept more responsibility and claim fewer rights vis-à-vis their subjects. The commitment to parity realigns the relationship of subject to narrator and changes the way each is seen. As connection is emphasized, control recedes. A feminist approach to "objectivity" can lead the narrator to efface herself and let the subject speak for herself.[4] However, the biographer who elects to let her subject speak for herself and adopts a respectful, "hands-off" attitude may be criticized for taking a "weak" position. In a zero-sum model, power "added" to the subject is "subtracted" from the narrator.

> The biographer producing such a work often pretends that he is allowing the character to speak for himself or herself. This is an ingenuous way of avoiding biographical responsibility. (Edel 1979, 18)

So we see that when biography focuses on the narrator/subject relationship, familiar controversies arise. Biographers write frankly about the intensity and complexity of the bond between themselves and their subject.[5] But in biography as in the social science traditions, identification is often perceived as a threat to objectivity. The narrator's commitment to engage in acts of rescue or advocacy revives conflicts concerning objectivity.[6] Intersubjectivity can thus be seen as either an asset or a threat. For many biographers a conflict about closeness versus distance arises around their identification with the subject. For some, closeness signals the threat of fusion and the eclipse of objectivity. The biographer fears that a relationship that is "too close" might obliterate his analytic capacity.

> When a biographer identifies with the subject the emotions are bound to be more intense and the result is the blindness that resides in idealization. . . . intrusive emotions can enter into the. . . . job. (Edel 1984, 286)

Closeness and distance are heavily implicated in gender scripts, as we have seen in Chapter 4. It is therefore not surprising that female and male biographers view identification in a different light. Dissenting from Edel's biographical practice, Bell Gale Chevigny (1983) drew closer to Margaret Fuller instead of seeking to increase the distance between herself and her subject. Chevigny utilized a recognizably feminine style of relationship work in subjecting her feeling of identification to self-scrutiny. She chose to work through her identification rather than abandoning or stifling it. In order to do this Chevigny had to fight feelings of dismay at the intensity of her engagement with Fuller, and suspicion that her feminist commitments were a possible source of bias. She attained a more powerful insight without sacrificing feeling, and came to define objectivity as enriched by subjectivity. For her, the dangers of feeling psychologically connected were balanced by

> the promising possibility that by engaging the identification with the subject (rather than fleeing it) one can achieve a deeper and clearer understanding of her than that vouchsafed by "objectivity." (1983, 81)

The idea of an activist narrator is not new in biography. Biographers often express a desire to cheat history, to reverse obscurity, to save the subject from mortality. The biographer becomes the sponsor of a life; he has a drive "to save, if not a soul, then a personality for the company of future generations" (Pachter 1979, 4). Feminist biographers in particular appreciate that the possibility of a viable future depends, at least in part, on securing a usable past.

> Feminist biographers often see themselves as engaged in an act of rescue, trying to restore to their rightful place foremothers who have been ignored, misunderstood, or forgotten. (Hall 1987, 23)

Feminist biography is positioned to recast the biographer's classic dilemmas, beginning with a redefinition of the narrator. Feminist biographers go beyond the activist narrator to show the reader a narrator in relationship. Feminist biographers declare themselves in a number of ways. Sometimes they rely on the selection of a biographical subject to make their feminist point. Lucy Sprague Mitchell's biographer frames the life with an account of her own identification with her subject, situating herself as an academic woman in whose life work and love are both central (Antler 1987). A more forceful presence is that of Carol Ascher, Simone de Beauvoir's biographer, who addresses her subject directly. In writing a letter objecting to the lack of reciprocity between herself and de Beauvoir (1984), Ascher illustrates a new protocol of narrator and subject. She violates the cultural pretense of objectivity, emphasizing her demand for mutuality by preemptively revealing herself. She extends narratorial reflexivity further by including a self-dialogue in which she explores the transgression of femininity her self-revelation involves, wrestling with the knowledge that a good girl would not expose herself in that way.

Ascher's insertion of herself, her demands, and her apprehension profoundly alter the biography: the relationship becomes part of the text and part of the subject matter. The text now includes a relationship that itself has a theme of conflict (Minnich 1985). In "personalizing" the biographer's task the narrator incurs risks but also gains. Ascher's personal passion for equality brings an advantage to the biography: it provides the grounds for a startlingly apt intellectual apprehension of her subject (Minnich 1985, 293). Another feminist biographer who recognizes the active, situated narrator is Wendy Mulford, the biographer of Sylvia Townsend Warner and Valentine Ackland (1988). As a biographer Mulford sees herself mediating lives, and reflexively allows the reader to witness her struggle with her dislike of Valentine Ackland.

In addition to reshaping the received agenda of biography, feminist biographers have begun to import insights deriving from gender scholarship in social science and literature. Indeed, a profound understanding of the gender system is one of the strengths of feminist biography. The biographer of women must be able to tell her subject's life within the powerful but often elusive iron cage of gender. This has meant analyzing the distinctive positioning of women vis-à-vis socially significant constructions such as achievement, sexuality, and worth. The accepted polarity of public and private has been a major target of feminist critique. Biographies of public women have often stumbled when their authors become entrapped in this dualism of public and private that masks sex role stereotyping.[7] Feminist biographers reject the sequestering of women in "the private sphere." In tracing the development of Susan B. Anthony's political consciousness Kathleen Barry shows a new relation between public and private, establishing consciousness as the endpoint, rather than the origin, of Anthony's amazing career.[8] A political consciousness accompanied this reversal, and produced an awareness of the possibilities that could transcend the limitations of this term (1988, 31). Another biographer attempts to blur the distinction between public and private life, redefining "feminism as life process" and questioning the restriction of feminism to public action to change society (Antler 1987).

The Social Production of Obscurity

The gendered distinction between public and private underlies the classification of women's lives as "notable" or "obscure." In telling women's lives we go head-to-head with a gendered intellectual and literary tradition that presents us with the question, Why have there been no great women artists/writers/philosophers? Feminist biography gives us a way to reconceptualize the question. The seeming paucity of women subjects is a manifestation of gender dynamics, for the "shortage" of female subjects is manufactured by the social production of obscurity. We begin to recognize that women's lives are caused to disappear. It is the social production of obscurity that renders women's lives invisible, unintelligible, and/or insignificant.

In every age, women geniuses have gained access to the academy, the platform, or the printing press. They have created work that could guarantee them fame in perpetuity. But great women have been lost in every epoch, and their great works mislaid. As the generations turn, as records are kept or discarded, as work is attributed or appropriated, as reputations and contributions are assessed, as critics speak—and others, perforce, fall silent—women are erased from history. Twenty years of women's history have restored to us some of our female geniuses and heroines—Hypatia, La Malinche, Virginia Woolf, Christine de Pisan, and Frida Kahlo, among others.[9] The historical studies were needed to demonstrate that the invisibility of women results from an active process of omission operated by human judgment and human agency. Understandably, history has restored to us mainly notable women, leaving the great majority unknown and undocumented. We should not, however, take obscurity for granted; rather, we should examine its dynamics.

In viewing obscurity as the product of an active process of exclusion we should examine "obscure" as a verb. To obscure, according to Webster, is to darken, to dim, to make less conspicuous, to overshadow.[10] The fate of Christine de Pisan and her work illustrates the operation of such processes. Few authors can have been lost and rediscovered as often as she was (Lawson 1985). In her own lifetime (1365–1430?) Christine de Pisan was a respected writer. Her reputation survived her for a century, but then was eclipsed. She was rediscovered in the early seventeenth century, but a plan to publish some of her books miscarried. Rediscovered again in the eighteenth century, Christine de Pisan was the subject of a biography and later yet was anthologized. She received critical acclaim in 1838, and again when her lyric poetry was published fifty years later. In this century, nonetheless, some of her works cannot be found in print. Such lives as hers have been forcibly submerged, usually through the agency of male scholars, critics, and publishers (see Schibanoff 1983; Lawson 1985).[11]

The social production of obscurity renders women's lives invisible, unintelligible, and/or insignificant. The most general form of obscurity is simple invisibility. Most women's lives are obscure in the sense of being unrecorded. Throughout history, the majority of women have lived undocumented lives.[12] Even today, amid the thousands of statistics we take for granted in a post-Weberian world, the fact, and certainly the facts, of many women's lives are still obscured.

According to Webster,[13] that which is obscure is in an inconspicuous position, hidden, hence not well-known. Obscurity in a second sense, insignificance, is related to the *perceived* dimness of uncounted and unremarked obscure lives. They are thought to be of no importance. The privileging of the public over the private is reflected even in women's self-reports. The perception of insignificance results from an active process of peripheralization of women's concerns, joined with a privileging of male experience, the institutionalization of narrative conventions shaped to male accounts, and staffing patterns that recruit males to gatekeeping positions. Lives that seem insignificant to the gatekeepers are consigned to obscurity. Judgments of "significance" are made by a restricted class of readers: critics, professors, editors. Peripherality, in turn, reflects the judgment of the subject who positions himself at the center.

A third aspect of obscurity is unintelligibility, which can refer to a life or to the text that memorializes it. But unintelligibility is a judgment that is rendered, rather than an attribute of the text. In judging intelligibility the subjective reaction of the reader is projected onto the text: a text that I understand is "clear"; a text I do not understand is "obscure." The judgment of unintelligibility may simply signal a failure of intersubjectivity, but its consequence is the expulsion of the subject from the community of shared discourse. The dynamics of the social production of obscurity can be seen in three biographies of contemporary women: Barbara McClintock, Manya Wilbushewitz Shohat, and Mabel Dodge Luhan.

Barbara McClintock, an Obscure Woman

Barbara McClintock was an "obscure" biologist who became visible to the public through her biographer, Evelyn Fox Keller (1983), and the tardy award of a Nobel Prize for her scientific achievements.[14] In the 1970s, when Keller began her project, Barbara McClintock was a poor candidate for biography. She was a talented, dedicated, and quirky woman of a type that big-time science had made obsolete; she was a misfit, a failure, a loser. Barbara McClintock had become obscure, a footnote to history. From the perspective of microbiology as the field had developed over the past twenty-five years, she was insignificant.

McClintock was not born to fame. She was not the daughter, consort, or mother of a famous man. She was a reclusive, solitary scientist whose life was her work, and whose work was completely inaccessible to the general public. Her field, plant genetics, was an atypical choice for a woman. Family tradition holds that McClintock was a self-contained individual from infancy. An early and sustained separation from her parents may have contributed to a lifelong relish of solitude and a lack of intense emotional relationships with human beings.[15] Her family supported the principle of self-determination, if not her goal of a career in science. McClintock was in fact well suited to the highly nontraditional career that she sought. Even the institutionalized sexism of Cornell University's plant breeding department, which refused to admit her for graduate study, presented no permanent obstacle. McClintock's exceptional ability won her scientific recognition, and her career grew up along with the discipline. By 1944, when she was elected to the National Academy of Science and elected president of the Genetics Society of America, she was at the pinnacle of her career. Then she began the work on genetic transposition that was to be her "downfall."

Following the publication of a paper on transposition in 1950, McClintock prepared to present her full results and model at the annual Cold Spring Harbor Symposium. Her apprehension of this event was more than justified: her presentation was greeted with silence, snickers, mutters, and a few slurs on her mental health. Five years later she tried again, presenting the even greater complexity her succeeding research had revealed. The rejection was even more pronounced. McClintock was devastated. Her peers' reaction reversed a lifetime's experience of confident, self-directed activity and the appreciation with which it had been received. In a typical consequence of unintelligibility, McClintock herself blamed for the "failure of communication." She was shunned; her reprints were no longer requested; she was not invited to give seminars.[16]

McClintock stopped talking about her work; she stopped publishing, and became "wary" about audiences and visitors. She "retreated into obscurity" (E. Keller 1983, ix). Keller analyzes this cataclysm as a crisis of intelligibility. There is no indication that the award of the Nobel Prize to McClintock in 1983 reversed or eradicated the effects of this experience. Barbara McClintock died in 1992.

Manya Wilbushewitz Shohat, an Unintelligible Woman

The life of Manya Wilbushewitz Shohat illustrates another aspect of 'obscurity.' An activist, terrorist, and pioneer who should be remembered as the inventor of the kibbutz, Shohat is largely unknown today.[17] Making sense of her political history has posed a biographical challenge. Manya's political development was influenced by the contradictions of Jewish life in late nineteenth-century Russia. Born in 1880 to a family with an Orthodox, landowning father and a more secularly oriented mother, Manya had among her siblings a diverse spectrum of political reactions. Her own trajectory took her from the place assigned to women in Orthodox Judaism, to Russian populism, to police socialism, to terrorism, Zionism, and finally agricultural collectivism. Manya first became concerned about poverty in the lives of the Russian peasants, and became committed to social change. She ran away from home at fifteen and found work as a carpenter in her brother's factory in Minsk. There she organized a strike against him, and the special oppressions under which Jews worked.

The Bund and Zionist organizations competed for the allegiance of Jewish workers at this time. Manya was closely related to proponents of Zionism and of terrorism. Extending her political commitment to all working people, Manya journeyed to the Tartar area to aid victims of famine and cholera, in defiance of an edict banning Jews from traveling there. She became acquainted with the Russian communal system, and on her return to Minsk organized an urban commune there.

Arrested in 1899 in a police crackdown on the Bund, Manya was kept in solitary confinement and compelled to engage in political debates with the chief of security police. According to her account, she taught him the basics of police socialism. They came to an agreement that she would be released from prison to organize the Jewish Independent Labor Party, which indeed came into a brief existence in 1901.

Manya first visited Palestine in 1904, and began to work on the problem of an economic base for Russian Jews who would immigrate to Palestine. She now traveled in Europe seeking support for the establishment of agricultural collectives. She began to collect and transport arms for Jewish self-defense groups in Russian cities. On one of these trips Manya was cornered by a secret police officer who had been following her. Manya shot him, packed up his body in a trunk, mailed it to a fictitious address, and continued on her way. After spending some months with a terrorist group, changing her address every day, Manya returned to Palestine in 1906, went to America to study collective settlements, and returned to Palestine to begin her experiments. She formed an alliance with Israel Shohat, who wanted to establish a camp to train men to defend Jewish settlements, and married him in May 1908. In their experimental collective, equal participation by women was a fundamental principle.[18]

From the beginning Manya was difficult to classify using the conventional categories of political activism. The progression of political commitments made by this passionate activist is "unintelligible" from the perspective of established political theories of Left and Right. In such theoretical anomalies the difficulties are more frequently attributed to limitations of the individual than to those of the paradigm. Pointing out the limitations of the taken-for-granted paradigm of "political man," Shulamit Reinharz (1984b) solves the "problem" of Shohat's political inconsistency by elucidating a "women's praxis" that differs from that of men. The seeming inconsistency of Shohat's changing political commitment was no more than the development of ideology continuously defined through experience mediated by relationships (Reinharz 1984b, 276).[19]

Ambiguities of Gender: Mabel Dodge Luhan

A third example illustrates a paradox of obscurity: how a famous woman, the focus of extensive attention in fiction and nonfiction, can still elude understanding. The life of Mabel Dodge Luhan was not obscure. Mabel, undeniably a "mover and shaker," immersed herself in the spirit of her times, supporting, writing, and speaking about the various causes that promised to liberate her and her fellow men and women from the spiritual and psychological shackles of the past.[20] Mabel was conscious of constructing herself and adopted a sequence of identities—the androgynous daredevil and hardhearted vamp of her youth in Buffalo, the sustained impersonation of a medieval aristocrat in Florence, and the muse to male genius, to name just a few. The challenge of Mabel's life illustrates the central problematic of gender, and indicates the need for further development.

Mabel's life was well publicized and well documented. Yet two current biographies offer contradictory accounts of her, underscoring the complexities of interpreting gender.[21] It appears that both biographers had access to roughly the same sources and neither had the advantage of a personal relationship with her subject. Their substantially different accounts arose from the persons and perspectives of the biographers. Both biographers were women, but they came to the task equipped with different repertoires of gender. One narrator took gender as a central problematic for the life. The other operated with an implicit theory of gender that was no less influential for being unexamined.

One biographer (Hahn 1977) views Mabel in a context of relationships with men. Hahn's Mabel is a self-serving, hardhearted rich woman who cared little for her husbands, lovers, or son. She is lacking in the feminine virtues of nurturance, warmth, self-sacrifice, loyalty, and service to others.[22] Hahn's most serious criticism of Mabel is in terms of work and worth. In this third-person account the narrator's subject-positioning remains unacknowledged and unanalyzed. Hahn portrays Mabel as an unproductive, no-talent hanger-on in the councils of the gifted and celebrated. In Hahn's harsh judgment Mabel is parasitic and somehow inauthentic because she did not seek to achieve in the same ways as the men she so admired. Mabel is also castigated for her class position; Hahn presents her as a parasite and a "capitalist." In Hahn's treatment, Mabel is unpatriotic to boot.[23]

The other biographer, Lois Palken Rudnick, constructs Mabel as a figure in history, as a representative of women, and as an exemplar of a gender dilemma:

> Mabel. . . . speaks to those who are seeking to understand the roles of women in the American past and to define them for the future. She wished to reveal, think about and change the universe, but believed the desire 'to found the world anew' could only be accomplished by men.   (Rudnick 1984, xii)

For this biographer Mabel is a "common denominator" whose life connects important social and intellectual issues in late nineteenth- and early twentieth-century European and American life.[24] The central dilemma of Mabel's life is defined within a discourse of gender. For beneath the image of the sexually liberated "New Woman," Mabel found women (and herself) emotionally and intellectually reliant on men.[25] She saw herself as possessing vision but lacking puissance. She believed she needed to be completed by a doer: he would be the agent, she the inspiration.[26] By allowing the powerful men she collected to draw upon her feminine essence, Mabel expected to control the process and direction of their creative energies (1984, xii).

Issues of authorship and authority are central to Mabel's life and work, and to the different interpretations of her biographers. What Rudnick saw as Mabel's personal myth, Hahn accepted as fact. Hahn saw Mabel much as the admittedly self-centered male artist might have seen her—as a source of services. Whether viewed as "earth mother" or sex object or handmaiden, her role definition is always with reference to the male subject. Hahn seems to apply sexual scripts originating in her own culture, without problematizing them. She relies on stereotypes that are incapable of carrying the biography. Rudnick is able to relate Mabel's essential ambivalence to prevailing discourses of gender. The "vicariousness" of Mabel's ambition was a reflection of the limits placed on women's ambition and assertion in her time; this makes Mabel *more* representative of her times than women she knew who were doers (Willa Cather, Emma Goldman, Margaret Sanger).[27]

The case of Mabel Dodge Luhan shows that more attention needs to be paid to gender scripts that underwrite self-evaluation. Mabel was not a conventional woman nor confined in the private sphere; femininity did not provide an adequate script for her life. In her life and writing Mabel directly engaged the gender system; inescapably her biographers are led to grapple with it in seeking to tell her life. Certain challenges in Mabel's life underscore the need for new narratives deeply informed by research and theory on gender.

Women are positioned in a distinctive way vis-à-vis dominant themes of their culture, such as achievement. Empirical research on achievement motivation is an area where sex differences have been repeatedly documented and often underinterpreted (see Atkinson 1958). When Matina Horner brought women into this tradition (1969), the gendered nature of achievement became visible for the first time.[28] Situations of achievement, structured as they were, confronted women with a classic approach/avoidance conflict, where achievement outcomes carried both reward and punishment.

Societal expectations for achievement prescribe that male success is the norm and female success the anomaly. Sexual scripts affect the interpretation of successes and failures, as research shows. In the U.S., young people learn a gendered style of attribution that they use to interpret their own and others' success and failure (Deaux and Emswiller 1974; Deaux et al. 1975).[29] The individual's chances for occupational success are colored by the way others interpret their performance. In the context of gendered attribution, it is the narrator's task to put the subject's muted claims and self-doubts in the perspective of the society in which she lives. The narrator must temper the subject's individualistic interpretation of failure. The two biographies of Mabel Dodge Luhan diverge in how the narrator responds to the challenge of self-deprecation. Hahn in particular is taken in by her surface self-denigration, failing to ask to what expectations or intimidation that self-presentation is a response. Possibly Mabel's own self-belittling definition corresponds to the narrator's assessment, hence is not problematized.[30]

Apart from issues of ambition and achievement, Mabel Dodge Luhan's life highlights the need for a more nuanced understanding of gender scripts that shape self-presentation. Neither Rudnick nor Hahn problematizes Mabel's struggles with the narratives available to her.[31] Mabel was an unusual woman in making a claim on posterity and in recognizing herself as an agent in history. When she began writing her memoirs in 1924, her goal was to present her life as a paradigm.[32] Yet Mabel had difficulty in finding a pattern for her self-narrative. She became dissatisfied with borrowed ways of perceiving and expressing experience.[33] In the last volume of her autobiography Mabel struggles with dilemmas of self-expression.

> Was one to be forever reminded of something else and never to experience anything in itself at first-hand? My mind seemed to me a waste-basket of the world, full of scraps that I wanted to throw away and couldn't.
>
> (Luhan 1937, 301–2)

Mabel's self-reproach can be read as the protest of a woman dead-ended by a received patriarchal culture, for whom no language exists. She was doubly balked, as biographical and autobiographical subject, by the inherited language and images of an androcentric tradition. In formulating her view of herself as subject, she was impeded by otherness as defined by men's eyes. As a subject of autogynography, she was grappling with the enduring dilemmas of telling women's lives.

These issues do not exhaust the biographical potential of Mabel Dodge Luhan. The complexities of Luhan's life call out for future biographies that explore more deeply Mabel's relationships with women, her sexuality, the identity of "rich woman," and connectivity.

Conclusion

In concluding this chapter, we can recognize the achievements of feminist biography even while acknowledging the need for further development. Strands of feminist method seen in other genres have come to fruition in biography. Thus recognition of the importance of the second person has paved the way for a developing theory of the narrator. A more static view of the narrator/subject relationship has given way to expression of an ongoing, unpredictable relation of two subjectivities. The principle of parity, central to feminist methodology, has led to abandoning control and allowing connection to reemerge.

When subject and narrator are less separated the "space" between them can be explored, elaborated, theorized. Authors write of empathic leaps, of joining their horizon with that of the subject. Communication is flowing in both directions. When both subject and narrator are seen as subjects, and neither holds a monopoly of interpretation, the text is radically restructured. It may appear as a consultative process or contain elements of dialogue, as where Fay Weldon addresses Rebecca West in the second person (1985), or Ascher writes to de Beauvoir (1984). The narrator's insertion of herself into the text often produces experimental forms. Both subject and authorship are unconventional in Wendy Mulford's joint biography of Sylvia Townsend Warner and Valentine Ackland (1988).[34] Mulford selects a dual subject, and also acknowledges the possibility of more than one narrator, as she shares authorship with Sylvia's close friend. The text itself becomes unconventional, disordered, and once again, "messy." The inclusion of the biographical relationship in the text increases the narrator's burden[35] and points toward more complex interpretation (Minnich 1985, 288).

Other distinctive features of feminist biographies are less experimental while still advancing the practical understanding of intersubjectivity. Feminist biographers, sensitized to women's preoccupations, refract in their texts content that we previously discovered in women's autobiographies. The form and framing of feminist biography reflect connection, dailiness, and emotion work. Friendship between women provides a paradigm for feminist biography. Writing the life of another woman requires some of the same qualities or conditions as a good conversation with a friend:

> mutuality, as interdependence risked, respected, and enjoyed; equality, guaranteeing the grounds for and so allowing the celebration of difference; familiarity, knowing enough about each other in the various worlds we inhabit to hear what is said and to comprehend what is meant.
>
> (Minnich 1985, 287)

The feminist principle of parity that has revolutionized the narrator/subject relationship redefines the reader as well. When the relationship of subject and narrator is present it is easier for us, as readers, to achieve and maintain a relation of mutuality, equality, and familiarity. Feminist biography is characterized by an explicit recognition and concern for the reader. So in feminist biography the reader often appears as a co-participant in the relationship of subject and narrator,[36] and is frequently included by means of the first-person plural. The link between subject, narrator, and reader is affirmed in language that valorizes a familiar form of relationship work. Reading women's lives is like

> the best sort of gossip, a really good talk about interesting friends in the course of which we touch on their lives, our own lives, our continuing efforts to understand women's lives and life itself.   (Minnich 1985, 292)[37]

Other emphases also highlight relationship.[38] Attempts to write the biography of a relationship may be the harbinger of a revival of prosopography (Rose 1985; Ware 1987; Mulford 1988; Butler and Rosenblum 1991). Previously neglected or "obscure" women may enter the literature of biography in the form of collective biographies (Rose 1985). Another direction for future development in feminist biography is intersectional studies exploring differing constellations of race, class, and gender. The difficulty of such a focus can be seen in a biography of Jessie Ames where Jacquelyn Dowd Hall (1979) struggled with her subject's triple marginality as she sought to place Ames in regional history where men dominated; in a women's movement lacking a southerner's perspective; and as an individual whose talents and sensibility were at odds with her circumstances and times. Hall accepted the task of struggling against the hegemonic discourses and patriarchal intellectual tradition, factors that are part of Ames' *and* Hall's stories.

Some writers see far-reaching effects of the new feminist biography. By undermining the constructed polarity of public and private life women's biography changes history (Barry 1988). By creating a relation of woman to woman across time and cultures, feminist biography helps establish the public space so long denied to women (Minnich 1985, 288).

8

A Feminist Approach to Telling Women's Lives

Now the blindness in human beings. . . . is the blindness with which we are all inflicted in regard to the feelings of creatures and people different from ourselves. . . .

Hence the stupidity and injustice of our opinions, so far as they deal with the significance of alien lives. Hence the falsity of our judgements, so far as they presume to decide in an absolute way on the value of other persons' conditions or ideals. . . .

It absolutely forbids us to be forward in pronouncing on the meaninglessness of forms of existence other than our own; and it commands us to tolerate, respect and indulge those whom we see harmlessly happy and interested in their own ways, however unintelligible these may be to us.

—William James (1899, 229; italics mine)

William James's quote is applicable to all endeavors that take human beings as their subject-matter. It is a plea for empathy and respect in the face of difference. It is also a warning against arrogance in interpretation, against chauvinism and against universalizing one's own subject-positioning. Above all, it is a reminder that there is never only one narrative, a reminder that we must bear in mind in this chapter, as we look forward and backward at the challenges of telling women's lives.

The task of this book has been to identify the elements of a woman-centered methodology for telling women's lives, and indicate the direction of its further development. Inevitably, we have looked backward at the history of life-telling, at canons and conflicts. Established traditions of life-telling have been fruitful in pointing toward changes that are needed if existing genres are to accommodate women's narrative. In the context of established traditions, contradictions and reversals that are unavoidable in woman-centered scholarship have serendipitously opened many unsuspected pathways. The S/N/R/T framework developed from the study of existing traditions, transformed by feminist advances. These developments have created a sense of forward momentum that dominates this book. But I would be remiss to understate the conservative power of genres and gatekeepers that continue to shape the future of life-telling. Consequently, in concluding this book these innovations are viewed from two sides, what has been as well as what may be.

In the conjunction of old and new scholarship the stage was set for a creative conflict that changed every term of the S/N/R/T framework, resulting in a revisioned subject; a researcher transformed into a narrator; increased inclusion of some readers but a distancing from the critic/reader; and a text that often includes the voice of the narrator. The general outline of a feminist methodology for telling women's lives is now apparent. Elements of an emerging feminist praxis include reversing abstraction and context-stripping; affirming relationship and avowing a biographically real narrator; demystifying the researcher and moving toward parity with the informant; discarding dissociative methods in favor of a feminist praxis of connection; embracing "messiness" and abandoning a monistic linear narrative. A researcher transformed by reflexivity into a narrator emerges as the central actor in this developing praxis. Changes in the narrator, in turn, produce changes in the subject/narrator relationship; in the subject and in the text; and they produce new relationships with readers.

The Narrator

Reflexivity is the essential trigger for the transformation of researcher into narrator. In feminist life-telling the subjectivity of the narrator is not only acknowledged and brought into the frame but also analyzed and developed as a tool. Feminist explorations of narratorial subjectivity are characterized by (1) going toward (into) feelings, (2) getting close to the subject, (3) self analysis, and (4) treating feelings as information. Feminist scholars regard their feelings as invaluable guides that lead them further into the phenomenon (and incidentally, closer to the subject). Self-avowal is necessary in order to permit the development of disciplined subjectivity. This is what Krieger (1983) did when she opened herself to her reaction to her experience in the field. She did not abandon analysis to wallow in her feelings; rather, by restoring them to their context in interaction she used feelings to cast light on the issues of the study.

Adopting a principle of going toward feeling, women narrators examine and work with their attraction to (or, more rarely, their dislike of) the subject. Following an ethos of connection rather than separation, feminist biographers valorize affinity, as we have seen in the work of Chevigny. Instead of trying to suppress her initial reaction or fake neutrality, Jacqueline Dowd Hall treated her dislike of Jessie Ames as information about herself and their relationship, utilizing her reaction to articulate a dynamic of gender that applied both to subject and narrator. Matter-of-factly, these scholars have treated feelings as information and used them to shape the tools of an original analysis.

Feminist researchers do not view their personal attributes as contaminants. Instead, they recognize the contribution of their own qualities to a unique and situated account. This narrator does not feel the need to manage or deceive the subject.[1] She is not compelled to don the cloak of invisibility or the platform shoes of scientific detachment. She is more likely to shed "scientist drag" and appear before her subject in a recognizable everyday identity,[2] with significant implications for the narrator/subject relationship. A more peer-like self-presentation of the narrator in turn facilitates reciprocity in the subject-narrator relationship. Instead of viewing researcher and informant as roles, and emphasizing the corresponding protocol, feminist researchers have focussed on the self and subject in relationship, a relationship of collaboration rather than control. This approach is particularly apt where the aim of the research is imparting or sharing the reality of another's experience.[3]

Female culture provides signposts for some narrators to turn toward innovation. Thus the emotion work that is valorized in female culture provides a pattern for the narrator's task of working with subjective responses in a disciplined and goal-directed way. The development of a praxis of empathy in telling women's lives rests upon this foundation in female culture. The narrator's subjectivity, joining feeling with cognition, enables her to understand the other's experience as though it were her own.

Women's willingness to do work on themselves, to bring themselves into the frame, has made possible a new kind of understanding. Studying women's ways of knowing, Mary Belenky and her collaborators have examined strategies women employ to "stretch the outer boundaries of consciousness" in the pursuit of understanding.[4] Such reflexive work plays a major part in readying narrators for an empathic connection with the subject. Narrators' intellectual exploration of their own responsiveness to and connection with their subject was a major underpinning in the development of a praxis of empathy, a feminist method for telling lives.

The Subject

A striking characteristic of the feminist approach to life-telling is an upgraded conception of the subject. The active, agentic subjects sometimes glimpsed in earlier biography and life history were often overshadowed by the narrator. A revisioned subject emerges clearly in accounts of feminist methodology, which assumes a subject who is eager to explore how she constructs meaning and who feels as much in control of the research situation as does the researcher (Reinharz 1984a, 181). Now accounts focus on the subject as agent (Hall 1987; Chevigny 1983), operating in an expanded sphere. The consequences of thinking of subjects in this way can be seen in Gluck and Patai's (1991) book on women's personal narratives, which provides ample evidence that subjects claim an active, agentic role. With an upgraded subject meaning is constructed in the dialogue between researcher and subject, and the data gathering process is one of recording it. The subject plays a role in analysis and interpretation along with the narrator; in some instances her interpretation may prevail over that of the narrator.

The Narrator/Subject Relationship

Inserting the self into the frame increases the importance of the relationship between narrator and subject and changes its focus. A redefined subject complements a narrator who operates on feminist principles, who does not try to bind or deny her subject's capacities. Rather than seeking to neutralize the active, problem-solving orientation of a fellow human being, the feminist narrator enlists her as a collaborator. Thus Pat Taylor sustained a collaborative relationship with Jewell Babb, the subject of her oral history. This partnership went beyond the boundaries of formal interviews, for Mrs. Babb continued to send notes to the narrator as her process of recollection continued. Following an interview Mrs. Babb often extended the dialogue by adding handwritten notes (Reinharz 1992, 140). In this kind of association the data gathering process is seen as one of recording of meaning constructed in the dialogue between researcher and subject. The knowledge that constitutes the subject matter is itself a social emergent, created rather than merely accessed in a focussed interaction between two members of the same species.

Feminist methodology creates a link between the regained subjectivity of the narrator and that of the subject. Intersubjectivity is both the ground and the product of this connection. The way feminist research is built upon intersubjectivity involves a premise of parity and a methodology built upon connection. The narrator forges the essential link between her own subjectivity and that of the subject through a conscious practice of empathy. Empathy permits the narrator to expand her experiential base by acquiring vicarious knowledge or "second-hand first hand" experience (Belenky et al. 1986).

A Feminist Praxis of Empathy

Feminist perspectives refine connection, empathy, and parity into the tools of a new approach to telling women's lives. The feminist method for life-telling depends on the deliberate exercise of empathy, consciously developed as a method of research.

> In the experience of empathy there is a certain immediacy, a quickening sense of correspondence, a leap of vitality, an insight that catches one up in the interaction itself, and, eventually, a compelling interest in the fates of other people. (Frank 1979)

In Frank's definition, affinity and identification, fundamental building blocks for understanding human lives, are refined as intellectual tools. The joining of thinking and feeling in empathy sparks an accelerated movement back and forth from insight to involvement. This process leads finally to the point of caring—and, let it be said, to an unconventionally passionate scholarship. But empathy is distinct from the spontaneous, untransformed sense of identification that biographers remark, and must be consciously fostered. This empathy is a disciplined, cognitive activity based on an intentional connection. Empathy, the participation in another's reality, requires activity and the exercise of will (Sartre, quoted in Crapanzano 1980). It is achieved through the narrator's disciplined use of her own subjectivity.[5]

One approach is the method Belenky et al. call "connected knowing": where the knower seeks to enter into a union with that which is to be known. She seeks to see the other in her own terms,[6] accepts the subject as real, and maintains her integrity in seeking to know her. In order to gain understanding of the other, the subjectivity of the narrator is turned receptively toward the subject. Her stance is one of respectful attentiveness.

Women's culture provides the roots for a praxis of connection in feminist research. Feminists rely on a continuity between their activities as researchers and the daily life of women. Thus feminist scholars have discovered resources for their research in the discourse of women's daily lives, emphasizing continuities between the biographer's skills and the skills of normal social interaction.

> All our encounters involve interpreting each other during an interaction; the biographer is in interaction with her subject. Here is where we begin to touch the subjectivity of others, and they ours. . . . We begin to know our subject the way we do others in our lives.   (Barry 1990)

Intersubjectivity is the term Barry uses to refer to this deeper level of understanding. This intersubjectivity forms the core of social life, creates the connections among individuals, and is the means by which we are located in the social world. It is the reader's basis for interpreting biography.

The Reader

The subject/narrator relationship redefined in feminist terms evokes a different reader and authors a different sort of text. In making herself known to the subject the feminist narrator also makes herself known, in her particularity, to the reader. To some degree she may rely on a shared female culture that connects subject, narrator, and reader. Increasingly, she may make use of the extensive research on women and gender that has been produced in the past quarter-century—knowledge that the reader may also share.

A hallmark of the new feminist methodology is the narrator's avowal of her woman's experience. Accounts that are characterized by a self-reference permit women narrators to call upon everyday life as a source of explanatory models. Women's everyday associations often provide the models for theory. Theoretical contributions are thus characterized by accessibility. Bell Gale Chevigny selects everyday images to express her insights. She recasts the narrator/subject relationship in terms of a symbolic mother-daughter bond in which each becomes a surrogate mother for the other in an ideal reciprocity. In such a relationship, both intellective and empathic, an author can be in possession of, and possessed by, her subject in such a way that the embrace enhances the autonomy of both (Chevigny 1983, 81). In the trope of the mirror Chevigny chooses another element from women's everyday life, developing the image in a way that portrays the simultaneous agency of two subjects.[7] She combines both images in the observation:

> When we are the writing daughters of women who do not write or otherwise articulate our aspirations for autonomy, we will probably be tempted in writing to create our own maternal, mirroring, sanctions and precedents. (1983, 95)

We should note that under the "old rules" of life-telling such narratorial strategies may entail new risks. For while the "common reader" may welcome a closer relationship with both subject and narrator, the critic/reader may be disapproving, even scandalized.[8] Professional judgment may deal harshly with innovative texts.

The Text

The centrality of the narrator/subject relationship is reflected in the way feminist life-tellers shape their texts. The emphasis on this relationship may produce a text with two or more voices, as where Susan Tucker juxtaposes the accounts of southern black women domestic workers with those of their employers, retaining the dialogic structure.[9] These texts can convey a sense of process, a lack of fixity, and reflect the openness of dialogue.

The retention of natural speech, with all its hesitations, produces unconventional texts. Reflecting the form of face-to-face interaction, the text may incorporate the interruptions and contestation that are excised from most published texts. A feminist life history may include the subject's disagreement with the narrator's interpretation: for example, Beatrice Hanson repudiated the feminist interpretation of her folklorist granddaughter, Katherine Borland.[10]

A number of narrators have combined different forms in order to communicate information in a new way.[11] A dialogue between doctor and patient is rendered in two forms: as a sociology article and as a dramatic reading (Paget 1990). A dramatic reading with an audience of professional sociologists was the vehicle for a dialogue between Carolyn Ellis and Art Bochner (1992). Other social scientists share a desire to find narrative forms that permit a freer, more complex, less linear, less univocal expression.

A text made dimensional by the presence of the narrator can take many forms; ingenuity is the byword. Some writers borrow from neighboring traditions.[12] Others have fashioned research modalities from everyday life. One researcher organized, then led a consciousness-raising group whose discussions she used as a source of data for her research on the lives of women between forty and sixty (Mary Gergen, in Reinharz 1992, 221). If the consciousness-raising group was the invention of the 1970s, the electronic bulletin board is the invention of the 1990s. Terry Kramer used this medium to generate data in activist research (Reinharz 1992, 222).[13]

The principle of narratorial reflexivity can lead to recording changes in oneself and in the emerging understanding of the other. The text may go through revisions that reflect these changes; some writers choose to include this history in their text. An open-ended text can reflect feminist epistemology. The narrator leaves the door open to disputability, refusing to cover up the lack of fixity in the reality that is being discussed. Rejecting pretensions to a single right answer, the narrator repudiates the authoritative narratorial voice.[14]

Implications of Feminist Life-Telling

Feminist methodology has transformed the elements of the S/N/R/T framework at a theoretical level. Equally, feminist principles have wrought changes in the larger project of life-telling as a whole. In turn, the project of feminist life-telling carries the potential for reconceiving social science. Life-telling provides a paradigm for a new study of humans, with implications for metatheory and metamethodology. I have argued that in social science, the reciprocal humanity of the partners imposes distinctive requirements on the fundamental character of inquiry. Solving the "problem" of intersubjectivity is crucial to a re-vision of social science. Of course, intersubjectivity ceases to be a problem if we abandon the belief that thinking and feeling must be polarized, and hence represent a dichotomous choice.

The challenge when we are dealing with "our equals," human beings, is to devise a methodology based on sympathy (Bachelard, in Frank 1979). A feminist praxis of empathy is the only method with the potential for managing difference or "otherness." Only empathy, by making understanding possible, contradicts "that certain blindness" that makes others unintelligible. Under previous epistemologies the "danger" of identification, fusion, and loss of objectivity seemed to demand a distancing response and a defensive objectification of the other. But this is not the only possibility: intersubjectivity, re-visioned, yields solutions to the conflicts that perennially divided subject and narrator. It resolves both the fusion "issue" and the distance issue by means of empathy. It restores the sentient narrator to the research encounter and opens up new areas of inquiry.

Re-visioning Objectivity through Intersubjectivity

Objectivity is not completely abandoned but rather re-visioned, calling for the integration of thinking and feeling.[15] Real objectivity is sought by decreasing psycho-social distance between the narrator and the subject. Devereux re-visioned objectivity in terms of "the creative control of consciously recognized irrational reactions, without loss of affect" (1968, 101–2). The requirements of the new objectivity are thus avowal, retention of affect, and control. Avowal refers to the narrator's conscious recognition of her own subjectivity, a subjectivity that persists in the text. As feminist life-telling demonstrates, the new objectivity begins with reflexivity. Retention of affect requires the narrator not to indulge in denial, in "shutting down," or invoking invisibility. Retaining affect, the narrator does not abdicate in the face of emotion. Control in this context requires avowal, not disavowal of self and feeling. A move toward "strong" objectivity means moving into feelings, not fleeing or banishing them.[16]

With the avowal of affect and subjectivity, new content is added to the research enterprise. The creative use of this new material will be a challenge to future generations of researchers.

Feminist Methods: Challenge and Reaction

Innovations in life-telling have emerged in a seemingly natural way. But every forward step has been accompanied by conflict and resistance. The earliest authors who sought to inscribe women's lives were caught between the inadequacy of approaches sanctioned by the canon and the risks of deviation and dissent. In exploring women's autobiography, biography, and life history we discovered that women scholars trained to traditional paradigms encountered a number of obstacles when they began telling women's lives: dissociative methodology, androcentric narrative traditions, and theories that universalized men's experience. Telling a woman's life has required researchers to reorient themselves vis-à-vis the traditions of their disciplines. Placing oneself as a woman within the frame and attempting woman-centered scholarship disrupted the taken-for-granted premises of the discipline.

Powerful imagery of re-visioning has been employed by feminist scholars in many disciplines to refer to changes in their approach to research. Women operating within patrilineal paradigms were experiencing a kind of double vision: when the traditions and training of their discipline were in focus, women were invisible, but when they sought to place women in the foreground, the discipline blurred. This double vision of women, the perennial gift of marginality, produced valuable innovation once gender was analyzed. Before this could happen, however, the woman scholar experienced a painful separation from her training and the conventions of her discipline. A "line of fault" divided the traditions of her discipline from her experience as a woman (D. Smith 1979).

Concretely, women's methodological dissent from their disciplinary traditions has led to reversals of many established principles of patriarchal practice. The line of fault, and women's ways of struggling with it, account for a divergent development of feminist methodology and epistemology. The practices that emerged challenge the authority and the exclusivity of traditional paradigms at a metamethodological level. The future of feminist life-telling depends not only on new inventions—these feminist reversals—but also in the reaction to them.

The centrality of intersubjectivity in feminist methodology challenges the convention of the disembodied scientist, contradicting the valued detachment required by objectivity-as-distance. The feminist practice of inserting the narrator into the frame constitutes a fundamental reversal of social science orthodoxy.[17] The biographical presence of the narrator violates norms of disembodiment and distance. Concluding that methodologies based on dissociation cannot produce objectivity, feminist researchers have, in fact, turned their backs on the tradition of disavowal and dissociation. The narrator's presence brings about a further reversal by healing the imposed division between self and subject matter and permitting the space between them to be explored.

Acknowledging personal involvement and pursuing its guideposts represents a powerful reversal of separative ideology. Inserting the narrator into the text can trigger overt conflict in one's professional life. In Krieger's book *Social Science and the Self,* "Myra" records the result of her experiment with writing in the first person:

> Then it became a point of struggle with a close colleague, my editor, and
> some others.   (1991, 193)

Avowal of self is subject to censure in patriarchal social science, and those who dare it are subject to strong feelings of transgression and intimidation. Resistance to subjectivity in general is likely to manifest itself in response to female subjectivity in particular. So simple a departure as writing in the first person becomes the focus of intense reaction in academic circles. It is the red flag signaling the eruption of subjectivity (female subjectivity at that). The prescient Susan Krieger explored the significance of first-person writing in a recent study (1991). Krieger's respondent "Myra" reports:

> The people who object to the personal material are not especially articulate about their objections. They just don't like it. I think they are embarrassed by it. They think it unseemly. They think it is inappropriate. It is not social science. It's not academic and authoritative. It's too confessional. It's self-indulgent, narcissistic, unnecessary, and superfluous.   (1991, 194)

By inverting the valuation of objectivity and subjectivity, feminist methodology achieves another reversal. Not surprisingly, feminist scholars report feelings of transgression, of being in the wrong when they study women, "get personal," or use the first-person singular. The use of the first person, in the context of scholarship, has the political connotation of disruption or subversion. The female first person, in addition, opens the door to the return of female "messiness" and a threat to control and order. For scholars who use more of the self than just the pronoun, the sanctions may be correspondingly more severe. The narrator who practices self-avowal should be prepared to have her work interpreted as confessional, and to be criticized as self-indulgent, emotional, and so on. Work that is by, for, and about women continues to be judged insignificant by many professional peers; work that is, in addition, written in the first person can be dismissed as anecdotal and unprofessional.[18]

Another powerful reversal is the rejection of dissociative methods in favor of methods based on connection. Recognition of the theoretically compelling reality of intersubjectivity necessitates the adoption of such methods. Achieving intersubjectivity requires a praxis based on association rather than dissociation. But the adoption of the associated premise of parity is profoundly unconventional; it irreparably ruptures the dominance relation between the researcher and the subject.

Viewing the methodological innovations of feminist life-telling in their professional and organizational context, we are forced to recognize that they were achieved at considerable personal and professional cost. The experience of deviating from the pattern has been a harrowing one for innovators. And the obstacles encountered by the pioneers are by no means ancient history; the risks and penalties are in force today. Feminist scholars continue to work in the shadow cast by methodological orthodoxy, and feel intimidated and penalized in so doing. These dynamics have serious consequences for the recruitment, persistence, and survival of succeeding generations of women writers.

Under the rule of dominant paradigms, an atmosphere of censure affects the confidence and intellectual assertiveness of female writers. Women's intellectual capacity and thinking are invalidated. From the reports of the younger scholars Krieger studied, it is clear that gatekeepers' attacks on women's writing, aimed at eliminating the first person, tended to suppress subjectivity. Writing was the focus of struggles these younger women encountered in trying to reconcile their sense of the phenomena they studied with the established forms of social science.[19] "Ruth" reports the way her self-expression was disciplined:

> In psychology class, I was taken to task because I did not write like a social scientist. I was told to write in the passive intransitive voice and to have no presence. *I had thought I was going to be a writer, but I found that everywhere I turned, my writing was wrong.*   (1991, 223, italics mine)

Krieger's study makes it clear that graduate training serves as a focus for sanctions experienced by feminist life-tellers in social science. For her informants following professional standards seemed to require an opposition between subjectivity and disavowal. "Kathleen," an educational sociologist, describes an obligatory formula for professional communication:

> My writing style changed very drastically in graduate school. It became very stilted. . . . There is clearly a formula where you start out a paper saying, "Many studies have been done but this is where the hole is." Then you provide some theory, then data, conclusions, and suggestions for future research.
> (1991, 206)

Not surprisingly, her sense of professional expectations blocked what and how she wanted to write. In succumbing she feels she is sacrificing originality:

> The formula is very comforting, but, to me, it is constraining. I do not let myself spin a thought out in that formula, or really do intellectual work.
> (1991, 203)

Following the formula blocks the writing these authors want to do. Challenging this orthodoxy, however, exposes the writer to professional penalties. "Kathleen" says:

> The formula style is not the way I want to write. However, acceptable journals require it. . . . people . . . suffer if they do not write in this way, using the formula. They suffer disdain from colleagues. . . .
> What I feel in writing social science is a frustration, a desperation. . . . I feel frustrated, desperate, out of place. . . . In the process of trying to put it into the formula, I sometimes feel disgust. I hate that process. I hate what I try to squeeze my material into. It no longer says clearly what needs to be said about my subject. I never want to read back on it.   (1991, 206)

Today, examining the consequences of practicing feminist reversals has brought us back to our point of origin. The gender politics we find in reactions to the first person recapitulates the fears and penalties we found in subjects of autobiography, biography, and life history. The most radical innovators in telling women's lives find themselves, like generations before, in fear of the male reader/critic. The dilemmas reported by Krieger's respondents echo the accounts of an earlier generation of feminist scholars. These are not intrapsychic conflicts, but rather reflect social structure: routine practices that, if they remain unchanged, will continue to silence the voices of many women artists and intellectuals. Women are still writing within a context of examples and methods, deliberately taught and consciously enforced, that do not reflect or resonate with women. In these pages we are quoting only the survivors of such training. We cannot forget those whose voices were permanently lost in these processes, the numbers of voices stilled of those who did not persevere.

Throughout the book I have argued against a naturalistic, overly individualistic view of the act of telling lives. I have emphasized the material and symbolic context of women's writing, the sources of threats and sanctions. The accounts of women's experiences in graduate school spotlight one site where change is needed. For Krieger's informants graduate training was a battleground, the focus of a cruel choice between validity and legitimacy. Krieger's respondents, all graduate school survivors, identified their professional socialization as a process of invalidation and alienation that introduced a division between self and work. Graduate schools remain extraordinarily influential; they continue to dominate the professional context in which tellers of women's lives must operate. Even for writers who are located outside the academy, they are the source of images of the discipline and of internalized standards. Graduate schools may not train all the writers, but they train the gatekeepers.

Krieger's respondents are a generation or more younger than the pioneers quoted earlier, but they report parallel experiences. "Diana" says:

> In all my schooling, I have felt that I do not think exactly right. I do not think in a sedate way. I feel as if I am going to be in trouble any minute. It scares me. Yet I can only think of something the way I think of it. I do not really know how to accommodate. . . .
>
> What I am trying to say with this is that I feel I am always in trouble. . . . I feel that somebody else has to do it for me and I better be quiet . . . . My experience is that nobody understands me, or they correct me. Then someone else says the exact same thing a few days later. It pisses me off when that happens. I have wondered if maybe there is some unique way that I present that causes me problems. (1991, 213, 214)

She is encouraged to think the problems lies with her. The conflict between authenticity and conformity seems inescapable. Following her judgment of what feels right puts the woman scholar in the wrong. "Diana" observes:

> When I want to write something my way, I have felt there is something wrong with me, with my style of thinking. . . . I feel I almost cannot do something the way the authorities want it done. It goes so against the grain of me. (1991, 208)

Conclusion

It is tempting to end this long journey in a flurry of progress and promise. Having seen the error of patriarchal ways, we might hope that prevalent distortions of the past could be magnanimously assimilated to a gloriously opening future where feminist perspectives and praxis could lead to a new, improved synthesis and the study of men's lives. But writing as a feminist who works in the male-defined academic tradition, I doubt that the conversion is complete. Even when we revision ourselves as narrators, and enter new texts as we invent them, we do not by these acts alter the patriarchal traditions of knowledge; we do not at a stroke replace all the critics and professors. A "line of fault" still divides the traditions of academic disciplines from our experience as women. The fate of this line of fault must be our focus as we speculate about the future of feminist life-telling.

Today, the outlines of gendered intellectual production remain in place. Failing substantial change in graduate training, conflicts will persist for practitioners who want to join self and work. Instead of being exposed to new styles of work as a matter of course, students who are drawn to innovative methods are made to feel deviant and inferior. They grope their way without institutional support and in the face of professional penalties. In the past, the feminist vision arose only as the product of tortuous processes of re-vision and second sight; infrequently, and against long odds. Restricting change to the individual's effort is harrowing for her and costly to the profession. When intergenerational transmission of knowledge is lacking or blocked, the burden rests with the individual. As long as new generations are denied access to tools and knowledge they must continue to seek it in priceless renegade texts. The essential guideposts to the new objectivity will continue to be first-person accounts of transformation and re-vision, which will continue to be peripheralized in organized training.

The attributes most characteristic of feminist life-telling are practices that, singly and collectively, continue to be transgressive. Writers who want to survive in academia and set their own intellectual agenda feel themselves at risk. Lacking models and mentors, the necessity of invention falls on them. As students they will bear the double burden of having to be "bilingual." "Ginger," a communications researcher who writes plays as well as social science, says:

Because the distanced way is how social science has always been done, and men fucked us up, and it's boring, and they were trying to imitate a model that is not really true: logical positivism. . . . I think we are all trained with the traditional forms. To think of new ones, it is like you are being asked, "What if this wasn't an eagle, what would it be?" then you have to imagine an eagle in a chicken suit.   (Kreiger 1991, 220)

Future generations are condemned not only to accept the challenge of imagining the eagle but also must be prepared to deal with the guys in the chicken suits.

Some readers may feel that the current generation of writers will be exempt from these pressures and conflicts. Certainly the presence of feminist mentors and a feminist canon must mitigate the penalties for woman-centered scholarship and for narratorial self-avowal. In the experience of social scientists quoted in Krieger, the existence of an alternative canon encourages writing in the first person.[20] However, it is questionable whether feminist scholars are yet in a position to control the reward structure in their departments and disciplines. Career risks persist. Resistance to self-avowal, which is based in deep gender conditioning, will not disappear until gender socialization changes.

Without change, texts that incorporate the elements of feminist life-telling will continue to meet resistance. Texts that are marked by female intensity, that overflow with feelings, that arm emotions with reason and vice versa—these will still be difficult or impossible to assimilate. Such texts will never be candidates for the canon. They will be excluded early, dismissed smartly, forgotten expeditiously. The counter-canon will remain a vital necessity.

But are these the only possibilities? Graduate education could become the crucible for a new objectivity, simply by putting into operation the hard-won principles of feminist method. Imagine an alternative future where reflexivity is taught as a fundamental aspect of research methods. Learning would mean training in empathy paired with reflexivity. Imagine the teaching of empathic technique, by alternating or combining affinity and analysis. Beginning researchers would closely examine affect as well as cognitions produced by their learning experiences, freed from the necessity of concealing or denying them. When the learner's reactions of discomfort are expected and examined rather than stifled, peer support can be mobilized in the service of learning. The powerful group dynamics of the classroom can support moving toward an objectivity that incorporates subjectivity. Reflexivity and group support can increase trust of self and others, perhaps contributing an unanticipated improvement in academic climate.

Detachment, so long mistrusted, can be replaced with a more nuanced sense of answerability that acknowledges the narrator's multiple audiences and obligations. A scholar trained to take responsibility for her/his reactions would likely be a more principled researcher. Ethics would come alive in a process of paying attention to the relationships between subject and narrator, narrator and reader as an integral part of the various points in the production of knowledge. Such learning would provide a never-to-be-forgotten demonstration of professional ethics.

Operationalizing the principles of feminist method in training researchers implies adjustments at the metatheoretical and metamethodological levels. Taking multiple relationships as fundamental to research suggests using communication rather than experimental control as the paradigm for research. Different skills would be required, stimulating the development of new curricula. Deliberate scrutiny of natural speech, emphasizing conversation and dialogue, would lead to cultivation of listening techniques. A parallel problematization of reading might focus on the relationship between subject, narrator, and reader rather than on the text in isolation. Such a focus could benefit from deconstructive techniques of reading. We can imagine that the author's subjectivity could be routinely recouped and the resonance between narrator and reader revived.

Graduate training could easily make greater use of reciprocity between informant and researcher and extend that insight to the parallel relationships between narrator and reader. Students would recognize that they and their professors are equally capable of taking on the functions of subject, narrator, and reader. Many aspects of graduate training could be transformed by this insight. The style and impact of critique could be dramatically altered when the critic/reader can concede an identification with and affinity for the writer. Taking this connection as fundamental would result in more enthusiastic and mutually respectful teaching and learning.

In a book that has emphasized an unconventional and inclusive approach to narrative, concern with graduate training may seem an anomalous note with which to close. Some readers may think that it is of interest to only a tiny number of writers and readers; others that it is irredeemably elitist. But it is hard to dismiss the power of gatekeeping, to deny that forms and standards of evaluation continue to be learned in educational settings, to think and write entirely outside the influence of the canon. Possessing the outlines of a method for telling women's lives, we find the task is not complete. What is lacking is an infrastructure that would routinely provide all students with access to women's narratives, with all the reach provided by diversity of place, person, and time. To neglect these needs is to contribute to the age-old social production of obscurity which has for so long devoured women's work.

Notes

NOTES TO CHAPTER I

1. Lini de Vries worked in Paterson's silk mills as a child, served as a nurse in the Spanish Civil War, and worked as a public health pioneer in Mexico, where I first knew her in the 1970s.

2. Michael V. Angrosino reports that two narrators differing in race, age, and degree of familiarity with her culture elicited two different accounts of her life from Rebecca Levenstone, a native of Saba (1989).

3. At the same time, this tradition remains a strong influence on readers and writers of social science. For this reason, Chapter 5 contains a strong critique of the rhetoric of scientific objectivity and research methods in the social sciences.

4. Virginia Woolf speaks of readers as hearers of the long forgotten appeal, rescuers, life-givers (1925).

5. By text I mean any social action or document that can be represented through the use of narrative.

6. Gelya Frank has remarked that "the tendency to compare ourselves with others is always close at hand when reading a biography or writing one" (1985, 189).

7. First-person accounts of women's lives may be rare; it is equally possible, however, that women's accounts are simply hidden from our eyes by gendered edifices of discipline and canon.

8. This is too often the case even in the scholarly literature of the social sciences and in biography, where third-person accounts are the standard.

9. This critique of the third-person treatment of women is not meant to deny all validity to such treatments of information about women. However, an unnecessary polarization of first-person and third-person accounts introduces distortion. The valorization of "objectivity" results in suppression of the subjectivity of both subject and narrator. The orthodoxy of third-person accounts accounts for the disappearance of the second person at the time the text is written.

10. Françoise Lionnet observes that constructing "race" so as to exclude women results in the inability of some black male writers to see contestation in the works of black female writers. Since women's politics is "different," it is invisible to people who are speaking for blacks (1989, xii). Lionnet's discovery re-

capitulates Mary Helen Washington's analysis of the critical neglect of Gwendolyn Brooks's *Maud Martha* (Washington 1984). See also Hull et al. (1982).

11. Anne Moody (1968) tells the story of her childhood in segregated, dirt-poor Mississippi. Her coming of age coincided with the beginning of the struggle for racial equality. Anne Moody was a student at Tougaloo College when the NAACP and SNCC began organizing in Mississippi. She participated in one of the first lunch counter sit-ins. Her account is that of a participant in history, her report a bulletin from the battle line.

12. Angela Davis, lecturing at Syracuse University in April 1992, noted the rewriting of the history of the Civil Rights Movement in such a way that women have disappeared.

13. See Bingham (1989).

14. Kath Weston has taken the subject-positioning of lesbians and gay men as a starting point for analyzing a generic problem. She analyzes coming out stories in order to illuminate the way "family" is constructed in the United States (1991).

15. See Arnold (1975, 1987); Krieger (1983); Ponse (1978).

16. For the most part, a woman writing as subject is immune from criticism: her narrative is read as incorporating the particulars of sexuality, class, race, and age that situate her. The reader also remains out of range; although she is accorded personal qualities, they are not used to invalidate her. A woman writing as narrator or critic, however, may be targeted for attack.

17. The problem may lie with our habits of reading rather than with the text itself. The obsession with purity, the reliance on binary oppositions, and above all the judgmental, hierarchizing response are not native to feminist scholarship. This kind of attack may reflect our education and training in patriarchal institutions and traditions. "Universalism" as a disvalued practice may be in the eye of the beholder. In reading women's writing we should be sceptical of oversimplifying responses; the diversity of women's lives should lead us in the direction of increasingly complex understandings.

18. Readers and would-be narrators can learn from the experience of Euro-American women who became aware of culturally derived expectations that they carried into the field with them. In reflexively examining their responses to difference American authors discovered their unavowed cultural assumptions (Briggs 1970; Myerhoff 1980; Shostak 1981).

19. Other women of color talk back to collective Others: to the canon, the discourse, the theorists, and critics. See hooks (1981, 1984, 1989, 1992); Lionnet (1989).

20. Salazar (1991).

21. See, for example, Tanaka (1981); Lee (1991).

22. Again, it is Françoise Lionnet who claims that the advantage of our "minority" status as women is that we will never be deluded into thinking that we can represent anyone but ourselves (1989, 6).

23. Indeed, if we took published autobiography as an index, we would seriously underestimate women's motivation for reflexive writing. As recently as 1980, the large field of criticism in autobiography ignored women almost entirely (Jelinek 1980).

24. A public woman may be defined in terms of her relationships with a man, but her daily life and work as a housewife are deemed insignificant by definition. Patricia Spacks makes this point, observing, "housewives and average men seldom write their autobiographies" (Spacks 1972, 3). Autobiography as the public record of a public life demands a certain kind of narrative. By implication, there is nothing in the life of a housewife or average man that merits the telling.

25. An extended discussion of this conflict about authorship can be found in Gilbert and Gubar (1979). It is discussed in more depth in Chapter 2.

26. Hall (1987, 27). The woman subject is a double deviant: she must possess the valorized attributes of the dominant group (to which she cannot belong), but she cannot shed the stigma of primary deviance (the group to which she does belong). For analysis of the double deviant see Laws, (1975). For further application of the concept of double deviance, see Schur (1983).

NOTES TO CHAPTER 2

1. Constructing the autobiography involves strategies of dissociation: elision, excision, editing. The accepted conventions act to "clean up the act." Life may be "messy," but art is not. In its transformation to autobiography the life is shorn of repetition, confusion, and interpersonal hubbub. Superfluous personages are pruned away. Relationships are muted. Contradictory voices are stilled. Daily routines and bodily events are suppressed. Whiskers are shaven and shorn. The life's trajectory is smoothed toward a known outcome. A linear and chronological organization is imposed. A personal destiny is discovered and linked with history. Design and intention are enhanced. These attributes of generic autobiography are so well established as to seem entirely natural.

2. The life we read has been shaped, fictionalized, and universalized. As readers we are dependent upon this account for access to the life; only through it do we come to know the life, or imagine that we do. The life as lived is eclipsed; only the account survives. Readers and critics focus on this creation, rather than on the life that has receded beyond our reach.

3. Elements of masculine culture, with its emphasis on suppression of affect, its impersonality, its predilection for control or asymmetrical power relations, find yet another reflection in the principles of social science methodology. Good form, in this masculine tradition, requires the excision of the personal and emotional. In parallel, excision of personal attributes and feelings is considered a virtue in orthodox social science research procedure (see Chapter 5). These characteristics of masculine self-presentation, evident in scholarship as well as fiction,

have only recently been analyzed in terms of gender significance; see, for example, Evelyn Fox Keller (1985).

4. Sandra Gilbert and Susan Gubar have analyzed the ways in which authorship and authority are imbricated with the masculine tradition of the subject (1979).

5. Sidonie Smith points out the link between the privileged cultural fictions of male selfhood and the judgment of "significance" in life stories (1987, 93).

6. The emphasis on individualism, however, evokes the problematic concept of the subject. The subject in autobiography is construed in specific ways. Michael Ryan expresses reservations about the central role of the subject in conceptualizations of autobiography (1980). Ryan, reading for gender, notes that the autobiographical subject is to be taken as male. In reviewing Philippe Lejeune's *Le Pacte autobiographique* (*On Autobiography*) Ryan notes that Lejeune formalizes and absolutizes the white male subject. Such a standard excludes those who do not write (oral histories), persons who take another's name (slaves, wives), illegal aliens, and others barred from certain legal transactions. Here the reader/critic seems to assert the identity of autobiographical subject and property-owning male. This tradition presents obvious difficulties for the inclusion of women as subjects (Ryan 1980, 14).

7. Other separative techniques employed by Adams include the use of the third person. James Goodwin (1983) has analyzed Henry Adams's reliance on the third person in his autobiography, *The Education of Henry Adams*. Adams depicts the self as object rather than agent; he refers to himself in nonhuman terms and elaborates a theory of history which presupposes his own death.

Henry Adams identifies himself with two extra-personal entities: with history, and with the tradition of Harvard graduates (Goodwin 1983, 122). Goodwin describes Adams's autobiography as an exercise in belittling himself and, ultimately, in suicide (1983, 127).

8. Ryan's deconstruction of "self-evidence" holds for any absolutized idea, such as generic autobiography. When difference is interpreted as anomaly or deviation, instances of difference can be distanced and devalued, placed at the periphery and forgotten. From this subject-positioning, the lack of correspondence between women's accounts of their lives and the generic standard can be interpreted as a fault or inadequacy of female autobiography, which can then be dismissed. This is the method of reading patriarchy.

9. Regrettably, the understanding in which Olney is interested is limited to one sex.

10. In parallel to this personal history, Olney constructs a jocular genealogy of autobiography as a genre. It is a selective and personal history, not directed by concern for inclusivity or exhaustiveness. Olney identifies Scargill's *Autobiography of a Dissenting Minister* (1834) as the first autobiography, but fails to consider Margery Kempe (1432) or Margaret Cavendish (1656). He cites Anna

Robeson Burr, whose book *The Autobiography: A Critical and Comparative Study* appeared in 1909, only in passing. Olney emphasizes Dilthey, Misch, and Gusdorf, confessing that his high opinion of the latter's thinking derives mainly from its similarity to his own. The attraction to similarity and rejection of difference is a leitmotif in *Metaphors of Self* (Olney 1972).

11. Krupat's book is titled, ironically, *For Those Who Come After*. Those who come after, whether Native American readers who seek to know earlier generations, or scholars who will be the next generation of critics, will learn that Krupat "regrets" the omission of women from his study. Such omissions decisively affect the adequacy of understanding available to scholars in the field. It is particularly regrettable that Krupat, whose book is designed to counteract the neglect of Native American voices in the canon of autobiography, feels justified in neglecting those of women.

12. From the subject positioning of male inheritance, autogynography is an act of war. Nathaniel Hawthorne acknowledged this in denouncing the "d——d mob of scribbling women" who were invading the lucrative market of popular writing in his time. While women writers tried to pacify the critics by denying that they were men's competitors, Hawthorne was mobilizing battleground metaphors, referring to them as "ink-stained Amazons" triumphing on a field of battle (Wood 1971, 9).

13. In this, autobiography serves as the paradigm for understanding what is happening in other traditions of life-telling. In biography, life history, and oral history as in autobiography, current developments reflect the contradictory pressures of gender and genre.

14. This is not to deny that the fiction of the impervious male subject has deceived or confused both subject and critic. Emma Goldman was taken in by the fiction of the male subject, and believed that the male revolutionaries who were her peers were "heroic, and hewn all of a piece"—not divided, as she felt herself to be. In commenting on Goldman, Spacks also appears to take literally the traditional male self-presentation of unruffled, unfeeling, goal-directed living. She, like Goldman, compared women with this fictive standard.

15. Jelinek has noted a critical consensus on the requirement that the subject (and not others) be the focus of the autobiography (1980, 4). Thus if others play too great a role in one's account of her life, it will be downgraded to a memoir or reminiscence.

16. Domna Stanton suggests that the "typical" female narrative is a partial inscription, perhaps an intentional disguise. Seemingly conventional women's narratives may harbor an unexpected ambiguity: in revealing what is permitted and expected of her (e.g, a "domestic dailiness," a prosaic and limited round, a preoccupation with close relations), the female autobiographer is simultaneously concealing what is not permitted (1984).

17. Janet Gunn comes out forthrightly for the position that genre is an in-

strument for reading, not for writing (1982, 21). It links the text with the world readers inhabit (and, I might add, the subject as well).

18. Critics tend to be polarized along lines of sex as well as gender concerns. Thus while the feminist critique paints autobiography as too restrictive and too limiting, at least one leading male critic deplores a lack of limits.

19. At one time the project of autobiography was viewed as impermissibly messy. Janet Gunn (1982) notes that only the decline of formalism permitted autobiography entrée as a literary genre; previously it had been "too unruly" to fit in.

20. Northrop Frye observes that black history tends to be preserved in autobiography rather than standard histories—but does not analyze why this might be the case, or question whether the boundaries of literary genres might constitute similar filters in regard to outsider groups generally (1957).

21. Lady Sarashina (1971).

22. For a discussion of the obscuring of Christine de Pisan's reputation, see Chapter 7.

23. Patricia K. Addis has published an extensive annotated bibliography of American women's autobiographical writings (1983).

24. Typification is a central issue in the social sciences, where individuals are often selected to "stand for" a culture or people.

25. Ironically, it may be that women who have been privileged to study in universities are most hampered by exposure to the male canon. As Dorothy Smith says, "The penetration of the society by the ideological process includes, particularly for the highly educated, an 'in-depth' organization of consciousness" (1979, 144). The more educated the individual, the more she thinks like the authorities in "her" field.

26. This belief is paralleled in literature, social science, and behavioral science.

27. Independent-minded scholars could, of course, abandon the canon and discover primary texts that give the lie to this distorted scholarship. The majority of scholars will, regrettably, follow their leaders.

NOTES TO CHAPTER 3

1. Margery Kempe was a fifteenth-century Englishwoman whose narrative is considered to be the first full autobiography in English. It is the account of her mystical relationship with God, and is written in the third person (1940).

2. Current scholarship casts doubt on the candor of Nin's diary. Nevertheless she articulates the ideal that in private writing one can be totally honest.

3. See, for example, Carrighar (1973); Carr (1966); Luhan (1933, 1935, 1936, 1937).

4. Fanny Fern was the pen name of one of the first American women to sup-

port herself by writing, whose publication of the novel *Ruth Hall* in 1854 created a scandal for its unfeminine protagonist and author.

5. Beatrice Webb became the collaborator and wife of Sidney Webb, the British economist and socialist of the late nineteenth century.

6. Phyllis Rose recounts the successful execution of this project by Jane Carlyle, whose secret diaries contained devastating reproaches directed toward her husband (1984).

7. These narrative strategies are found in first-person accounts, but they can also be found in third-person traditions such as biography and life history.

8. For a continuing discussion of women's silences, see Shulman (1979). Current discussions of duplicity and truth-telling in personal narrative problematize the female subject's distinctive "voice" and the sex of the reader (D. Smith 1987; Peterson 1990).

9. In female memoirs of the Victorian period Nord discovers two strategies which attempt to resolve the contradiction between telling one's life and feminine self-effacement. One strategy denies the female self, supplanting it with an implicitly nongendered identity as a writer. The other strategy denies the contradiction between self-assertion and self-effacement by minimizing the public life and achievements of the woman subject.

10. Kingston (1976); Arnold (1975, 1987); Lord (1982); Millett (1990).

11. Deborah Norris Logan (1761–1839) was a member of an influential Pennsylvania family and hostess to the artists, politicians, and historians of her time. She was the first woman member of the Historical Society of Pennsylvania, and a published poet. She undertook her four thousand-page diary at the age of fifty-four, and continued it for twenty-four years, until her death (Barr 1985).

12. Cavendish combined several strategies for "telling it slant." At the same time she was writing a dutiful and admiring account of the duke's life, Cavendish was creating a parallel world of imagination in *The Blazing World*. In this female utopian fantasy, Margaret cast herself as empress (warrior-goddess, "angel . . . or Deity") and scribe to the empress. In the fictional account Margaret appropriated the roles of warrior, author, scholar, and leader that she had previously lauded in her husband.

13. Women's first-person accounts provide the major means of access to women's subjectivity. It is precisely this expression of subjectivity that constitutes the first challenge to the traditions that exclude women. Kathleen Barry notes that the ideological construction of womanhood created under patriarchy excludes women's subjectivity. Essentializing ideologies effectively remove women from history. Women's subjectivity, she holds, is the most fundamental challenge to the ideological construction of womanhood created under patriarchy (1990).

14. Schibanoff observes in women writers a desire to circumvent the male gatekeepers and make direct contact with their female readers (1983, 476).

15. Women's writing "in code" makes possible covert communication via a

subtext, often rebellious or subversive, lurking beneath the manifest text (N. Miller 1980).

16. By emphasizing the constraints that exist outside the writer herself, I do not mean to suggest an iron necessity to the communicative strategy of indirection. To view "telling it slant" as an imperative under patriarchy might lead to undesirable outcomes. One effect might be acceptance of the ghettoization of women's work and its alienation from the canon. Other possibilities exist, including alternative narrative strategies employed by women in their autobiographical writings.

17. Elizabeth Foote Washington gazed upon the frowning face of posterity when she wrote in 1792:

> Now that it is probable that I may not have any children, so of course this book and all my other manuscripts must fall into the hands of some relative, who may laugh at them and think as my servants, and may not give them a reading—but throw them into some old drawer as waste paper, or give them to their children to tear up, as is too often the case with many people, they give their children books to play with and destroy.   (Evans 1975, 354)

18. To insert oneself into history—as is required by the autobiographical act—implies a sense of entitlement, a sense of belonging. Alfred Kazin observed, "To have a sense of history one must consider *oneself* a piece of history" (1979, 85; italics in original).

19. See "Autogynography: Is the Subject Different?" in Stanton (1984, 15).

20. Throughout this book, my references to written texts and reading are haunted by the oral narrative and the need to emphasize listening. We still know very little about the shape of women's lives, and still less about how they are experienced. It is vital to listen intensely, and comment minimally.

NOTES TO CHAPTER 4

1. See de Jesus (1962); Schlissel (1982); Culley (1985); Hampsten (1982).

2. Although important literary figures visited the household during the time Harriet Jacobs was writing her book, she was separated from them by the boundaries of race and class: they did not know she was a writer, and she did not seek encouragement or information from them. Her status as a servant, and her race, made her identity as a writer both invisible and unspeakable.

3. In discussing connection as an important theme in women's self-writing, my focus is on the way (some, but not all) women choose to present themselves, not on "how women are."

4. The developmental dimension of women's sense of connection is emphasized in Carol Gilligan's work on a distinctively female "ethic of care" that centers on activities of relating: seeing and responding to need, and sustaining the web of connection (1982, 62). In its aspects of oceanic identification and care for

the social and physical world, the ethic of care resembles Erik Erikson's concept of generativity (1950).

5. Gilligan observes that, in women's belief system, activities of care make the world safe (1982).

6. This ethic of care appears also in the lives of women who work in isolation and do not form families in adulthood. The manner of their care is apparent in Sally Carrighar's work as a naturalist, and Barbara McClintock's way of relating to the Indian corn on which her research was based (Carrighar 1973; E. Keller 1983). Erik Erikson has noted that his character trait of generativity, linked in its narrowest expression to reproduction, can be developed into an oceanic concern for the generations and the world (1950).

7. A number of social scientists have speculated about the antecedents of women's orientation to connection (Chodorow 1978; N. Miller 1980). Janet Lever (1976), studying primary-age children at play, found that girls and boys handle conflicts in ways that seem to prefigure the moral differences of young adulthood. Lever observed that boys had learned ways of adjudicating conflicts that arose during games, in such a way that the game could continue. Girls would sacrifice the game to preserve a relationship if conflict threatened to disrupt the relationship.

8. Relationship work is, of course, invisible in the public world of work. It does not produce a product, generate surplus value, or lend itself to claims of authorship. Its contribution to the GNP cannot be quantified. More to the point, feeling work is not normatively defined as part of the masculine role. Unlike women, men are not judged in terms of relationship work, its quality, or its outcome.

9. Women's accounts expose essentialist theories as articulating the subject-positioning of males. Such theories are part of the ideological apparatus that, insisting on fundamental differences between women and men, evades the question of why men do not commit to costly and important relationship work.

10. Sociologists have repeatedly scouted the boundaries of this territory when they analyze social relations in terms of reciprocity, courtship in terms of exchange, and work relationships in terms of equity. Recent scholarship in the sociology of emotions develops the concept of feeling work (Gouldner 1970; Blau 1964; Hochschild 1983).   .

11. Women writing about peace or the environment often convey this sense of power and energy (see Macy 1983; Mayerding 1984).

12. Efficacious feeling work can be a source of pride and power for women. Relationship skill or "affective competence" figures in women's idea of maturity and in their self-evaluations. Gilligan holds that women's self-evaluation is tied to their ability to care (1982, 17). Caring involves demanding and effortful activity; hence women rightly regard relationship work as requiring skill. Caregiving is experienced as personal power.

13. To be sure, women are not supposed to "profit from" their emotion work. On the contrary: societal norms prescribe a heavily asymmetrical investment of care for women (Long and Porter 1980). Nevertheless, some women's writing reveals an awareness of tradeoffs: too much taking care of others may preclude taking care of oneself. When an individual disregards the tradeoff between self-care and other-care, alienation and exploitation can result. Lives devoted to caretaking are often lives where the caregiver neglects to take care of herself. Marcia Westkott has commented on the potential contradiction between women's inner feelings and external conduct (1979). Spacks comments on the inside/outside contradiction when she notes "the omnipresence of anger as the corollary of 'goodness' in the autobiographies of women who devote their lives to caretaking" (1972, 267).

14. Narcissism, a term bearing powerful negative connotations from its appropriation by Freud, might better be deconstructed into its components of self-love and self-assertion.

15. Barbara Ehrenreich traces the development of masculine sex role scripts in the United States from the post–World War II years (1984). Bellah et al. discuss a dilemma that is seen from the subject-positioning of men (1985).

16. Other daughters who have chronicled a relationship in writing a biography of a parent are Mary Catherine Bateson (1984) and Susan Cheever (1984).

17. Butler and Rosenblum (1991).

18. This characteristic of women writing lives crosses disciplinary limits: biographers, too, seek to tell relationships. In other traditions of life-telling, the narrator's self-inscription into the text is an innovation of form. In such texts a plural subject is created via narratorial agency.

19. A nascent revival of prosopography is one of the directions of innovation in women's autobiography and biography.

20. Pauli Murray, a lawyer and feminist, was one of the first women ordained in the Episcopal clergy.

21. Fields (1983); Murray (1956).

22. Sarah Kirsch (1989) created a mixed form, "a collaborative, rudimentary artwork" in which the boundaries between herself and her subjects could not be discerned. Her instrument was the tape recorder. Sistren and Honor Ford Smith created a text inadvertently, as their theater project evolved from performance to written text (1987).

23. Critics can be relied on to reject this private (female, messy) self: conventionally, only the public self is worthy of attention. Juhasz reports that reviewers literally hated *Flying*. The work is explicitly likened to soap opera; Juhasz points out that dailiness and melodrama can only evoke ridicule as a response (1980).

24. Women writing about the personal can expect to be criticized as "self-indulgent." In *Flying* Kate Millett (1990) deliberately employed the diary mode.

Critics accused Millett of taking herself too seriously: of thinking that her personal doings are important to the rest of us (Juhasz 1980).

25. Critics of women's plays complain about the lack of plot and loose, episodic structure. Women's poetry is characterized as open, intimate, particular, involved, engaged, committed. The form of the poetry is explicitly seen as an extension of the female self (Gilligan 1982, 22). In the social sciences, in addition to literature, telling women's lives involves similar innovations in form and elicits similar critical judgments. Both messy content and messy form, expressing women's experience, are judged negatively.

26. Marjorie DeVault (1991) has documentented a similar revision in critics' readings of Nadine Gordimer's *The Late Bourgeois World* (1966). At publication the novel was clearly undervalued by critics who found it unintelligible. Literary critics of the mid-to-late 1970s had the benefit of feminist, political, and academic discourses that rendered the protagonist more intelligible.

NOTES TO CHAPTER 5

1. Social science texts follow the convention of being written from the perspective of an invisible third person, an Archimedean position located outside of space and time.

2. Sociologist Alvin Gouldner's term refers to underlying, taken-for-granted premises, cultural baggage that the social scientist brings with him from the society at large. Domain assumptions are learned much earlier than the official knowledge covered in graduate training, and are usually left untouched by this training.

3. Experimental research provides the closest approximation to researcher invisibility. Experiments can actually be designed in such as way that the scientist is spared all contact with the subjects who provide data. In the interests of avoiding contamination or influence of the Ss toward the experimental hypotheses, the investigator can employ functionaries, who are themselves "blind" to the hypotheses of the study, to conduct the experiment ("run the Ss"). In other designs the experimental stimuli are presented mechanically, or delivered by computer, to further purge the social from the experiment.

4. The ideology of value-freedom and objectivity has been directly challenged by the sociology of knowledge perspective, which holds that social theory is grounded in the social position of its theoreticians (Berger and Luckmann 1966). Recent studies confirm that the social composition of the academic profession—the sex, race and social class of its practitioners—materially affects the knowledge that is created, preserved and imparted by them. The body of knowledge that is passed down to succeeding generations of social scientists reflects the social character of its creators. Not surprisingly, the most incisive and fundamental

critique of the cult of objectivity is to be found in current feminist scholarship (Harding 1991; E. Keller 1985).

5. The misleading model of physics opposes thinking and feeling, creating a dualism that casts the narrator as one who thinks and the subject as one who feels. This premise conveniently denies the researcher's subjectivity and subordinates the subject. The dualism is reinforced by professional socialization that distances the two.

6. Even in the experiment subjects meet the researcher more than halfway. Since the subject is capable of the same cognitive processes as the experimenter, deception is employed to make the odds more unequal. Experimental design routinely involves deception in the form of a "cover story" invented to conceal the true purpose of the experiment. Data indicate that the experimenter's inventiveness is often outstripped by that of the subjects, as they in turn circumvent the "cover story" and attempt to uncover the experimenter's true goal.

7. People who try to study people without being human themselves face an unenviable predicament (La Barre 1968, viii).

8. Peer review does not necessarily offer a corrective to the researcher's self-deception. On the contrary: other researchers who share the researcher's anxiety are easily convinced by methods which assert objectivity through denial. Social scientists nourished in the professional literature come to believe their own propaganda. Freeman and Krantz observe wryly:

The fiction of the invisible observer led to a fallacious . . . assumption . . . that a social science could exist without an observer. In fact, what developed was a social science in which all participating investigators agreed where the observer should stand. (1980, 10).

9. It can be seen that, at a deeper level, "value-freedom" is a trope for a phobic response to the reality, the uncontrollability, the *thereness* of others, the exigent fact of two subjectivities.

10. Manuals used in training social scientists emphasize the instrumental treatment of subjects, and establishment of an asymmetrical relationship of control. Compartmentalization is presented as the "correct solution" to the threat of intersubjectivity.

11. Unacknowledged, the separative self underlies the typical power dynamics of traditional research methods. In Keller's words, "Power *over* the other then makes up for the lost sense of relation *with* the other (C. Keller 1986, 138; italics in original).

12. The idea of "value-free" inquiry contradicts the basis of our ability to perform it. Learning to engage in systematic inquiry, whether *in vivo* or *in vitro,* involves learning to make discriminations and differential valuings. Moreover, the tasks of the professional social scientist require the conscious and careful application of values. The selection of a topic for research, the election of a canon, evaluation and peer review, hiring and promotion, differential reward and suc-

cess, the dominance of paradigms undeniably result from the application of values.

13. Crapanzano is plagued by the inability to control unilaterally the research relationship from which "his" data came. Yet he recognizes that taking total possession results in extinction of the other or his reduction to a specimen.

14. See, for example, Hill and Stull (1987) Stokes et al. (1980); Hendricks (1981).

15. In preparing a monograph the author must go carefully through it and remove all telltale traces of the ethnographer writing it (La Barre 1968, ix). Such editorial practices of disavowal make possible the illusion of an Archimedean point where the observer "stands." The power relationship between narrator and subject is also obscured by the narrator's failure to disclose himself, to register his subjectivity in the text.

16. For accounts of ethnographic fieldwork, see Golde (1970); Rabinow (1977). For an account of oral history research see Rosengarten (1979). See also Rosengarten (1975).

17. Gadamer (1975).

18. Crapanzano reports that he feels in control when he is writing but out of control when he is in the forcefield of the face-to-face relationship (1980).

19. A rereading of the classic life history text, *The Polish Peasant in Europe and America* (Thomas and Znaniecki 1918), gives plentiful evidence of an erupting narratorial presence that continually contradicts the subject's account.

20. Gouldner points in a direction he cannot follow, however; the taboo against self-revelation is so fundamental that he cannot bring himself to enter the text in his particularity (1970).

21. A number of scholars have commented on the creative potential that is released *in the subject* by the occasion of being interviewed. The presence of the observer imparts significance to the life, and stimulates self-reflection. The face-to-face situation provides the subject with a stimulus and opportunity to create a life story. As Crapanzano writes of his subject Tuhami, "I became, I imagine, an articulatory pivot about which he could spin out his fantasies *in order to create himself as he desired.* I was created to create him" (1980, 140; italics mine).

22. Loewenberg, who is both a historian and a psychoanalyst, emphasizes countertransference ("the emotional and subjective sensibility of the observer") as a tool for enhancing understanding (1969, 3).

23. I do not regard empathy as a spontaneous and unmediated response to another, but rather as a conscious approach to understanding her. Empathy does not originate "from the gut," nor from the ovaries. The practice of empathy is not "doing what comes naturally" but is a learned professional skill.

24. In conventional graduate training, taking statistics (for example) is thought to prepare the researcher for a lifetime of work. The practice of empathy, in contrast, is not a one-time, in-depth training experience. Learning empa-

thy is an ongoing process, more like undergoing psychoanalysis than like passing graduate statistics. In order to "stay" psychoanalyzed one must continually exercise the skill.

25. Asymmetry in power and communicative relationships works against such feelings, with predictable effects on the quality of research. The research encounter involves extended dyadic exchanges under conditions of privacy and confidentiality that become intimate when personal information is exchanged. The potential for intimacy increases with diffuse or extended relationships.

26. In the conventional mode, the researcher is not thinking of reciprocity. His assignment is to manipulate the subject's responses so as to facilitate his goals.

27. Ann Oakley (1981) criticizes the paradigm for social science interviewing as set forth in methodology textbooks that are used to train researchers. The textbook interview is structured so as to minimize resemblance to ordinary conversation and obscure everyday attributes of both participants. The interviewer's goals must be adopted as the goals of the interaction. The interviewer is limited to question-asking and rapport-promoting behaviors; self-disclosure and reciprocal discourse are proscribed.

28. Sandra Harding has contrasted "strong objectivity," which includes the researcher, with the more traditional "weak objectivity" that disavows him (1991).

29. Contesting this taboo may be more difficult for male social scientists than for female.

30. Problems of intersubjectivity may take different forms for narrators of different sexes, for the meanings of connection and separation follow gender scripts. When female and male researchers discuss their relationships with the subject, they value, fear, and struggle with different elements.

NOTES TO CHAPTER 6

1. Hoboes were homeless people looking for work; bums were people who couldn't or wouldn't work because of addictions.

2. Bertha puzzled over the origins of the hobo women she met. As she sought to explain her own motivation, she sought to understand theirs. Half of them, she found, were impelled outward by a home situation where divorce, step-parents, or too many children made them redundant; many others had reached their majority in orphan asylums and been turned loose. Others came from other institutions, including jails and mental asylums. They chose the life of the road, with its hardships, over alternatives they had known (Reitman 1988, 70).

3. Some girls perfected the vocabulary and behaviors of the "saved" in order to appeal to religious agencies. Others presented fictional ancestry that made them eligible for benefits from one or another ethnic or religious agency. One

woman made a practice of driving straight to the town hall and, with her infant in her arms, striking a bargain with the mayor or sheriff. Claiming that the family was on the way to relatives down the road, she promised to get right out of town if they would give her money for gas or a new tire. If not, the town would have to take responsibility for them.

4. Ben Reitman was a considerable personage. Studs Terkel dubbed him "Chicago's most eminent clap doctor." Chicago's red-light district was his childhood home, which he left to travel with two hoboes and become a "road kid." He tramped and bummed across the United States, Mexico, and Europe. He became a doctor and, at twenty-five, opened an office to treat the people with whom he had lived and traveled. Periodically he would close down that office and return to the road. Later he opened a "hobo college." He was Emma Goldman's lover and comrade, and traveled with her for ten years.

5. Bertha's grandfather was an abolitionist and publisher of *The Woman's Emancipator*. An advocate of votes for women and freedom from marriage, he was jailed for sending birth control information through the mail. He was called upon to defend his unmarried and pregnant daughter to the authorities, who thought she should either be arrested or forced to marry. All four were imprisoned. Bertha describes a family that might appear in one of George Bernard Shaw's comedies: mama does the cooking and sewing for the jail population, studies socialism and Esperanto, and nurses her baby; papa catches up on his reading, and grandpa writes articles for publication.

6. Jenny had died before her letters came into Allport's hands. Allport's account does not specify how the correspondence became his property.

7. Jenny's correspondence with Glenn and Isabel was an invention mothered by necessity. Glenn had been Ross's roommate at Princeton, where Jenny had met him during happier times. Their desultory relationship was transformed by Jenny's great need for a confidant during a period from 1926 to 1937. This flow of letters was Jenny's lifeline, "fired by hot necessity."

8. The official position of the Church of England was that divorce was invalid, hence a marriage like Jenny's constituted adultery.

9. "The Bridge" is Jenny's personal code word for the idea of suicide. In the correspondence Jenny repeatedly mentions jumping from a bridge. It is not clear whether this idea signifies an assertion of ultimate control over life or an expression of self-pity.

10. Where gatekeepers cannot see women as typifying their society, female voices continue to be marginalized or silenced. The politics involved in typification and judgments of typicality had a major impact on the history of *The Fantastic Lodge*.

11. The few women who appear in *The Polish Peasant* are made invisible by being excluded from sociological analysis.

12. Despite its literary quality, *Letters from Jenny* has received much less at-

tention from sociologists than the better-known life histories of men. Jenny's accounts of work in hospitals and asylums is revelatory, the quality of her analysis on a par with Stanley's account of penal institutions in *The Jack-Roller*. Ironically, Jenny's has received no professional mention, while Stanley's contribution has been recognized and applauded by sociologists.

13. This vocabulary of denigration is the more striking when contrasted with the masculine virtues Allport saw in Jenny.

14. As Janet was an uncommon subject, so the sociologist who was to become her advocate was an uncommon narrator. At the time they met, Howard S. Becker was a *wunderkind* who had just received his Ph.D. from the University of Chicago at the age of twenty-three. He was a quick-thinking, streetwise professional who supported himself playing piano in jazz clubs around Chicago. Janet and her husband were part of Becker's circle of musician acquaintances. In contrast to the dominance relationship of Clifford Shaw and "Stanley," Becker treated "Janet" as a peer. They were close in age: Janet was twenty-one to Becker's twenty-three. The life history interviews were conducted in Becker's home; in addition, "Janet" was a babysitter for the Becker family.

15. The Institute for Juvenile Research in Chicago undertook a major research impetus on drug use from 1947 to 1953. "Janet Chase" was interviewed in connection with this larger study.

16. In accounts where the narrator's subjectivity is effaced or disavowed, these elements are often projected onto the subject. The narrator may denounce in his subject the qualities he must deny in himself. Negative judgments of the subject are particularly revealing in this way.

17. The witch/bitch vocabulary that Allport (1965) employs when he discusses Jenny's character contrasts dramatically with the sympathetic tone in which (male) juvenile delinquents are presented in other well-known life histories. See Marcia Millman for a commentary on the unacknowledged identification of male ethnographers with society's "bad boys" (1975).

18. When it was published in 1961, *The Fantastic Lodge* contained a glossary. Drug terms which have entered today's mainstream were assumed to be unknown to most readers then.

19. The British edition of *The Fantastic Lodge* includes some of Janet's poetry.

20. Howard Becker, personal communication, November 1990.

21. The traditional life history paired a young, uneducated, white ethnic teenage delinquent with an authoritative, respectable, middle-class professional who was decisively older and decisively dominant. Clifford Shaw, for example, was ten years older than the sixteen-year-old "Stanley" when their association began.

22. Repercussions from that voice began to be felt as soon as it was captured on tape. Janet's profanity alarmed the women who typed her life history, and

their complaints reached the ears of the researchers at IJR (Bennett, personal communication, November 1990).

23. Janet's early years also included a troubled relationship with her mother, a history of sexual delinquency, and a baby given up for adoption.

24. One proposal was to bracket her text by authoritative social science commentary (as Wladek's account had been in *The Polish Peasant*). Another alternative was to solicit an introduction by Janet's psychiatrist. Either would have the effect of taming Janet and diluting her voice. As the negotiations continued, it appeared at times that the parties were close to agreement. Ultimately, however, Clifford Shaw's resistance prevailed: *The Fantastic Lodge* was suppressed.

25. For example, the issue of ownership of the interview was conventionally settled by an hourly payment of five dollars to the interviewee. Evidently this token payment was not sufficient to contain Janet's possible claims to authorship. Shaw went further. He executed a legal agreement with Janet in 1953, which assigned all rights to IJR on condition that her real name not be used and that she would get royalties. On this occasion she received ten dollars.

26. It may be that in presenting Clifford Shaw with a *fait accompli,* Becker challenged the authority of the powerful senior researcher of the Institute for Juvenile Research. Although the fate of Janet's text might be analyzed as a result of personal conflict between Becker and Shaw, James Bennett emphasizes the institutional forces that were brought to bear.

27. Autobiographical work by sociologists may offer a new perspective on the join between the personal and the structural, a perpetual focus of sociological analysis. Analyzing how sociologists position themselves as subjects and also as sociologists may indicate some of the limits of narratorial reflexivity as a research method. In addition to the two collections mentioned in the text, sociological autobiographies include Riley (1988); Coser (1977); Berger (1990); Oppenheimer et al. (1991). Other autobiographical subjects include G. Homans (1984) and Whyte (1994).

28. Goetting (1994).

NOTES TO CHAPTER 7

1. Much can be learned about the individual from the facts he invents about himself (Kaplan 1979).

2. "A secret myth, as well as a manifest myth . . . is hidden within every creative life. . . . the biographer who writes the life of his subject's self-concept passes through a facade into the inner house of life" (Edel 1979, 21). While the sexual nature of Edel's imagery has been overlooked, the potentially invasive nature of biography is acknowledged.

3. A potential subject, Vladimir Nabokov, repulses the threat of violation by scornfully defining biography as "psychoplagiarism" (Edel 1979, 21).

4. Although respect for the subject motivates many feminist biographers to efface themselves and their role, I would argue that the biographer has essential contributions to make to telling women's lives. The feminist biographer is uniquely capable of locating her subject in the framework of the gender system. Far from feeling apologetic about adding her own voice to that of the subject, she should recognize that failure to analyze gender is still common in scholarly work and requires correction.

5. A sense of identification is reported by biographers who never met their subjects, as well as by oral historians and biographers who have established face-to-face relationships with living subjects.

6. There is substantial disagreement about the role and visibility of the narrator. Some biographers insist that the factual material must be left unaltered; others think this is impossible. Biographers who mistrust the subject feel that the narrator must correct "self-serving" first-person narratives, while others mistrust the "putative objectivity (the absence of a point of view)" of the biographer.

7. Jacquelyn Dowd Hall found that her thinking was hostage by the private/public polarity, impeding her ability to provide an integration in her study of Jessie Ames (1979).

8. For her the personal was political. Barry (1988) emphasizes the importance of Anthony's positive choice not to marry. Her decision not to accept the role of "old maid" was a dramatic reversal of the social view of singlehood as nonchoice. Henry James had created a demonic image of the nonmarrying woman in *The Bostonians*. So powerfully negative was the "old maid" identity that Elizabeth Cady Stanton saw need for a countermyth to represent her friend Susan.

9. In excavating the paths of exceptional women, women's history has revealed more than the facts of their lives. It shows us how history is made: the underlying processes by which some events and actors are selected into history, and others selected out. The reclamation projects of women's history have taught us that notable women have been eclipsed as regularly as obscure ones.

10. In the context of gendered suppression of women's lives, making obscure suggests a close relationship with "obscurantism," defined *in Webster's New World Dictionary* as opposition to human progress and enlightenment.

11. Censorship and editorial interference are two ways in which a woman's thought can be dimmed, rejected, pushed to the periphery, and finally launched into oblivion, as illustrated by the vicissitudes of Christine de Pisan's work. Susan Schibanoff (1983) provides an account of how the *Book of the City of Women* was paraphrased, burlesqued, distorted, and even attributed to other authors. Subsequently the work itself was written out of history, and only recently rediscovered.

12. In past times women born to unpropertied families were never reflected in records kept of real property. If women never inherit, manage, or dispose of

land or wealth, they will remain invisible in censuses based on real estate. Women do not become military heroes and the subjects of military history. In the United States they have traditionally not gone to college on the GI Bill, enjoyed veterans' preference, or appeared in the records of the Veterans' Administration. Most will not be elected to public office.

13. *Webster's New World Dictionary* (1966).

14. Barbara McClintock, born in 1902, died in 1992.

15. Evelyn Fox Keller suggests that Phyllis Greenacre's psychological profile of the creative artist fits McClintock as a child (1983, 205).

16. In describing the general process of creating deviance, Edwin Schur (1983) lists practices of shunning, blaming, and trying to correct or treat.

17. Why she is forgotten is a question that has not yet been resolved. Shulamit Reinharz (1984b) addresses the theoretical issue of unintelligibility and perhaps provides a clue to Shohat's obscurity.

18. The record of this settlement is particularly important, as sexual equality was not incorporated as an organizing principle of the kibbutzim subsequently established as agricultural collectives in Palestine.

19. In this formulation Reinharz, a sociologist, incorporates the findings of the psychology of women, that relationships play a central role in women's moral judgments. Reinharz extends this conception to women's principled behavior in the public sphere of politics. The example of Manya Shohat demonstrates how taking a woman's life as the focus of scholarly work stimulates theory development.

20. Mabel repeatedly demonstrated her mastery of the issues of the day, and exhibited immense organizing power. She was a catalyst for thought and action (Rudnick 1984, 85). She was a planner of the epoch-making Armory Show of 1913, which many date as the dawn of modern art in America. Mabel was an organizer of the Paterson Pageant commemorating the Paterson silk mill strike; she contributed to *The Masses* and served on its advisory board. She was also a popularizer of Freudian psychology in a weekly column she wrote for the Hearst papers. Her salon provided a forum for revolutionaries and anarchists, for writers and artists. In New York she joined Heterodoxy. When she relocated to New Mexico, Mabel involved herself in Indian affairs.

21. Hahn (1977); Rudnick (1984).

22. Neither biographer would dispute Mabel's neglect of her son, John Evans. There is, in addition, an emotional coldness that is manifested in Mabel's turning away from Maurice Sterne (her third husband) after his near drowning; her seeming lack of feeling in connection with the suicide of her friend Bindo in Florence, and the suicide attempt of "Clarence" in her home (Rudnick 1984, 216). In a chilling but little developed episode, Mabel acquired a child, Elizabeth, to console her after the end of her love affair with John Reed. This pretty but apparently not brilliant little girl seems to have been mislaid shortly thereafter, and vanishes from the story.

23. On the eve of World War I, Mabel published an anti-war piece, and wrote an open letter to Woodrow Wilson. She interviewed soldiers and their wives and was involved in the founding of the Women's International League for Peace and Freedom and the Women's Peace Party.

24. Chief among these was the issue of the "New Woman" and her relationship to modern America's emergence from the Victorian age. Through her own writings and activities and the words of newspaper reporters, painters, poets, and fiction writers, Mabel became a leading symbol of the New Woman: sexually emancipated, self-determining, in control of her own destiny. "To many she heralded Woman as World Builder" (Rudnick 1984, ix).

25. "The selves and worlds she tried to build always had to be 'authorized' by men" (Rudnick 1984, xii). Mabel's self-imposed limitation reflects Spacks's "corruption of female imagination," as when a potential woman artist who, lacking permission to *do,* transforms *herself* into a work of art (Rudnick 1984, 41).

26. It should be noted that Mabel herself did not adopt a Freudian formula of powerlessness, of peripherality, of wistful penis envy in thinking about her relationship with the creative man. Her vision was better expressed in the revived formula of *mutterrecht:* beyond all others flesh and spirit, idol, inspiration, muse; painters and sculptors will want her as a model; she will feed the dreams of poets; in her the intellectual will explore the treasure of feminine "intuition" (Rudnick 1984, 332n).

27. Many women suffered this confusion, and the ambivalence of a strong desire for self-assertion coupled with a belief in women's dependence on men (Sochen 1972).

28. What "counts" as achievement, the established measures of achievement motivation, the societal reward structure—in short, the whole achievement industry—has been based on male patterns of separation and competition. Achievement itself is sex-typed; women express unease and a sense of transgression when they admit being attracted to success defined in the masculine manner.

29. Early research demonstrated a strong effect of gender on individuals' interpretations of success and failure. Men were more likely to explain their success by reference to internal or enduring attributes like ability, and their failure by reference to transitory or external attributes like luck. Their failures do not stick. Women exhibited the converse pattern, imputing their successes to transitory or external attributes and their failures to internal or enduring ones. Gendered patterns of attribution were found in employers' tendency to reward one pattern of self-attribution—taking credit for success—more lavishly than the other. Current research on causal attribution sustains the importance of gender (Ashkanasy 1989, 1994).

30. An ear sensitive to gender might detect a similarity between Mabel's disclaimer and that of Caroline Lee Hentz in Chapter 3. Spacks (1980) has sug-

gested that a narrative of self-deprecation is common in women's autobiographies; bowing to gender expectations might well motivate "telling it slant" in this manner.

31. Carolyn Heilbrun has noted that men have had permission to live many kinds of lives, and have had many life stories and many narrative strategies available. Women, in confronting these, feel guilty, inauthentic, unentitled (1985).

32. Hahn (1977) had to overlook or discount this aspect of Mabel's personal myth in order to present her as an essentially trivial, parasitical female.

33. Her first view of southwestern life reminded her of the gothic worldview of Europe; the Indians resembled Maxfield Parrish illustrations; the singing of Mexican Penitentes sounded like Gregorian chant (Nelson 1980, 249). Every perception had reference outside the new world she was trying to encounter.

34. Textual innovation may, however, be hard on the reader. While acknowledging that Mulford's bumpy text fits the erratic trajectory of women's lives, the reader may resist it, objecting to the awkwardness of having to jump from one subject's life to that of the other.

35. Of course, such inclusions may violate accustomed distances between the reader and the subject, or reader and narrator. The critic/reader may feel claustrophobic or imposed upon by a degree of (unsought, unanticipated) intimacy such as Ascher's narrator creates (Minnich 1985, 291).

36. Sometimes the reader is called upon to mediate the conflict between narrator and sources. Joyce Antler discovered, in interviewing Lucy Sprague Mitchell's children, that their recollection of her was as an absent and unaffectionate mother. Confronted with the evidence of their mother's daily work on their behalf, the children remained unpersuaded. Antler appeals to her readers to confirm her interpretation. She also appeals to the reader to provide some plausible interpretation in gender terms of this undervaluing of a devoted mother (1984).

37. In her view, gossip is a fine and subtle mode of analysis developed primarily by women as a result as well as essential ingredient of our "interactional work" and our need to develop a feminist understanding of everyday life (Minnich 1985).

38. Mulford experimented with language in seeking to express her subjects' dailiness and domesticity, their rootedness in place. The materiality of her approach is emphasized by her taking up residence in the subjects' house in Dorset.

NOTES TO CHAPTER 8

1. In Reinharz's approach, for example, it is the researcher who must demonstrate trustworthiness, must convince the subject of her *bona fides*.

2. In a two-way dialogue information is exchanged rather than elicited. This reciprocity is illustrated in Ann Oakley's chronicle of her research experience (1981). Rather than turning aside the respondents' questions, Oakley disclosed herself in a dialogue with the subject. Questions her respondents asked Oakley

indicate clearly that they perceived and valued her as a peer, rather than as an impersonal authority figure. Oakley contrasts her feminist methodology, and the data so obtained, with the orthodox research interview. She notes that her credibility was enhanced, not destroyed, by avowal.

3. Life history and biography, for example, both require a method capable of retaining the dual subjectivity of narrator and subject.

4. Among them are making the unconscious conscious; consulting and listening to the self; voicing the unsaid; listening to others; staying alert to all the currents and undercurrents of life around them; and imagining themselves inside that which they are seeking to understand (Belenky et al. 1986, 141). By such a process of avowal and self-examination the narrator's subjectivity is brought to a new level of understanding which itself shapes the product.

5. The narrator transforms her subjective experience via a range of self-analytic techniques, creating thereby an instrumentality for heightened understanding of the subject. "If the researcher's self is the instrument by which the investigation proceeds, then that instrument must be well understood" (Reinharz 1984a, 356). Self-analysis must include the narrator's knowing her own values and preferences, and knowing how she shapes her experience. In Reinharz's method consultation and listening to the self takes the form of a written diary kept throughout the research process; this record of the researcher's feelings is also data. In accounts of her own research experiences Reinharz demonstrates that the narrator's subjectivity can be an asset. Her approach requires a disciplined subjectivity that can be "homed in" on the subject (in the manner suggested by Loewenberg) to intensify insight.

6. Belenky et al. describe connected knowing in terms that speak of a purposive empathy. The stance of connected knowing involves preparation, concentration, will, and above all, abstention from controlling. Vis-à-vis the subject, the narrator takes an attitude of receptiveness. Truly attending to the subject requires emptying the self of its contents so it can receive. Connected knowing requires patience and forbearance (1986, 117).

7. Chevigny (1983) saw that growth and mastery require a validating mirror—prototypically, the delighted face of a supportive mother. As a biographer, Chevigny came to the realization that she was creating in Fuller a mirroring self, and was simultaneously providing such a mirror for her subject. Her work of empathy and agency was creating a mutually supportive intersubjectivity.

8. See the discussion, below, on penalties for writing in the first person.

9. Tucker (1988).

10. Hanson (1991).

11. The transformation of method can be seen in such current works as Gluck and Patai (1991), in which the familiar techniques of oral history are transformed by feminist practices and questions. See also Taylor (1981).

12. "Myra," the pseudonymous sociologist quoted in *Social Science and the Self,* adopted field-notes as a narrative form, imaginatively shaping them to por-

tray a situation and extend her analysis beyond the empirical observations (Krieger 1991, 195–96).

13. The anonymity of the electronic bulletin board and the testimonies of others made it possible for subjects to speak out about sexual harassment, a problem in which victims fail to complain because they fear blame and retaliation.

14. Jacquelyn Dowd Hall believes that interpretation of a woman's life must be open-ended. She says, "We have challenged the illusion of objectivity and relinquished the arrogance of believing we can get our foremothers right, once and for all" (1987, 35).

15. Recognizing that thinking and feeling are continuous, Peter Loewenberg has written about the necessary incorporation of emotion into the researcher's work. A disciplined subjectivity does just that. In incorporating feelings into the calculus, it brings affect together with cognition.

16. Sandra Harding has discussed the program for "strong" objectivity, in contrast with the weak objectivity that is sought in traditional positivist approaches to social knowledge (1991).

17. Susan Krieger explores the use of the first person in professional writing. In her recent book, Krieger says, "Writing personally has become a way that I can feel I am doing social science in a responsible manner" (1991, 1).

18. Several of the social scientists interviewed by Krieger reported that their training involved fundamental invalidation of their thinking and means of expression. The resulting alienation attaches to the work, the profession, and the self.

19. These conflicts drove them to nontraditional forms: journal writing, letters, conversation, fictive field-notes, and other models that provide some space for a narrator.

20. It was exposure to feminist writing that gave Krieger's respondents "permission" to write personally. To "Eleanor," cultural feminist literature

> felt personal to me to read it. It also gave me permission to talk personally in my own writing in a way that was hard to find within history. . . . I sat down to write my introduction, expecting it to be a miserable experience, and it wrote very comfortably and almost immediately.   (1991, 198)

Reading first-person writing reconnects the narrator with the reader inside herself. Inspired to write in the first-person in her turn, she gains a sense of liberation and empowerment. "Eleanor" found that she could go beyond the conventional limits and avow her values.

> I wrote the introduction in the first person. . . . I was elated. The first person was a voice I was happy with. It felt comfortable to me. For the first time, the work jelled for me. Then I rewrote the body of the text to accompany the introduction. *I wrote a conclusion that had a moral.* (Krieger 1991, 196; italics mine)

Bibliography

Abel, Elizabeth. 1981. "(E)Merging Identities: The Dynamics of Female Friendship in Contemporary Fiction by Women." *Signs* 6, 3: 423–25.

Acker, Kathy. 1988. Introduction to *Boxcar Bertha,* by Dorothy Reitman. New York: AMOK Press.

Adams, Timothy Dow. 1990. *Telling Lies in Modern American Autobiography.* Chapel Hill, NC: University of North Carolina Press.

Addis, Patricia K. 1983. *Through a Woman's I: An Annotated Bibliography of American Women's Autobiographical Writings, 1946–1976.* Metuchen, NJ: Scarecrow Press.

Allen, Paula Gunn. 1983. *The Woman Who Owned the Shadows.* San Francisco: Spinsters, Ink.

Allen, Paula Gunn. 1986. *The Sacred Hoop: Recovering the Feminine in American Indian Traditions.* Boston: Beacon Press.

Allport, Gordon W. 1942. *The Use of Personal Documents in Psychological Science.* New York: Social Science Research Council.

Allport, Gordon W. 1965. *Letters from Jenny.* New York: Harcourt, Brace and World.

alta. 1974. *Momma: A Start on All the Untold Stories.* New York: Times Change Press.

Anderson, Rufus. 1825. *Memoirs of Catherine Brown, a Christian Indian of the Cherokee Nation.* Boston: Crocke and Brewster.

Angrosino, Michael V. 1989. "The Two Lives of Rebecca Levenstone: Symbolic Interaction in the Generation of the Life History." *Journal of Anthropological Research* 45, 3 (Fall): 315–26.

Antler, Joyce. 1984. "Was She a Good Mother?" In *Women and the Structure of Society: Selected Research from the Fifth Berkshire Conference on the History of Women,* edited by B. J. Harris and J. K. McNamara, 53–66. Durham, NC: Duke University Press.

———. 1987. *Lucy Sprague Mitchell: The Making of a Modern Woman.* New Haven, CT: Yale University Press.

Anzaldúa, Gloria. 1987. *La Frontera: The New Mestiza.* San Francisco: Spinsters/Aunt Lute.

Aptheker, Bettina. 1989. *Tapestries of Life: Women's Work, Women's Consciousness, and the Meaning of Daily Experience.* Amherst, MA: University of Massachusetts Press.

Ardener, Shirley, ed. 1975. *Perceiving Women.* New York: John Wiley.

Argyris, Chris. 1975. "Danger in Applying Results from Experimental Social Psychology." *American Psychologist* 30, 4: 469–86.

Armitage, Susan. 1983. The Next Step. *Frontiers* 7, 1: 3–9.

Arnold, June. 1975. *Sister Gin.* Plainfield, VT: Daughters, Inc.

———. 1987. *Baby Houston.* Austin, TX: Texas Monthly Press.

Ascher, Carol. 1984. "On 'Clearing the Air': My Letter to Simone de Beauvoir." In DeSalvo, and Ruddick 1984, 85–103.

Ascher, Carol, Louise DeSalvo, and Sara Ruddick, eds. 1984. *Between Women.* Boston: Beacon Press.

Ashkanasy, N. M. 1989. "Causal Attribution and the Supervisor's Response to Subordinate Performance—The Green and Mitchell Model Revisited." *J. Applied Social Psychol.* 19, 4: 309–30.

———. 1994. "Automatic Categorization and Causal Attribution—The Effect of Gender Bias in Supervisor's Response to Subordinate Performance." *Aust. J. Psychol.* 46, 3: 177–82.

Atkinson, John W. 1958. *Motives in Fantasy, Action and Society: A Method of Assessment and Study.* Princeton, NJ: Van Nostrand.

Bachofen, Jacob. 1967. *Das Mutterrecht.* Translated by Ralph Manheim. Princeton, NJ: Princeton University Press.

Bair, Deirdre. 1990. *Simone de Beauvoir: A Biography.* New York: Summit.

Bakan, David. 1966. *The Duality of Human Existence.* Boston: Beacon Press.

Barr, Marlene. 1985. "Deborah Norris Logan, Feminist Criticism, and Identity Theory: Interpreting a Woman's Diary without the Danger of Separatism." *Biography* 8, 1: 13–24.

Barrios de Chungara, Domitila, with Molina Viezer. 1977. *Let Me Speak: Testimony of Domitila, a Woman of the Bolivian Mines.* Translated by Victoria Ortiz. Mexico City: Siglo Veintiuno Editores, SA.

Barry, Kathleen. 1988. *Susan B. Anthony, a Biography: A Singular Feminist.* New York: New York University Press.

———. 1990. "The New Historical Syntheses: Women's Biography." *J. Women's History* 1, 3: 75–105.

Bashkirtseff, Marie. 1899. *The Journal of a Young Artist: 1860–1884.* Translated by Mary J. Serrano. New York: Cassell.

Bateson, Mary Catherine. 1984. *With a Daughter's Eye.* New York: Pocket Books.

Bauman, Zygmunt. 1978. *Hermeneutics and Social Science.* New York: Columbia University Press.

Becker, Howard. 1966. Introduction to *The Jack-Roller*, by Clifford Shaw. Chicago: University of Chicago Press.

Belenky, Mary Field, Blythe McVicker Clinchy, Nancy Goldberger, and Jill Mattuck Tarule. 1986. *Women's Ways of Knowing: The Development of Self, Voice, and Mind*. New York: Basic Books.

Bell, Quentin. 1972. *Virginia Woolf: A Biography*. New York: Harcourt Brace Jovanovich.

Bellah, Robert N., Richard Madsen, William M. Sullivan, Ann Swidler, and Stephan M. Tipton. 1985. *Habits of the Heart: Individualism and Commitment in American Life*. New York: Harper and Row.

Benjamin, Lois. 1991. *The Black Elite: Facing the Color Line in the Twilight of the Twentieth Century*. Chicago: Nelson-Hall.

Bennett, James. 1987. *Oral History and Delinquency*. Chicago: University of Chicago Press.

Benstock, Shari, ed. 1988. *The Private Self: Theory and Practice of Women's Autobiographical Writings*. Chapel Hill, NC: University of North Carolina Press.

Berger, Bennett M. 1990. *Authors of Their Own Lives: Intellectual Autobiographies*. Berkeley, CA: University of California Press.

Berger, Peter, and Thomas Luckmann. 1966. *The Social Construction of Reality: A Treatise in the Sociology of Knowledge*. Garden City, NY: Doubleday.

Bernikow, Louise. 1980. *Among Women*. New York: Harmony Books.

———, ed. 1974. *The World Split Open: Four Centuries of Women Poets in England and America, 1552–1950*. New York: Vintage.

Bertaux, Daniel. 1981. *Biography and Society: The Life History Approach in the Social Sciences*. Beverly Hills, CA: Sage.

Bertaux, Daniel, and Martin Kohli. 1984. "The Life Story Approach: A Continental View." *Annual Review of Sociology* 10: 215–37.

Beyerchen, Alan D. 1977. *Scientists under Hitler*. New Haven, CT: Yale University Press.

Bingham, Sallie. 1989. *Passion and Prejudice: A Family Memoir*. New York: Knopf.

Bittner, Egon. 1980. "Autonomy and Technique: How Far May We Go before Professional Solutions for All Problems Will Begin to Diminish Human Life?" *Sociological Study of Social Problems Newsletter* 12, 4: 2–3.

Blau, Peter. 1964. *Exchange and Power in Social Life*. New York: John Wiley.

Blumer, Herbert. 1979. *Critiques of Research in the Social Sciences: An Appraisal of Thomas and Znaniecki's "The Polish Peasant in Europe and America."* New Brunswick, NJ: Transaction Books.

Bonaparte, Princess Marie. 1951–53. *Five Copy-books, Written by a Little Girl between the Ages of Seven-and-a-half and Ten, with Commentaries*. Translated by Erich Mosbacher and Nancy Procter-Gregg. London: Imago.

Booth, Alan. 1972. "Sex and Social Participation." *Am. Sociol. Rev.* 37: 183–92.

Borland, Katherine. 1991. "'That's Not What I Said': Interpretive Conflict in Oral Narrative Research." In Gluck and Patai 1991, 63–75.

Bradstreet, Anne. 1967. "To My Dear Children." In *The Works of Anne Bradstreet,* edited by Jeanine Hensley. Cambridge, MA: Belknap Press of Harvard University Press.

Briggs, Jean. 1970 [1944]. "Kapluna Daughter." In Golde 1970.

Brodzki, Bella, and Celeste Schenk. 1988. *Life/Lines: Theorizing Women's Autobiography.* Ithaca, NY: Cornell University Press.

Brooks, Gwendolyn. 1974. *Maud Martha, a Novel.* New York: AMS Press.

Brownstein, Rachel M. 1982. *Becoming a Heroine.* New York: Viking.

Bruss, Elizabeth. 1976. *Autobiographical Acts: The Changing Situation of a Literary Genre.* Baltimore, MD: Johns Hopkins University Press.

Buechler, Hans C., and Judith-Maria Buechler. 1981. *Carmen, the Autobiography of a Spanish Galician Woman.* Cambridge, MA: Schenkman.

Bulkin, Elly, Minnie Bruce Pratt, and Barbara Smith. 1988. *Yours in Struggle: Three Feminist Perspectives on Anti-Semitism and Racism.* Ithaca: Firebrand Press.

Bulmer, Martin. 1983. *"The Polish Peasant in Europe and America:* A Neglected Classic." *New Community* 10: 470–76.

———. 1984. *The Chicago School of Sociology: Institutionalization, Diversity, and the Rise of Social Research.* Chicago: University of Chicago Press.

Burgess, E. W. 1945. "Research Methods in Sociology." In *Twentieth Century Sociology,* edited by G. Gurvitch and W. E. Moore. New York: Philosophical Library.

Burr, Anna Robeson. 1909. *The Autobiography: A Critical and Comparative Study.* New York: Houghton Mifflin.

Buss, Fran Leeper. 1980. *La Partera: The Story of a Midwife.* Ann Arbor, MI: University of Michigan Press.

———. 1985. *Dignity: Lower Income Women Tell of Their Lives and Struggles—Oral Histories.* Ann Arbor, MI: University of Michigan Press.

Buss, Helen M. 1990. "The Different Voice of Canadian Feminist Autobiographers." *Biography* 3, 2: 154–68.

Butler, Sandra, and Barbara Rosenblum. 1991. *Cancer in Two Voices.* San Francisco: Spinsters.

Campbell, Joseph. 1949. *Hero with a Thousand Faces.* Princeton, NJ: Princeton University Press.

Carr, Emily. 1946. *Growing Pains: An Autobiography.* Toronto: Irwin.

———. 1966. *Hundreds and Thousands: The Journals of Emily Carr.* Toronto: Clarke, Irwin.

Carr, Helen. 1988. "Native American Women's Autobiography." In Brodzki and Schenk 1988, 131–53.

Carrighar, Sally. 1973. *Home to the Wilderness*. Boston: Houghton Mifflin.

Cavendish, Margaret, Duchess of Newcastle. 1886. *The Life of William Cavendish, Duke of Newcastle, to Which is Added the True Relation of My Birth, Breeding and Life*. London: J. C. Nimmo.

Chanfrault-Duchet, Marie-Françoise. 1991. "Narrative Structures, Social Models, and Symbolic Representation in the Life Story." In Gluck and Patai 1991, 77–92.

Cheever, Susan. 1984. *Home before Dark*. Boston: Houghton Mifflin.

Chernin, Kim. 1983. *In My Mother's House: A Daughter's Story*. New York: Harper and Row.

Chevigny, Bell Gale. 1983. "Daughters Writing: Towards a Theory of Women's Biography." *Feminist Studies* 9, 1: 79–102.

Childress, Alice. 1986. *Like One of the Family*. Boston: Beacon Press.

Chodorow, Nancy. 1978. *The Reproduction of Mothering: Psychoanalysis and the Sociology of Gender*. Berkeley, CA: University of California Press.

Clifford, James L. 1970. *From Puzzles to Portraits: Problems of a Literary Biographer*. Chapel Hill, NC: University of North Carolina Press.

Clinchy, Blythe, Mary Belenky, N. R. Goldberger, and J. M. Tarule. 1985. "Connected Education for Women." *J. Education* 167, 3: 28–45.

Codere, Helen. 1973. *The Biography of an African Society, Rwanda 1900–1960*. Tervurem, Belgium: Musée Royal de l'Afrique Centrale.

Coser, Lewis A. 1977. *Masters of Sociological Thought: Ideas in Historical and Social Context*. New York: Harcourt Brace Jovanovich.

Crandall, V. J., R. Dewey, W. Katkovsky, and A. Preston. 1964. "Parents' Attitudes and Behaviors and Grade School Children's Academic Achievements." *J. Genetic Psychol*. 105: 53–66.

Crapanzano, Vincent. 1980. *Tuhami: Portrait of a Moroccan*. Chicago: University of Chicago Press.

Culler, Jonathan. 1982. *On Deconstruction: Theory and Criticism after Structuralism*. Ithaca, NY: Cornell University Press.

Culley, Margo. 1992. *American Women's Autobiography: Fea(s)ts of Memory*. Madison, WI: University of Wisconsin Press.

———, ed. 1985. *A Day at a Time: The Diary Literature of American Women from 1764 to the Present*. Old Westbury, NY: The Feminist Press.

Daly, Mary. 1973. *Beyond God the Father: Toward a Philosophy of Women's Liberation*. Boston: Beacon Press.

Davies, Margaret Llewelyn. 1975. *Life as We Have Known It*. New York: Norton.

———. 1978. *Maternity: Letters from Working Women*. New York: Norton.

Deaux, Kay, and T. Emswiller. 1974. "Explanations of Successful Performance on Sex-Linked Tasks: What Is Skill for the Male Is Luck for the Female." *J. Personality and Social Psychol*. 29: 80–85.

Deaux, Kay, L. E. White, and E. Farris. 1975. "Skill vs. Luck: Field and Laboratory Studies of Male and Female Preferences." *J. Personality and Social Psychol.* 32: 629–36.

de Beauvoir, Simone. 1970. *The Second Sex.* Translated by H. M. Parshlay. New York: Bantam.

Deegan, Mary Jo. 1988. *Jane Addams and the Men of the Chicago School, 1892–1918.* New Brunswick, NJ: Transaction Books.

de Jesus, Carolina Maria. 1962. *Child of the Dark: The Diary of Carolina Maria de Jesus.* Translated by David St. Clair. New York: Dutton.

Deloria, Ella Cara. 1988. *Waterlily.* Lincoln, NB: University of Nebraska Press.

DeMallie, Raymond J. 1988. Afterword to *Waterlily,* by Ella Cara Deloria. Lincoln, NB: University of Nebraska Press.

Derlega, V. J., and J. H. Berg, eds. 1987. *Self-Disclosure: Theory, Research and Therapy.* New York: Plenum.

DeVault, Marjorie. 1990. "Novel Readings: The Social Organization of Interpretation." *Am. J. Sociology* 4: 887–921.

———. 1991. *Feeding the Family.* Chicago: University of Chicago Press.

Devereux, Georges. 1968. *From Anxiety to Method in the Behavioral Sciences.* The Hague: Mouton.

Dickinson, Emily. 1935. *Complete Poems.* Boston: Little, Brown.

Dollard, John. 1935. *Criteria for the Life History.* New Haven, CT: Yale University Press.

DuPlessis, Rachel Blau. 1985. *Writing beyond the Ending.* Bloomington, IN: University of Indiana Press.

Duras, Marguerite. 1981. "Interview with Susan Husserl-Kapit." In *New French Feminisms,* edited by E. Marks and I. de Courtivron, 174–76. New York: Schocken.

Edel, Leon. 1979. "The Fugitive under the Carpet." In Pachter 1979, 16–34.

———. 1984. "Transference: The Biographer's Dilemma." *Biography* 7, 4: 283–91.

Egan, Suzanna. 1984. *Patterns of Experience in Autobiography.* Chapel Hill, NC: University of North Carolina Press.

Ehrenreich, Barbara. 1984. *Hearts of Men: American Dreams and the Flight from Commitment.* New York: Doubleday.

Eisenstein, Hester. 1983. *Contemporary Feminist Thought.* Boston: G. K. Hall.

Ellis, Carolyn, and Arthur Bochner. 1992. "Telling and Performing Personal Stories: The Construction of Choice in Abortion." In Ellis and Flaherty 1992, 5–20.

Ellis, Carolyn, and Michael Flaherty. 1992. *Investigating Subjectivity.* Newbury Park, CA: Sage.

Elmendorf, Mary. 1976. *Nine Mayan Women: A Village Faces Change.* Cambridge, MA: Schenkman.

Empey, LaMar T. 1968. *American Delinquency: Its Meaning and Construction.* Homewood, IL: Dorsey Press.

Erikson, Erik. 1950. *Childhood and Society.* New York: Norton.

Evans, Elizabeth. 1975. *Weathering the Storm: The Women of the American Revolution.* New York: Scribners.

Fern, Fanny. 1855. *Ruth Hall: A Domestic Tale of the Present Time.* New York: Mason Brothers.

Fetterley, Judith. 1978. *The Resisting Reader: A Feminist Approach to American Fiction.* Bloomington, IN: University of Indiana Press.

Fields, Mamie Garvin. 1983. *Lemon Swamp and Other Places: A Carolina Memoir.* New York: Free Press.

Finger, Matthias. 1989. "L'Approche biographique face aux sciences sociales: Le Problème du sujet dans la recherche sociale." *Revue Européenne des Sciences Sociales* 27, 83: 217–46.

Fischer, C. 1976. "Undercutting the Scientist-Professional Dichotomy: The Reflective Psychologist." *Clinical Psychologist* 29: 5–7.

Fish, Stanley. 1980. *Is There a Text in This Class? The Authority of Interpretive Communities.* Cambridge, MA: Harvard University Press.

Flynn, Elizabeth A., and Patrocinio P. Schweikart, eds. 1986. *Gender and Reading.* Baltimore, MD: Johns Hopkins University Press.

Foucault, Michel. 1978. *The History of Sexuality.* New York: Random House.

Frank, Gelya. 1979. "Finding the Common Denominator: A Phenomenological Critique of Life History Method." *Ethos* 7, 1: 68–94.

———. 1985. "Becoming the Other: Empathy and Biographical Interpretation." *Biography* 8, 3: 189–210.

Freeman, James M., and David L. Krantz. 1980. "The Unfulfilled Promise of Life Histories." *Biography* 3, 1: 1–13.

Friedman, Susan Stanford. 1988. "Women's Autobiographical Selves: Theory and Practice." In Benstock 1988, 34–62.

Frye, Joanne S. 1986. *Living Stories/Telling Lives: Women and the Novel in Contemporary Experience.* Ann Arbor, MI: University of Michigan Press.

Frye, Marilyn. 1985. "Arrogance and Love." In *For Alma Mater: Theory and Practice in Feminist Scholarship,* edited by Paula A. Treichler, Cheris Kramarea, and Beth Stafford. Urbana, IL: University of Illinois Press.

Frye, Northrop. 1957. *Anatomy of Criticism.* Princeton, NJ: Princeton University Press.

Gadamer, Hans-Georg. 1972. *Truth and Historicity.* The Hague: M. Nijhoff.

———. 1975. *Truth and Method.* Translated by Garrett Borden and John Cumming. New York: Seabury Press.

Geiger, Susan N. G. 1986. "Women's Life Histories: Method and Content." *Signs* 11, 2: 334–51.

Geis, Gilbert. 1982. "The Jack-Roller: The Appeal, the Person and the Impact."
In Snodgrass 1982, 121–34.

Gilbert, Sandra M., and Susan Gubar. 1979. *The Madwoman in the Attic: The Woman Writer and the Nineteenth-Century Literary Imagination.* New Haven, CT: Yale University Press.

Gilligan, Carol. 1982. *In a Different Voice: Psychological Theory and Women's Development.* Cambridge, MA: Harvard University Press.

Gluck, Sherna. 1977. "What's So Special about Women? Women's Oral History." *Frontiers* 2, 2: 3–14.

Gluck, Sherna, and Daphne Patai, eds. 1991. *Women's Words: The Feminist Practice of Oral History.* New York: Routledge.

Goetting, Ann. 1994. "Helping Sculpt Life Stories: Musings of One Coeditor." Paper presented at the annual meetings of Sociologists for Women in Society, Los Angeles.

Goetting, Ann, and Sarah Fenstermaker. 1995. *Individual Voices, Collective Visions: Fifty Years of Women in Sociology.* Philadelphia: Temple University Press.

Golde, Peggy. 1970. *Women in the Field: Anthropological Experiences.* Chicago: Aldine.

Goodwin, James. 1983. "The Education of Henry Adams: A Non-Person in History." *Biography* 6, 2: 117–35.

Gordon, Lyndall. 1984. *Virginia Woolf: A Writer's Life.* New York: Norton.

Gottschalk, Louis, Clyde Kluckhohn, and Robert C. Angell. 1942. *The Use of Personal Documents in History, Anthropology, and Sociology.* New York: Social Science Research Council.

Gouldner, Alvin. 1960. "The Norm of Reciprocity: A Preliminary Statement." *Am. Sociol. Rev.* 25: 161–78.

———. 1970. *The Coming Crisis of Western Sociology.* New York: Basic Books.

Goulianos, Joan, ed. 1974. *By a Woman Writ: Literature from Six Centuries by and about Women.* Baltimore: Penguin Books.

Greenacre, Phyllis. 1971 [1957]. "The Childhood of the Artist: Libidinal Phase Development and Giftedness." In *Emotional Growth: Psychoanalytic Studies of the Gifted and a Great Variety of Other Individuals.* New York: International Universities Press.

Gunn, Janet V. 1982. *Autobiography: Toward a Poetics of Experience.* Philadelphia: University of Pennsylvania Press.

Gusdorf, Georges. 1980. "Conditions and Limits of Autobiography." In Olney 1980.

Hahn, Emily. 1977. *Mabel: A Biography of Mabel Dodge Luhan.* Boston: Houghton Mifflin.

Hall, Jacquelyn Dowd. 1979. *Revolt against Chivalry: Jessie Daniel Ames and the Women's Campaign against Lynching.* New York: Columbia University Press.

———. 1987. "Second Thoughts: On Writing a Feminist Biography." *Feminist Studies* 13, 1: 19–37.

Haller, Evelyn. 1988. "Review of *Lucy Sprague Mitchell: The Making of a Modern Woman.*" *Biography* 11, 4: 331–36.

Hampsten, Elizabeth. 1982. *Read This Only to Yourself: The Private Writings of Midwestern Women, 1880–1910.* Bloomington, IN: University of Indiana Press.

Hanson, Beatrice. 1991. "That's Not What I Said: Interpretive Conflict in Oral Narrative Research." In Gluck and Patai 1991.

Harding, Sandra. 1991. *Whose Science? Whose Knowledge? Thinking from Women's Lives.* Ithaca, NY: Cornell University Press.

Harris, S. L. 1972. "Who Studies Sex Differences?" *American Psychol.* 27: 1077–78.

Hawthorne, Nathaniel. 1913. *Works of Nathaniel Hawthorne,* vol. 12, edited by George Parsons Lathrop. Boston: Houghton Mifflin.

Heilbrun, Carolyn. 1985. *Women's Review of Books* 2, 12: 12.

———. 1988. *Writing a Woman's Life.* New York: Norton.

Hendricks, S. S. 1981. "Self-Disclosure and Marital Satisfaction," *J. Personality and Social Psychol.* 40: 1150–59.

Hentz, Caroline Lee. 1856. *Ernest Linwood.* Boston: J. P. Jewett.

Hill, C. T., and D. E. Stull. 1987. "Gender and Self-Disclosure: Strategies for Exploring the Issues." In Derlega and Berg 1987.

Hochschild, Arlie. 1983. *The Managed Heart: Commercialization of Human Feeling.* Berkeley, CA: University of California Press.

Hoffman, Leonore, and Margo Culley. 1975. *Women's Personal Narratives: Essays in Criticism and Pedagogy.* New York: Modern Language Association of America.

Homans, George Caspar. 1984. *Coming to My Senses: The Autobiography of a Sociologist.* New Brunswick, NJ: Transaction Books.

Homans, Margaret. 1983. "'Her Very Own Howl': The Ambiguities of Representation in Recent Women's Fiction." *Signs* 9, 2: 186–205.

hooks, bell. 1981. *Ain't I a Woman?* Boston: South End Press.

———. 1984. *Feminist Theory from Margin to Center.* Boston: South End Press.

———. 1989. *Talking Back: Thinking Feminist, Thinking Black.* Boston: South End Press.

———. 1992. *Black Looks: Race and Representation.* Boston: South End Press.

Horner, Matina. 1969. "Women's Will to Fail." *Psychology Today.* November: 36–41.

Horney, Karen. 1967. *Feminine Psychology,* edited by H. Velman. New York: Norton.

Huf, Linda. 1983. *A Portrait of the Artist as a Young Woman.* New York: Frederick Unger.

Hughes, Helen MacGill, ed. 1961. *The Fantastic Lodge: The Autobiography of a Girl Drug Addict*. Boston: Houghton Mifflin.

Hull, Gloria T. 1984. "Alice Dunbar-Nelson: A Personal and Literary Perspective." In Ascher, DeSalvo, and Ruddick 1984, 105–11.

Hull, Gloria T., Patricia Bell Scott, and Barbara Smith. 1982. *All the Blacks Were Men, All the Women Were White, But Some of Us Are Brave*. Old Westbury, NY: The Feminist Press.

Jacobs, Harriet. 1987. *Incidents in the Life of a Slave Girl*. Cambridge, MA: Harvard University Press.

James, Adeola, ed. 1990. *In Their Own Voices: African Women Writers Talk*. Portsmouth, NH: Heineman.

James, William. 1899. "On a Certain Blindness in Human Beings." In *Talks to Teachers*. New York: Henry Holt.

Jay, Paul. 1987. "What's the Use? Critical Theory and the Study of Autobiography." *Biography* 10, 1: 39–54.

Jelinek, Estelle. 1980. *Women's Autobiography: Essays in Criticism*. Bloomington, IN: Indiana University Press.

———. 1986. *The Tradition of Women's Autobiography from Antiquity to the Present*. Boston: Twayne.

Juhasz, Suzanne. 1980. "Towards a Theory of Form in Feminist Autobiography: Kate Millett's *Flying* and *Sita*; Maxine Hong Kingston's *The Woman Warrior*." In Jelinek 1980.

———. 1985. "Maxine Hong Kingston: Narrative Techniques and Female Identity." In Rainwater and Scheick 1985, 173–89.

Julian of Norwich. 1978. *Showings*. Translated by Edmund Colledge and James Walsh. New York: Paulist Press.

Kamel, Rose. 1992. "'In Retrospect these Journeys Loom Large': Carobeth Laird's *Encounter with an Angry God*." *Biography* 15, 1: 49–66.

Kaplan, Justin. 1979. "The Naked Self and Other Problems." In Pachter 1979, 37–55.

Kazin, Alfred. 1979. "The Self as History: Reflections on Autobiography." In Pachter 1979, 74–89.

Keller, Catherine. 1986. *From a Broken Web: Separation, Sexism and Self*. Boston: Beacon.

Keller, Evelyn Fox. 1983. *A Feeling for the Organism: The Life Work of Barbara McClintock*. New York: W. H. Freeman.

———. 1985. *Reflections on Gender and Science*. New Haven, CT: Yale University Press.

Kelley, Jane Holden. 1978. *Yaqui Women: Contemporary Life Histories*. Lincoln, NB: University of Nebraska Press.

Kempe, Margery. 1940. *The Book of Margery Kempe*, edited by Sanford Brown

Meech. London: Published for the Early English Text Society by H. Milford, Oxford University Press.

Kingston, Maxine Hong. 1976. *The Woman Warrior.* New York: Knopf.

Kirsch, Sarah. 1989. *The Panther Woman: Five Tales from the Cassette Recorder.* Translated and introduction by Marion Faber. Lincoln, NB: University of Nebraska Press.

Kluckhohn, Clyde. 1945. "The Personal Document in Anthropological Science." In Gottschalk, Kluckhohn, and Angell 1942, 79–176.

Kobrin, Solomon. 1982. "The Uses of the Life-History Document for the Development of Delinquency Theory." In Snodgrass 1982, 153–65.

Kohlberg, Lawrence. 1981. *The Psychology of Moral Development.* San Francisco: Harper.

Kolodny, Annette. 1980a. "A Map for Rereading: Or, Gender and the Interpretation of Literary Texts." *New Literary History* 11: 451–67.

———. 1980b. "Dancing Through the Minefield: Some Observations on the Theory, Practice, and Politics of a Feminist Literary Criticism." *Feminist Studies* 6, 1: 1–25.

———. 1980c. "The Lady's Not for Spurning: Kate Millett and the Critics." In Jelinek 1980, 238–59.

Kotre, John. 1984. *Outliving the Self: Generativity and the Interpretation of Lives.* Baltimore, MD: Johns Hopkins University Press.

Krieger, Susan. 1983. *The Mirror Dance: Identity in a Women's Community.* Philadelphia: Temple University Press.

———. 1985. "Beyond 'Subjectivity': The Use of the Self in Social Science" *Qualitative Sociology* 8, 4: 309–24.

———. 1991. *Social Science and the Self.* New Brunswick, NJ: Rutgers University Press.

Krupat, Arnold. 1985. *For Those Who Come After: A Study of Native American Autobiography.* Berkeley, CA: University of California Press.

Kuhn, Thomas S. 1962. *The Structure of Scientific Revolutions.* Chicago: University of Chicago Press.

Kuper, Hilda. 1978. *Sobhuza II, Ngwenyama and King of Swaziland.* London: Duckworth.

La Barre, Wesley. 1968. Preface to *From Anxiety to Method in the Behavioral Sciences,* by Georges Devereux, vii–x. The Hague: Mouton.

Ladner, Joyce. 1972. *Tomorrow's Tomorrow: The Black Woman.* Garden City, NY: Anchor.

Laird, Carobeth. 1975. *Encounter with an Angry God: Recollections of My Life with John Peabody Harrington.* Banning, CA: Malki Museum Press.

Lang, Candace. 1982. "Autobiography in the Aftermath of Romanticism." *Diacritics* 12: 2–16.

Langness, L. L. 1965. *The Life History in Anthropological Science*. New York: Holt, Rinehart, and Winston.

Langness, L. L., and Gelya Frank. 1981. *Lives: An Anthropological Approach to Biography*. Novalo, CA: Chandler and Sharp.

Laslett, Barbara. 1991. "Biography as Historical Sociology." *Theory and Society* 20: 511–38.

Lather, Patti. 1991. *Getting Smart: Feminist Research and Pedagogy with/in the Postmodern*. New York: Routledge.

Laws, Judith Long. 1975. "The Psychology of Tokenism." *Sex Roles* 1, 1: 51–74.

———. 1979. *The Second X: Sex Role and Social Role*. New York: Elsevier Scientific Publishing.

Laws, Judith Long, and Pepper Schwartz. 1977. *Sexual Scripts: The Social Construction of Female Sexuality*. Hinsdale, IL: Dryden.

Lawson, Sarah. 1985. Introduction to *The Treasure of the City of Ladies*, by Christine de Pisan. Hammondsworth, England: Penguin.

Lee, Joann Faung Jean. 1991. *Asian-American Experiences in the United States: Oral Histories of First to Fourth Generation Americans from China, the Philippines, Japan, India, the Pacific Islands, Vietnam, and Cambodia*. Jefferson, NC: McFarland.

Lejeune, Philippe. 1989. *On Autobiography*. Minneapolis, MN: University of Minnesota Press.

Lerner, Gerda. 1986. *Creating Patriarchy*. New York: Oxford University Press.

Lever, Janet. 1976. "Sex Differences in Games Children Play." *Social Problems* 23, 4: 478–87.

Levine, Donald N. 1971. *Georg Simmel on Individuality and Social Forms*. Chicago: University of Chicago Press.

Lifshin, Lyn, ed. 1982. *Ariadne's Thread: A Collection of Contemporary Women's Journals*. New York: Harper and Row.

Linderman, Frank Bird. 1972. *Pretty Shield: Medicine Woman of the Crows*. Lincoln, NB: University of Nebraska Press.

Lionnet, Françoise. 1989. *Autobiographical Voices: Race, Gender, Self-portraiture*. Ithaca, NY: Cornell University Press.

Lippard, Lucy. 1976. *From the Center: Feminist Essays on Women's Art*. New York: Dutton.

Loewenberg, Peter. 1969 *Decoding the Past: The Psychohistorical Approach*. Berkeley: University of California Press.

Long, Judy. 1981. "Female Sexuality over the Lifespan." In *Lifespan Development and Behavior*, vol. 3, edited by Paul Baltes and O. G. Brim, 208–51. New York: Academic.

Long, Judy, and Karen Porter. 1980. "Multiple Roles of Midlife Women: A Case for New Directions in Theory, Research and Policy." In *Between Youth and*

Old Age: Women in the Middle Years, edited by Grace Baruch and Jeanne Brooks-Gunn, 109–59. New York: Plenum.

Lord, Audre. 1982. *Zami: A New Spelling of My Name.* Trumansburg, NY: Crossing Press.

Lowie, Robert H. 1960. "Empathy, or 'Seeing From Within.'" In *Culture in History: Essays in Honor of Paul Radin,* edited by Stanley Diamond. New York: Columbia University Press.

Lugones, Maria, and Elizabeth V. Spelman. 1983. "Have We Got a Theory for You: Feminist Theory, Cultural Imperialism and the Demand for 'the Woman's Voice!'" *Women's Studies Int. Forum* 6, 6: 573–81.

Luhan, Mabel Dodge. 1933. *Intimate Memories: Background.* New York: Harcourt Brace.

———. 1935. *European Experiences.* New York: Harcourt Brace.

———. 1936. *Movers and Shakers.* New York: Harcourt Brace.

———. 1937. *Edge of Taos Desert: An Escape to Reality.* New York: Harcourt Brace.

Macy, Joanna. 1983. *Despair and Personal Power in the Nuclear Age.* Philadelphia: New Society.

Madge, C. 1963. *The Origin of Scientific Sociology.* London: Tavistock.

Marcus, Jane. 1988. "Invincible Mediocrity: The Private Selves of Public Women." In Benstock 1988.

Mason, Mary. 1980. "The Other Voice: Autobiographies of Women Writers." In Olney 1980.

Maurois, André. 1929. *Aspects of Biography.* New York: D. Appleton.

Mayerding, Jane, ed. 1984. *We Are All Part of One Another: A Barbara Deming Reader.* Philadelphia: New Society Publishers.

Mbilinyi, Marjorie. 1989. "'I'd Have Been a Man': Politics and the Labor Process in Producing Personal Narratives." *Interpreting Women's Lives: Feminist Theory and Personal Narratives,* edited by the Personal Narratives Group, 204–27. Blommington: Indiana University Press.

McCall, Michal, and Judith Wittner. 1990. "The Good News about Life History." In *Symbolic Interaction and Cultural Studies,* edited by Howard S. Becker and Michal McCall. Chicago: University of Chicago Press.

Mehlman, Jeffrey. 1974. *A Structural Study of Autobiography: Proust, Leiris, Sartre, Lévi-Strauss.* Ithaca, NY: Cornell University Press.

Miller, Jean Baker. 1986. *Toward a New Psychology of Women.* Boston: Beacon Press.

Miller, Nancy K. 1980. *The Heroine's Text: Readings in the French and English Novel, 1722–1782.* New York: Columbia University Press.

———. 1991. *Getting Personal: Feminist Occasions and Other Autobiographical Acts.* New York: Routledge.

Millett, Kate. 1990. *Flying.* New York: Simon and Schuster.

Millman, Marcia. 1975. "She Did It All for Love: A Feminist View of the Sociology of Deviance." In *Another Voice: Feminist Perspectives on Social Life and Social Science,* edited by Marcia Millman and Rosabeth Moss Kanter. Garden City, NY: Anchor.

Minnich, Elizabeth Kamarck. 1985. "The Friendship between Women: The Act of Feminist Biography (a Review Essay)." *Feminist Studies* 11, 2: 287–305.

Mitchell, David J. 1980. "Living Documents: Oral History and Biography." *Biography* 3, 4: 283–96.

Mitchell, Gillian. 1984. "Women and Lying: A Pragmatic and Semantic Analysis of 'Telling it Slant.'" *Women's Studies Int. Forum* 7, 5: 375–83.

Moffat, Mary Jane, and Charlotte Painter, eds. 1975. *Revelations: Diaries of Women.* New York: Vintage Books.

Moody, Anne. 1968. *Coming of Age in Mississippi.* New York: Dial Press.

Moser, C. A. 1958. *Survey Methods in Social Investigation.* London: Heineman.

Mulford, Wendy. 1988. *This Narrow Place: Sylvia Townsend Warner and Valentine Ackland: Life, Letters and Politics.* London: Pandora.

Murray, Pauli. 1956. *Proud Shoes: The Story of an American Family.* New York: Harper and Row.

Myerhoff, Barbara. 1980. *Number Our Days.* New York: Simon and Schuster.

Naples, Nancy. 1996. "A Feminist Revisiting of the Insider/Outsider Debate: The 'Outsider Phenomenon' in Rural Iowa." *Qualitative Sociology* 19, 1: 83–106.

Nelson, Janet. 1980. "Journey to the Edge of History: Narrative Form in Mabel Dodge Luhan's *Intimate Memories.*" *Biography* 3, 3: 240–52.

Neuman, Shirley, ed. 1991. *Autobiography and Questions of Gender.* London: Frank Cass.

Nin, Anaïs. 1966. *The Diary of Anaïs Nin,* vol. 1, edited by Gunther Stuhlmann. New York: Swallow Press.

———. 1967. *The Diary of Anaïs Nin,* vol. 2, edited by Gunther Stuhlmann. New York: Swallow Press.

———. 1969. *The Diary of Anaïs Nin,* vol. 3, edited by Gunther Stuhlmann. New York: Swallow Press.

Noddings, Nel. 1984. *Caring: A Feminine Approach to Ethics and Moral Education.* Berkeley, CA: University of California Press.

Nord, Deborah Epstein. 1985. *The Apprenticeship of Beatrice Webb.* Amherst, MA: University of Massachusetts Press.

———. 1986. "Female Traditions of Autobiography: Memoir and Fiction." In Estelle Jelinek 1986, 57–80.

Nussbaum, Felicity. 1988. "Toward Conceptualizing Diary." In *Studies in Autobiography,* edited by James Olney, 128–40. New York: Oxford University Press.

Oakley, Ann. 1981. "Interviewing Women: A Contradiction in Terms." In Roberts 1981.

Olney, James. 1972. *Metaphors of Self: The Meaning of Autobiography.* Princeton, NJ: Princeton University Press.

———. 1980. *Autobiography: Essays Theoretical and Critical.* Princeton, NJ: Princeton University Press.

Olsen, Tillie. 1961. *Tell Me a Riddle.* New York: Dell.

———. 1978. *Silences: Why Women Don't Write.* New York: Delacorte.

Oppenheimer, Martin, Martin J. Murray, and Rhonda F. Levine, eds. 1991. *Radical Sociologists and the Movement: Experiences, Lessons, and Legacies.* Philadelphia: Temple University Press.

Orlans, Kathryn P. Meadow, and Ruth A. Wallace. 1994. *Gender and the Academic Experience: Berkeley Women Sociologists.* Lincoln: University of Nebraska Press.

Pachter, Marc. 1979. *Telling Lives: The Biographer's Art.* Washington, DC: New Republic Books.

Paget, Marianne A. 1990. "Life Mirrors Work Mirrors Text Mirrors Life . . ." *Social Problems* 37, 2: 137–48.

Pascal, Roy. 1960. *Design and Truth in Autobiography.* Cambridge, MA: Harvard University Press.

Patai, Daphne. 1988. *Brazilian Women Speak: Contemporary Life Stories.* New Brunswick, NJ: Rutgers University Press.

Pearson, Carol. 1989. *The Hero Within: Six Archetypes We Live By.* San Francisco: Harper and Row.

Perry, William G., Jr. 1968. *Forms of Intellectual and Ethical Development in the College Years.* New York: Holt, Rinehart and Winston.

Personal Narratives Group, eds. 1989. *Interpreting Women's Lives: Feminist Theory and Personal Narratives.* Bloomington, IN: Indiana University Press.

Peterson, Linda H. 1990. "Female Autobiographer, Narrative Duplicity." *Studies in the Literary Imagination* 23, 2: 165–96.

Pleck, Joseph. 1981. *The Myth of Masculinity.* Cambridge, MA: MIT Press.

Plummer, Ken. 1983. *Documents of Life.* London: Allen and Unwin.

Pollak, S., and Carol Gilligan. 1982. "Images of Violence in Thematic Apperception Test Stories." *J. Personality and Social Psychol.* 42: 159–67.

Pollak, Vivian. 1984. *Dickinson: The Anxiety of Gender.* Ithaca, NY: Cornell University Press.

Ponse, Barbara. 1978. *Identities in the Lesbian Community: The Social Construction of Self.* Westport, CT: Greenwood.

Prescott, S., and K. Foster. 1972. "Why Researchers Don't Study Women: The Responses of 67 Researchers." Unpublished manuscript.

Rabinow, Paul. 1977. *Reflections on Fieldwork in Morocco.* Berkeley, CA: University of California Press.

Radin, Paul. 1926. *Crashing Thunder: The Autobiography of an American Indian.* New York: Appleton, Century, Crofts.

Rainwater, Catherine, and William Scheick, eds. 1985. *Contemporary American Women Writers: Narrative Strategies.* Lexington, KY: University Press of Kentucky.

Reinharz, Shulamit. 1984a. *Becoming a Social Scientist.* New Brunswick, NJ: Transaction Publishers.

————. 1984b. "Toward a Model of Female Political Action: The Case of Manya Shohat, Founder of the First Kibbutz." *Women's Studies Int. Forum* 7, 4: 275–87.

————. 1985a. "Feminist Distrust: Problems of Context and Content in Sociological Work." In *The Self in Social Inquiry: Researching Methods,* edited by David N. Berg and Kenwyn K. Smith, 153–72. Beverly Hills, CA: Sage.

————. 1985b. *Feminist Distrust: A Response to Misogyny and Gynopia in Sociological Work.* Unpublished manuscript.

————. 1989. "Teaching the History of Women in Sociology: Or Dorothy Swaine Thomas, Wasn't She the Woman Married to William I?" *American Sociologist,* 87–94.

————. 1992. *Feminist Methods in Social Research.* New York: Oxford University Press.

Reissman, Catherine. 1990. *Divorce Talk: Men and Women Make Sense of Personal Relationships.* New Brunswick, NJ: Rutgers University Press.

Reitman, Dorothy. 1988. *Boxcar Bertha: An Autobiography.* As told to Dr. Ben L. Reitman. New York: AMOK.

Rich, Adrienne. 1979. *On Lies, Secrets, and Silences: Selected Prose, 1966–1978.* New York: Norton.

————. 1986. *Of Woman Born: Motherhood as Experience and Institution.* New York: Norton.

Ricoeur, Paul. 1974. *Conflict of Interpretations: Essays in Hermeneutics.* Evanston, IL: Northwestern University Press.

————. 1984. *Time and Narrative,* vol. 1. Translated by Kathleen McLaughlin and David Pellauer. Chicago: University of Chicago Press.

————. 1985. *Time and Narrative,* vol. 2. Translated by Kathleen McLaughlin and David Pellauer. Chicago: University of Chicago Press.

————. 1988. *Time and Narrative,* vol. 3. Translated by Kathleen Blamey and David Pellauer. Chicago: University of Chicago Press.

Riley, Matilda White, ed. 1988. *Sociological Lives.* Beverly Hills, CA: Sage.

Roberts, Helen, ed. 1981. *Doing Feminist Research.* London: Routledge and Kegan Paul.

Roberts, Joan. 1976. *Beyond Intellectual Sexism: A New Woman, a New Reality.* New York: D. McKay.

Rollins, Judith. 1985. *Between Women Domestics and Their Employers.* Philadelphia: Temple University Press.

Rose, Phyllis. 1978. *Woman of Letters: A Life of Virginia Woolf.* New York: Oxford University Press.

———. 1984. *Parallel Lives: Five Victorian Marriages.* New York: Knopf.

———. 1985. *Writing Women: Essays in a Renaissance.* Middletown, CT: Wesleyan University Press.

Rosengarten, Theodore. 1975. *All God's Dangers: The Life of Nate Shaw.* New York: Knopf.

———. 1979. "Stepping over Cockleburs: Conversations with Ned Cobb." In Pachter 1979, 104–31.

Rudnick, Lois Palken. 1984. *Mabel Dodge Luhan: New Woman, New Worlds.* Albuquerque, NM: University of New Mexico Press.

Runyan, William McKinley. 1980. "Alternative Accounts of Lives: An Argument for Epistemological Relativism." *Biography* 3, 3: 209–25.

Russ, Joanna. 1983. *How to Suppress Women's Writing.* Austin, TX: University of Texas Press.

Ryan, Michael. 1980. "Self-evidence." *Diacritics* 10:1–16.

Said, Edward. 1978. *Orientalism.* New York: Pantheon.

Salazar, Claudia. 1991. "A Third World Woman's Text: Between the Politics of Criticism and Cultural Politics." In Gluck and Patai 1991.

Samelson, F. 1976. "From 'Race Psychology' to 'Studies in Prejudice.' Some Observations on the Thematic Reversal in Social Psychology." Paper presented at the Cheiron Society, Smithsonian Institution, Washington, DC.

Sampson, Edward E. 1977. "Psychology and the American Ideal." *J. Personality and Social Psychol.* 35, 11: 767–82.

———. 1978. "Scientific Paradigm and Social Value: Wanted—A Scientific Revolution." *J. Personality and Social Psychol.* 36: 1332–43.

Sarashina, Lady (Sugarawa Takasue No Musume). 1971. *As I Crossed a Bridge of Dreams: Recollections of a Woman in Eleventh Century Japan.* Translated by Ivan Morris. New York: Dial Press.

Sayre, Robert F. 1964. *The Examined Self: Benjamin Franklin, Henry Adams, Henry James.* Princeton, NJ: Princeton University Press.

Schibanoff, Susan. 1983. "Early Women Writers: In-scribing, or, Reading the Fine Print." *Women's Studies Int. Forum* 6, 5: 475–89.

Schlissel, Lillian. 1982. *Women's Diaries of the Westward Journey.* New York: Schocken Books.

Schur, Edwin. 1983. *Labeling Women Deviant.* New York: McGraw.

Schwabacher, S. 1972. "Male Versus Female Representation in Psychological Research: An Examination of the *Journal of Personality and Social Research* 1970, 1971." *Journal Supplement Abstract Service* 1972, 2: 20–21.

Scott-Maxwell, Florida. 1979. *The Measure of My Days.* Harmondsworth, England: Penguin Books.

Shaw, Clifford. 1930. *The Jack-Roller: A Delinquent Boy's Own Story.* Chicago: University of Chicago Press.

Short, James F. 1982. "Life History, Autobiography, and the Life Cycle." In Jon Snodgrass 1982, 135–52.

Shostak, Marjorie. 1981. *Nisa, the Life and Words of a !Kung Woman.* Cambridge: Harvard University Press.

Showalter, Elaine. 1975. "Review Essay: Literary Criticism." *Signs* 1, 2: 435–60.

———. 1977. *A Literature of Their Own: British Women Novelists from Brontë to Lessing.* Princeton, NJ: Princeton University Press.

———. 1985. *The New Feminist Criticism.* New York: Pantheon.

Shulman, Alix Kates. 1979. "Overcoming Silences: Teaching Writing for Women." *Harvard Educational Review* 49, 4: 527–33.

Shumaker, Wayne. 1954. *English Autobiography: Its Emergence, Materials and Forms.* Berkeley, CA: University of California Press.

Sistren with Honor Ford Smith. 1987. *Lionheart Gal: Life Stories of Jamaican Women.* Toronto: Sister Vision.

Smith, Dorothy. 1979. "A Sociology for Women." In *The Prism of Sex: Essays in the Sociology of Knowledge,* edited by Julia Sherman and F. Beck, 135–87. Madison, WI: University of Wisconsin Press.

———. 1987. *The Everyday World as Problematic.* Boston: Northeastern University Press.

Smith, Hilda. 1976. "Feminism and the Methodology of Women's History." In *Liberating Women's History,* edited by Berenice Carroll. Urbana, IL: University of Illinois Press.

Smith, Sidonie. 1987. *A Poetics of Women's Autobiography.* Bloomington, IN: Indiana University Press.

Smith-Rosenberg, Carroll. 1975. "The Female World of Love and Ritual: Relations between Women in 19th-Century America." *Signs* 1, 1: 1–29.

Snodgrass, Jon. 1982. *The Jack-Roller at Seventy: A Fifty Year Follow-up.* Lexington, MA: Lexington Books.

Sochen, June. 1972. *The New Woman: Feminism in Greenwich Village, 1910–1920.* New York: Quadrangle.

———. 1973. *Movers and Shakers: American Women Thinkers and Activists, 1900–1970.* New York: Quadrangle/New York Times.

Spacks, Patricia Meyer. 1975. "In Praise of Gossip." *Hudson Review* 35: 19–38.

———. 1972. *The Female Imagination.* New York: Discus (Avon Books).

———. 1980. "Selves in Hiding." In Jelinek 1980, 112–32.

Spengemann, William C. 1980. *The Forms of Autobiography: Episodes in the History of the Literary Genre.* New Haven, CT: Yale University Press.

Stacey, Judith. 1991. "Can There Be a Feminist Ethnography?" In Gluck and Patai 1991, 111–21.

Stanton, Domna. 1984. *The Female Autograph*. New York: New York Literary Forum.

Sterling, Dorothy, ed. 1984. *We Are Your Sisters: Black Women in the Nineteenth Century*. New York: Norton.

Stokes, J., A. Fuehrer, and R. Childs. 1980. "Gender Differences in Self-Disclosure to Various Target Persons," *J. Counselling Psych.* 27: 192–98.

Tanaka, Michiko. 1981. *Through Harsh Winters: The Life of a Japanese Immigrant Woman*. Novato, CA: Chandler and Sharp.

Tate, Claudia. 1983. *Black Women Writers at Work*. New York: Continuum.

Taylor, Pat Ellis. 1981. *Border Healing Woman: The Story of Jewell Babb as Told to Pat Ellis Taylor*. Austin, TX: University of Texas Press.

Thomas, W. I., and Florian Znaniecki. 1918. *The Polish Peasant in Europe and America,* vol. 1, vol. 2. Boston: Richard G. Badger, The Gorham Press.

Tolstoy, Sophie A. 1928. *The Diary of Tolstoy's Wife, 1860–1891*. Translated by Alexander Wertz. London: Victor Gollancz.

Tompkins, Jane P., ed. 1980. *Reader-Response Criticism: From Formalism to Post-Structuralism*. Baltimore, MD: Johns Hopkins University Press.

Tucker, Susan. 1988. *Telling Memories among Southern Women: Domestic Workers and Their Employers in the Segregated South*. Baton Rouge, LA: Louisiana State University Press.

Vigil, James Diego. 1988. "Group Processes and Street Identity: Adolescent Gang Members." *Ethos* 16, 4: 421–45.

Walker, Alice. 1983. *In Search of Our Mothers' Gardens*. San Diego: Harcourt Brace Jovanovich.

Ware, Susan. 1987. *Partner and I*. New Haven, CT: Yale University Press.

Washburne, Heluiz Chandler, and Anauta. 1940. *Land of the Good Shadows: The Life of Anauta*. New York: John Day.

Washington, Mary Helen. 1984. "'Taming All that Anger Down': Rage and Silence in Gwendolyn Brooks's *Maud Martha*." In *Black Literature and Literary Theory,* edited by Henry Louis Gates, Jr., 249–67. London: Methuen.

Watson, Lawrence C., and Maria-Barbara Watson-Franke. 1985. *Interpreting Life Histories*. New Brunswick, NJ: Rutgers University Press.

Webb, Beatrice P. 1926. *My Apprenticeship*. New York: Longmans Green.

Webster's New World Dictionary of the American Language. 1966. Cleveland, OH: World.

Weldon, Fay. 1985. *Rebecca West*. New York: Viking.

Westkott, Marcia. 1979. "Feminist Criticism of the Social Sciences." *Harvard Ed. Rev.* 49, 4: 422–30.

———. 1986. *The Feminist Legacy of Karen Horney*. New Haven, CT: Yale University Press.

Weston, Kath. 1991. *Families We Choose: Lesbians, Gays, Kinship*. New York: Columbia University Press.

White, Robert W. 1952. *Lives in Progress: A Study of the Natural Growth of Personality*. New York: Dryden.

Whyte, William F. 1994. *Participant Observer: An Autobiography*. Ithaca, NY: ILR.

Wood, Ann. 1971. "The 'Scribbling Women' and Fanny Fern: Why Women Wrote." *American Quarterly* 23 (Spring): 3–24.

Woolf, Virginia. 1925. "The Lives of the Obscure." *Dial* (May): 381–82.

———. 1976. *Moments of Being: Unpublished Autobiographical Writings*, edited by Jeanne Schulkind. New York: Harcourt Brace Jovanovich.

Zaretsky, Eli. 1984. *The Polish Peasant in Europe and America by William I. Thomas and Florian Znaniecki*. Urbana, IL: University of Illinois Press.

Zimmerman, Bonnie. 1983. "Exiting from Patriarchy: The Lesbian Novel of Development." In *The Voyage In: Fictions of Female Development*, edited by Elizabeth Abel, Marianne Hirsch, and Elizabeth Langland. Hanover and London: New England Universities Press.

———. 1984. "The Politics of Transliteration: Lesbian Personal Narratives." *Signs* 9, 4: 663–82.

———. 1990. *The Safe Sea of Women: Lesbian Fiction, 1969–1989*. Boston: Beacon Press.

Index

About the Author

Judy Long lives in Ithaca, New York, and Las Cruces, New Mexico. She is Professor Emerita of Sociology at Syracuse University. She has previously taught at the University of Chicago and Cornell University, and served as a consultant to the Equal Employment Opportunity Commission, the U.S. Commission on Civil Rights, and General Motors Corporation. Her previous work includes *Sexual Scripts: The Social Construction of Female Sexuality* and *The Second X: Sex Role and Social Role*. Judy Long is a graduate of Radcliffe College and the University of Michigan.

who is at stake is truth, ve... another ...
... the self ... during my ...
(in reading letters)
truth of an embodied subject of an experience
different for my own
a teacher who wanted ...

in my opinion, we implicitly listen to
the voice - not identify w/ her, but
objectify her to the extent we hear
a ...
can we imagine ... it? is that
2nd ... the way into understanding
her as a person who heard & ... /s
taught others & ... to say